Forecasting Methods
in Business and Management

Forecasting Methods in Business and Management

Michael Firth

Distributed Exclusively By

INTERNATIONAL IDEAS INC.
1627 Spruce Street
Philadelphia PA USA 19103

Edward Arnold

© Michael Firth 1977

First published in 1977 by
Edward Arnold (Publishers) Ltd.
25 Hill Street, London W1X 8LL

Boards edition ISBN: 0 7131 3371 6
Paper edition ISBN: 0 7131 3372 4

All Rights Reserved. No part of this publication may be reproduced, stored in a retrieval system, or transmitted in any form or by any means, electronic, mechanical, photocopying, recording or otherwise, without the prior permission of Edward Arnold (Publishers) Ltd.

Text set in 11/12 pt Photon Imprint, printed by photolithography, and bound in Great Britain at The Pitman Press, Bath

Preface

During the past ten years there has been a significant number of developments in formal forecasting techniques which can be applied to business decision situations. These developments have led to increased forecasting accuracy and have reduced, to some degree, the level of uncertainty that plagues decision-making. However, this rapid expansion has also meant that the general management literature relating to forecasting techniques has lagged behind and there is at present a lack of suitable textbooks. This book hopes to remedy that situation.

The book is specifically aimed at students intending to make a career in senior and middle management but who do not wish to specialize in operational research or forecasting. It will therefore be of interest to students studying for degrees in business and management administration and also those working for professional examinations such as accountancy. However, students who are specializing in operational research, statistics and forecasting will also find it useful as an overall introduction to business forecasting. Managers too will benefit from reading the book, both for purposes of revision and to bring themselves up-to-date on recent developments in forecasting.

The text is pitched at a general management level; that is, describing the applicability, usefulness and limitations of formal forecasting techniques. It does not set out to give a detailed description of the mathematics involved, this being something that need not involve general management. A comprehensive reference section is given at the end of each chapter, however, which enables the interested reader to follow up various topics in greater detail.

The book begins with two introductory chapters describing the role of forecasting in management and the broad characteristics of forecasting techniques. These chapters are important, since they offer a framework within which formal forecasting takes place. They are followed by chapters on the individual forecasting techniques, developing from quantitative time series and causal model methods through to subjective, qualitative techniques which involve using human judgement. Finally, there are two chapters concerned with the practical problems of obtaining data, the selecting of appropriate techniques and their implementation. It is hoped that this format will enable the reader to become thoroughly acquainted with formal forecasting techniques and also help in the application of the techniques to the reader's own forecasting situations.

M.F.

Notation

While this book does not involve itself with the mathematical basis of the various techniques, it does, nevertheless, introduce a number of formulae. These formulae are developed in the text, although four expressions need to be described here. Firstly, when an item can take a number of different values it is known as a variable. Daily rainfall is an example of a variable, since it can range from nothing to, say, two inches each day. Secondly, where we add a series of recordings of a variable together we use a summation sign, Σ. Thus if we have to add together the daily recordings of rainfall, 2″, 3″, 6″, 8″ and 5″, we describe this notationally in the text as

$$\sum_{i=1}^{5} Ri,$$

where Ri stands for rainfall on day i and the subscripts $i = 1$, and 5 tell us we add the recordings for days 1, 2, 3, 4 and 5 together (i.e. start at day 1, end at day 5). Therefore instead of saying

$$2″ + 3″ + 6″ + 8″ + 5″$$

we say

$$\sum_{i=1}^{5} Ri$$

This is a useful shorthand expression if the number of additions become large.

Thirdly, we often refer to the mean of a number of recordings for a variable. The mean is a statistical average which we obtain by adding the values of the variable together and dividing by the number of recordings. Thus the mean for the daily rainfall example above is

$$\frac{2 + 3 + 6 + 8 + 5}{5} = 4\cdot 8 \text{ or } \frac{1}{N} \sum_{i=1}^{5} Ri$$

where $N = $ the number of recordings.

viii *Notation*

Fourthly, it is useful to have some measure of the dispersion of the results around the mean value. The most commonly-used measure is the standard deviation, which is described notationally as σ. It is given by the formula

$$\sigma = \sqrt{\frac{\Sigma(R-\mu)^2}{N}}$$

where R = the value of the variable and μ = the mean of the variables. In the daily rainfall example, the standard deviation is calculated as follows:

R	μ	$R-\mu$	$(R-\mu)^2$
2	4.8	−2.8	7.84
3	4.8	−1.8	3.24
6	4.8	1.2	1.44
8	4.8	3.2	10.24
5	4.8	0.2	0.04
			22.80

$$\sigma = \sqrt{\frac{22.80}{5}}$$
$$= \sqrt{4.56}$$
$$= 2.14$$

Acknowledgements

The publisher thanks the copyright holders for permission to reproduce figures from the following sources:

Department of the Air Force, AFSC, Ohio, for Figure 12.12 from *Technological Forecasting* by R. C. Lenz, Jr.; Syndication International Ltd, London, for Figure 12.15 from *Science Journal*, October 1967; Dr Marvin J. Cetron and Gordon & Breach Science Publishers Ltd for Figures 12.2 and 12.3 from *Technological Forecasting*; McGraw-Hill Book Company, NY for Figure 12.5 from R. U. Ayres' *Technological Forecasting and Long-Range Planning*; Granada Publishing Ltd and Crosby Lockwood Staples for Figure 12.1 from Ashton and Simister's *The Role of Forecasting in Corporate Planning*; Holden-Day Inc. for Figure 5.1, adapted from a figure in Box and Jenkins' *Time Series Analysis, Forecasting and Control*; Her Majesty's Stationery Office for Tables 10.6 and 10.7 from *Economic Trends*, No 258, April 1975; Operational Research Society and Mr M. Batty for Table 6.1 from *Operational Research Quarterly*, 20, 1969 and the Institute of Electrical and Electronics Engineers, Inc. for Figure 12.16 from *IEEE Transactions on Engineering Management*, March 1965.

Contents

Preface

Notation

1 The role of forecasting in management   1
Forecasting, planning and decision-making. Uncontrolled environment. Building a model of corporate activities. Interrelationships. Uncertainty. Forecasting in practice. Summary. Suggested reading.

2 Forecasting situations and the characteristics of forecasting techniques   17
Requirements of a forecast. Forecasting techniques. The attributes of forecasting techniques. Time series patterns. Measurements of forecasting error. Summary. Suggested reading.

3 Time series forecasting: smoothing techniques   38
The first step—data examination. Moving averages. Weighted moving averages. Exponential smoothing. Smoothing techniques for trend analysis. Ratio trend. Deseasonalizing methods. Mathematical trend curve fitting. Summary. References.

4 Time series forecasting by classical decomposition analysis   61
Traditional factors in a time series. Classical decomposition models. Uses of decomposition analysis. The technique of decomposing a time series. Seasonal index. The trend factor. The cyclical factor. Making a forecast using classical decomposition analysis. Review of the methodology. Classical decomposition analysis in use. Summary. Suggested reading.

5 Adaptive methods of time series forecasting — 82
Adaptive filtering. Summary. References.

6 The monitoring of time series forecasting methods — 92
Summary. References.

7 An introduction to simple regression and correlation — 98
Causal models. Advantages of causal models in forecasting. Simple linear regression and correlation. Least squares method. Accuracy of the regression model. Simple correlation. Summary. Suggested reading.

8 Forecasting by multiple regression causal models — 117
Requirements involved in using least squares regression. An example of multiple regression. Simultaneous equations. Curvilinear analysis. Form of the variables. Additional techniques in regression. Procedures in building regression models for forecasting. Summary. Suggested reading.

9 The building of causal models — 141
Macroeconomic forecasting. Forecasting of demand. Other factors. Consumer durables. The assessment of market share. Relative price. Product quality. Distribution policies and after-sales services. Advertising. Market share estimated by salesmen. Summary. References.

10 Other techniques: input-output analysis, leading indicators — 160
Forecasting with input-output tables. A simplified example of input-output tables. Assumptions involved with forecasting from input-output tables. Forecasting with existing input-output tables. Input-output tables for 1971. Problems in utilizing input-output tables in forecasting. Summary of forecasting using input-output analysis. Leading indicators. References.

11 Subjective probabilistic forecasting and decision analysis techniques — 174
Probabilistic forecasts and other forecasting techniques. Objective and subjective probabilities. The basic interpretation of probabilistic forecasts. Expected values. The use of utility or preference theory in probabilistic forecasting. Probability trees.

Decision trees. Steps in building decision and probability trees. Risk analysis. Decision analysis. Deriving subjective probabilistic information. Summary. References.

12 Qualitative methods of forecasting 204
Explorative and normative models. The types of results given by qualitative forecasting. The adoption of qualitative forecasting methods. Extrapolation of trends. Time independent technological comparisons. Morphological analysis. Delphi method. Scenario. Normative relevance trees. Qualitative techniques in technological forecasting. Summary. References and suggested reading.

13 Data sources for forecasting 226
Data classification. Checking data sources. Data banks. Market surveys. Examples of types of market survey. The use of outside agencies in carrying out surveys. Sources of published data. References.

14 The selection and implementation of forecasting techniques 245
Requirements for implementing a forecasting technique. Examination of data. Qualitative forecasting. Using a number of forecasting techniques. Cost-benefits of forecasting. Summary of the guidelines to selecting an appropriate technique. Data output. Implementation of a forecasting system. Forecasting in practice and future developments. References.

Index 261

1

The role of forecasting in management

During recent years there has been considerable growth in the study of the theory of the firm. Underlying the various different theories, however, is the generally acknowledged structure of a company having one or several objectives towards which it strives by laying down and implementing plans. Planning involves making decisions which will have their effects and outcomes in the future and so an estimate of this future is required. This assessment of the future is termed forecasting and is a vital ingredient in any planning process.

In fact some authors make a distinction between the terms forecasting and prediction. For example, Brown in his book *Smoothing, Forecasting and Prediction of Discrete Time Series,* Prentice-Hall, 1963, defined forecasting as an objective computation, i.e. quantitative, while prediction was seen as a subjective estimate requiring managerial judgement and qualitative 'forecasts'. No such distinction is made in this book, with forecasting being the term generally used.

Forecasts have always been made in business planning, but until recently these were all too often purely subjective managerial or proprietorial 'hunches' which often amounted to little more than guesses. Management now, however, has a wide variety of techniques which can be incorporated into a formal forecasting system. This rapid expansion in the application of forecasting is the result of a number of factors:

1. The growth in forecasting techniques which are available for different problem situations and the growth in expert personnel to handle them.
2. The increasing size and complexity of business operations in which no one man can now adequately deal with decision-making. The resulting formalized management structures and planning arrangements have in turn encouraged the adoption of sophisticated forecasting methods. This contrasts with many small businesses run by a sole proprietor and marketing only a few simple products. In such cases it is possible for the

proprietor to have a fairly thorough understanding of the factors governing the business and so be able to make reasonable intuitive forecasts. This kind of enterprise, however, has declined enormously in its relative importance, giving way to larger organizations.

3. Management has become more aware of the benefits of forecasting. These include not only the accuracy of the single point forecast (i.e. a forecast consisting of a single figure, say £2453) but also

(a) The forecasting of a range of possible outcomes and their likelihood of occurrence. This acknowledges that most future business variables are uncertain and that they could take any of a number of quite likely values.

(b) The sensitivity testing of the results. Sensitivity testing measures the changes in the forecast for given changes in the assumptions that have gone into the forecast. For example we may expect growth in sales to be $X\%$ if the population continues its present growth rate; if we think that this growth rate could in fact increase to $Y\%$ then we can measure the impact of this on sales (hence testing the sensitivity of sales to changes in the population growth rate).

As an example a typical intuitive forecast of sales during a certain period by a manager may be 'a large increase is expected'. The application of statistical forecasting methods could, however, give a report along the following (simplified) lines: 'Expected sales in period X = 120% of this period's sales, with a 5% chance the sales could be up by 40% and a 5% chance sales could show no increase at all. This forecast assumes the following economic, fiscal and market circumstances.... If the conditions prevailing are changed by the following amounts ... the sales forecasts become....' The second type of report clearly gives much better information for decision making purposes: it gives figures on which to work, a range of outcomes and expresses the sensitivities of the results to changed environmental circumstances.

4. The resources that must be devoted to research and development and to capital expenditure have risen enormously in recent years, thus any mistakes in evaluating the eventual success of product development or the level of product sales can lead to significant losses and business failure. Additionally the lead time in research and development and in building large plants (i.e. the time taken for a product to get on to the market or for the plant to start producing) has been increasing in many industries, thus it takes longer for the success or failure to materialize, as well as involving greater sunk costs. This growth in the time and cost involved has considerably increased the riskiness of business, so the adoption of formal forecasting processes has become more important, in the attempts to reduce the uncertainty to bearable levels and aid decision-making throughout the company's life.

Forecasting, planning and decision-making

A company has one or more objectives, which are its *raison d'être*. It also has, at any one moment in time, various resources which can be utilized in achieving these objectives. The prevailing theories of the firm hold the company's objective to be the earning of a satisfactory return to the shareholders or the maximization of returns to the shareholders, subject to the constraints of employee satisfaction, government legislation, etc. While it is not the purpose of the book to discuss the philosophy of business enterprises, it is useful as a background structure to adopt the tenet that, subject to social and human constraints, the maximization of efficiency (expressed by profits in the competitive market place) is a major objective of the firm. The various resources that a business has include assets such as plant and machinery, cash, stocks, debtors, a skilled labour and managerial work force, and access to various markets including the capital market. These resources are used by the management to achieve the company's objectives; this includes redeploying assets in different areas, the transfer and sale of assets and the acquiring of additional funds with which to expand. This management of resources involves planning and decision-taking in order to achieve the company's objectives. Since the assets are capable of being used in various ways and at various efficiencies, management is faced with alternatives from which it is necessary to chose. Clearly the basis of

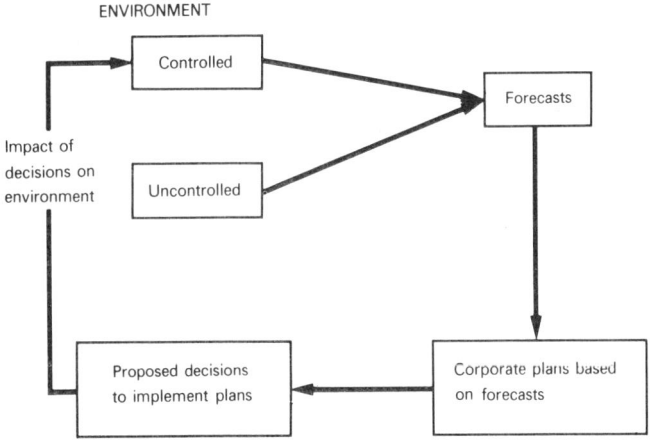

Figure 1.1 The forecasting loop

these plans, choices and decisions must be the expectations of future returns.

While forecasts of the future are a prerequisite to planning, it must be recognized that in many cases the implementation of the plans requires the forecasts to be revised. Forecasts are made with a specific set of assumptions in mind; the management may however make decisions based on these forecasts which alter the situation, so the forecasts need to be revised for the new circumstances (assumptions). This acts as a loop and is illustrated in Figure 1.1. The controlled environment relates to conditions over which the company has some influence such as advertising, promotional expenditure and after sales service. Thus forecasts are based on the controllable and the uncontrollable (i.e. consumer tastes, competitors' actions, government actions) environment. From these forecasts corporate plans are constructed and decisions made with the aim of achieving them. The forecasts must be revised if the proposed decisions have some significant impact on the business environment, and this in turn may cause plans to be altered, so the process becomes an iterative one. The main point to remember is that the impact of decisions must be measured on the company as a whole and not solely on an isolated division or functional area.

Example. The estimate of a company's forecasting department was that, with the existing economic, fiscal and controllable environment, cash proceeds from sales during the subsequent three month period would be £12·5 million. On seeing these figures the management became very concerned, as there was a short-term cash crisis looming: tax and dividend payments were due and the company accountant's figures based on the forecast sales revealed that the overdraft limit would be exceeded. The marketing manager claimed that an immediate increase in advertising expenditure and an immediate increase in credit terms would lead to a large increase in turnover of the company's major product. The forecasting department's assistance was again required to estimate the impact of these changed (controlled environment) circumstances on their estimates of profits and cash flows. Using these revisions the management looked at the advertising programme and credit facilities again and chose an appropriate course of action.

The above gives a very simplified example of the feedback loop involving forecasting and decision-making and it should be apparent that these situations are common in business. In well developed forecasting and planning departments a number of forecasts are often prepared on each occasion, each forecast relating to different assumptions regarding controllable and uncontrollable factors. This helps management to gain a quick, approximate idea of the sensitivity of the forecast as well as suggesting some of the possible decision alternatives.

Uncontrolled environment

The individual firm works within an industrial, national economic and international economic setting and these form broad parameters to its growth and prosperity. The firm has only a minor influence on these factors, so it is very much a case of the forecaster making his forecasts of the firm fit in with these parameters. Thus in preparing a forecast of, say, a firm's growth in the next ten years, the forecaster has to acknowledge and make forecasts of the general growth expected by the particular industry or the particular market and the growth in the national economy as a whole (which in turn will be partly influenced by the world economy). This especially applies to larger, mature firms which only have a limited scope to increase market share in the short term and are very reliant on a growth in the total market (which in turn greatly relies on the growth of the national economy). Smaller firms can of course buck the industrial and economic recessions, although this requires a lot of well-managed effort. The forecasting of industrial and economic trends is also vital for firms whose sales follow a cyclical pattern: wrong decisions at the turn of a cycle can and do have very serious consequences for such firms.

The forecaster therefore has to make an assessment of the total market for the firm's products and an assessment of the national economy. This can be done explicitly or semi-implicitly, with the forecaster making subjective assessments based on published information. A brief reference to macro-forecasting is made in Chapter 9 and, as will be seen, this in practice mainly utilizes existing published forecasts and statistics in the forecasting process. Major consideration must also be paid to the actions of the government, since these have a strong influence over business conditions and the economy (i.e. credit restrictions, public expenditure, investment incentives, indirect taxation, etc.). Again Chapter 9 gives a few guidelines in helping forecast government policies. In addition, other largely uncontrollable variables need to be assessed; examples include competitors' plans and strategies and changes in consumer tastes. The degree of forecasting that can be done varies enormously: in many cases the task can be so difficult that the forecaster must revert to using a purely subjective estimate. However, despite the difficulties of forecasting the uncontrollable environment, especially that relating to the actions of the government and their economic impact, it is necessary if useful forecasts of the firm are to be obtained. The forecaster must ensure that the forecasts of the firm are at least consistent with the macro-forecasts (for example, that the firm is not showing substantial growth during a year of economic recession unless sound reasons can be made out for such an expected performance).

Building a model of corporate activities

In implementing any forecasting system, it is necessary to build at least a rudimentary model of the business operations. A corporate model is one type, showing the various operations and interdependencies of a business system. The importance of the model is twofold. Firstly, it highlights the important factors in the achieving of the firm's objectives, so that the forecasting techniques can be applied directly to the significant items without expending the considerable costs that these techniques incur on trivial factors. It should be noted that forecasting techniques are generally only feasible when applied to disaggregated data; i.e. company profits and cash flows themselves are impossible to predict with any degree of accuracy. However, sales revenues and individual cost expenses are capable of being forecast and estimated future profits and cash flows can be derived from them. Secondly, a forecast of a specific item may lead to a decision taken by management which, apart from its obvious result, may in fact alter the outcome for another area of the business. If this is so then we need to evaluate the interdependency. The corporate model will help us determine the existence and the value of the association.

Example. A motor manufacturer forecast the sales of its various ranges over the following year. On receiving the forecasts, management was of the opinion that the sales of the recently introduced economy sized model could be increased substantially by a heavy advertising and promotional campaign. This proposed decision was investigated by the planning department and indeed increased sales could be expected. However, what was not considered was the impact this decision would have on the sales of the company's other products. The increased demand for the economy sized car in fact syphoned off some of the demand for the other types of cars sold by the firm and the forecasts for these makes were consequently too optimistic. The overall effect on the company's profits was that they were below what they would have been without having taken the decision to substantially increase the promotion of the new car.

By building a corporate model the planning department can more easily identify the inter-relationships between the various activities and the functional areas of the business. This helps prevent any decision being made without regard to the impact on the overall objectives of the firm.

The construction of the model will involve breaking the company down by its various activities (many companies have multi-product sales which are substantially different from one another) and by its cost structure. This breakdown will far exceed the information given in the annual accounts, but the data should be readily available within the company and the time involved in building the model should not be very great. In addition, the forecaster will call upon the knowledge and judgement of various managers in piecing together the corporate model and quantifying the relationships embodied in it. As will be obvious from the prior example, the forecaster should strive to quantify the possibilities of substitution and the complementary relationships of the products.

Figure 1.2 gives an example of a breakdown of a simple organization. The company's sales have been broken down between the three products it produces. Product C goes to two quite distinct markets and this has been shown in the figure. The various major classifications of costs relating to each subdivision of sales are then shown; fixed costs are assigned to sales on some accounting basis. By taking the difference between the annual sales proceeds (e.g. $S_A \times P_A$ for product A) and the total annual costs (e.g. $Z_A + Y_A + X_A$ for product A), we can obtain the profit earned from selling

Products	A	B	C	
			Automobile industry	Marine engineering
Customers	A	B	C_1	C_2
Sales volume (last year)	S_A	S_B	S_{C1}	S_{C2}
Sales price per unit	P_A	P_B	P_{C1}	P_{C2}
Major costs specified by type				
These can be sub-classified	Z_A	Z_B	Z_{C1}	Z_{C2}
into fixed, semi-variable	Y_A	Y_B	Y_{C1}	Y_{C2}
and variable expenses	X_A	X_B	X_{C1}	X_{C2}
Profits	W_A	W_B	W_{C1}	W_{C2}

Figure 1.2 A simple company breakdown

the product. The importance of the breakdown is that it shows all the important individual factors in a business. By forecasting the future outturn of these factors management can forecast future profits and can plan accordingly; for example, if it appears from the forecasts that plant capacity will be acting as the constraint on growth, then actions can be taken now. It must be stressed that Figure 1.2 is an extremely simplified example. In practice, the forecaster would probably have to contend with instances such as:

1. Interdependencies. The elasticities of sales between the various products should be quantified, as illustrated in the example on page 6.

2. The difficulties arising when products utilize common plant and machinery. In such cases the forecaster needs to evaluate the workload placed on these assets in case they become overburdened and act as a constraint on the growth of the business.

3. The supply of labour. This is a more qualitative factor but one which needs to be carefully considered in the corporate model.

4. The balance sheet items such as fixed and current assets and their financing. These should be evaluated and included in the overall corporate model. The uses and efficiency of the assets should be considered along

with the possibilities of raising additional capital monies to finance expansion.

All these and other factors should be included in the corporate model and interdependencies between any of them should be identified and measured. This will allow us to measure the complete impact on the firm of any decision taken or of any changes in the uncontrollable environment. It should be recognized that no corporate model can give a completely accurate representation of the firm's operations and, further, many of the inputs into the model may be of a subjective form (i.e. no quantification is possible or feasible, so management makes a subjective assessment). However, the building of a model, even with its various subjective and incomplete inputs, will almost certainly improve management's grasp of the various facets of the business, hopefully leading to superior forecasts and better decision-making.

Inter-relationships

It is very important that the inter-relationships in a business system be both identified and measured. Without this forecasting and decision-making can go considerably astray and lead, in many cases, to quite serious financial problems. The extent of the impact of a decision on the other operations in a firm can be surprising and the forecaster needs at least to acknowledge this impact. If the decision has a small impact on a lot of variables, then the forecaster may not try to measure this (because of the difficulty and expense involved) but just acknowledge its extent.

An example of the impact that a decision to increase advertising of a certain product will have on the various functional areas of management is shown in Figure 1.3. The figure gives plausible decisions that the individual managers may have to make to accomodate the impact of the increased sales. The corporate planning subdivision examines the impact of the proposed advertising campaign on the company's overall objectives.

The above sections have emphasized that decisions cannot be taken in a vacuum and that their impact on the business as a whole needs to be assessed. Hence the need for some sort of corporate model building where inter-relationships are recognized and measured. The actual methods of corporate model building can range from simple subjective types to sophisticated computer based models: see the reference to Grinyer and Wooller for a discussion of formal model building in larger companies in the UK.

Uncertainty

If the future was known with complete certainty then most of an organization's problems would disappear; the allocation of resources to

The role of forecasting in management

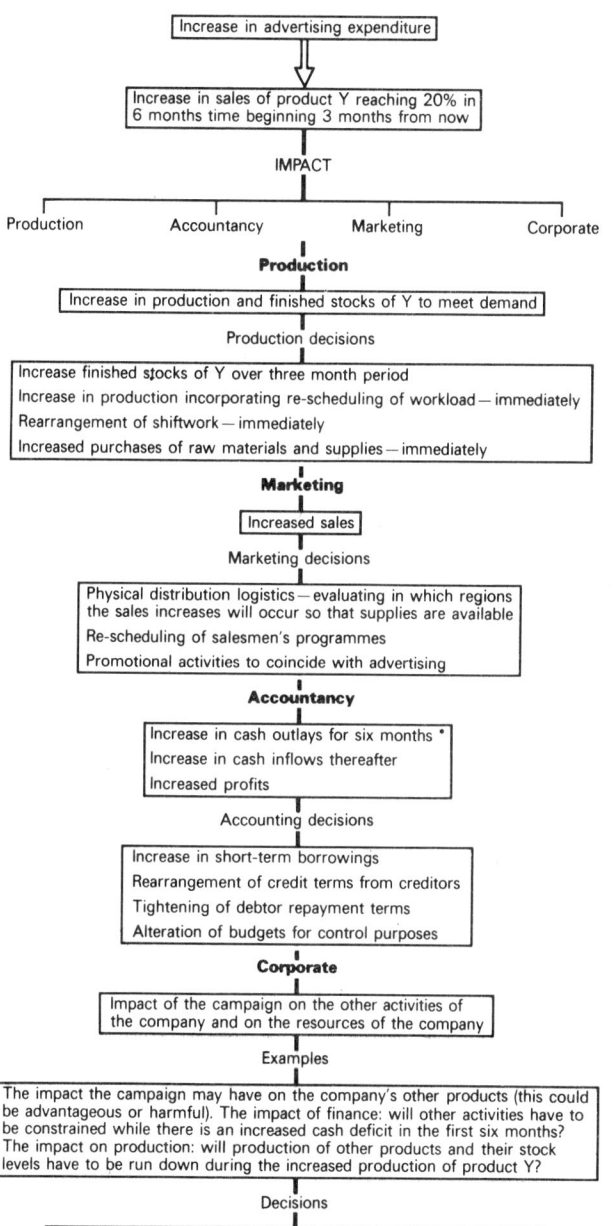

Figure 1.3

projects would be optimized and little or no control would be required in the running of them. However the future course of events is uncertain and the evaluation of this uncertainty is a major aspect of management's responsibilities. The purpose of forecasting is to reduce the uncertainty and give as much information as possible to the decision-taker. Obviously management must have some regard to the cost-benefits of forecasting, especially as the more sophisticated techniques involve substantial expenditure. (Chapter 14 deals with the evaluation of the cost-benefits of forecasting.)

As described earlier, the soaring capital costs and long lead time between initiating research and development and the marketing of a product have increased the riskiness of business operations. Without any methods to reduce the uncertainty this might lead to:

1. Increased bankruptcies.
2. A more cautious attitude by management, leading to a slowing down in the rate of progress.
3. The necessity for far higher profits on existing products to compensate for losses on new ventures.

All of these have the harmful socio-economic effects of increasing unemployment, lessening the rate of progress, increasing the cost of living and reducing the competitive nature of the market place. However, improvements in the techniques and the applications of forecasting have gone a long way in reducing the uncertainty of future events. The improvements consist of better quantitative methods, superior qualitative methodologies and a better understanding of business situations and the application of forecasting systems. Forecasting can give more accurate central values, supply ranges of outcomes and their probabilities of occurrence and specify the sensitivity of the results. This sort of information greatly assists management, who can marry their risk-bearing attitude to the estimated returns.

The forecasts will, in the vast majority of cases, be inaccurate to some degree and it is important for these errors to be monitored. The measuring of forecasting errors itself can provide valuable signals of turning points in business and economic statistics. Additionally the errors, although unpredictable, often follow standard statistical distributions which allow certain assumptions to be made and which can be incorporated in the forecasting technique (see for example Chapters 7 and 8).

Forecasting in practice

Although it is only during recent years that formal forecasting systems and identifiable planning departments have become popular, forecasting of some sort has always been done. The investment of resources, time and human energy for future returns has always involved at least some intuitive forecasting. Gradually, however, more techniques become available for forecasting the future and these have been adopted by companies in their planning departments. In addition, computer packages have been designed and management consultancies specializing in forecasting and planning have appeared providing services which even the smaller firm can afford.

As most firms are divided into functional areas, it is worth briefly examining some of their forecasting requirements. The various functional areas of an organization are typically responsible for a large amount of decision-taking, so it is they who directly need the information for decision analysis. The forecasting and planning departments usually work with the various decision-takers in designing a forecasting method for each particular situation. Figure 1.4 gives a brief example of the types of questions the functional managers ask and with which forecasting techniques and methods can help.

The marketing department needs forecasts of various kinds to help it determine customer requirements and plan distribution, promotional and advertising programmes. For example, forecasts of future sales of a particular product by geographical location over the subsequent three month period will be required by the marketing manager in preparing distribution schedules and planning the advertising campaign. The marketing department is the functional area which probably works closest with the forecasting team as regards sales estimates, especially those relating to existing products.

The production department requires forecasts of sales classified by product type, colour scheme, quality, etc. so that it can plan its workload in the most efficient manner and also establish its stockholding policies. There are various ways in which a production process can be made to operate and in order to determine what machines to run, what maintenance to do and when, what shiftwork to do, etc., the managers need information on sales volume. From the production forecasts the manager can then ascertain the input requirements and here again forecasts are required. For example, estimates of the costs and availability of raw materials are necessary, particularly where there are alternative materials or components that can be used in the process.

The personnel department has responsibilities for labour recruitment and training. Both of these require forecasts for various periods ahead so that the correct decisions can be made now. For example, the building of a plant at a new location is likely to lead to a big demand for skilled labour; the personnel department thus requires forecasts of the likely supply of labour in that location, the availability of labour who might be willing to

Marketing

What are the colour, quality, packaging and design requirements of our customers in the immediate future?

Which types of product are required in each location?

What sort of retail stocks do our customers expect us to maintain?

Where should our advertising and promotional campaign be concentrated and what should the total effort be?

At what stage is our product in its life cycle and what is the expected duration of each stage?

What is the likely market demand for each of our products in each of the next five years? What is our likely market share and what competitor innovation is likely?

How and in what areas should we concentrate the promotion of our new product?

What are our customer requirements likely to be five years from now and what socio-economic and technological changes are possible?

Personnel

What are our labour requirements in the immediate future, in which job specifications and at what level of experience?

What is the supply of labour position in the particular geographical and skill areas we are interested in and what is the likely demand from competitors?

What are the likely movements in wage rates, holiday entitlements and employee attitudes to physical conditions in which they have to work?

What is the likely demand for training facilities for employees and what types of skills will be required in future years?

Production

How much finished stocks should we keep of each type of product?

At what levels should we keep our raw material and bought-in component stocks?

What are the production requirements for each of the next twelve months?

What are the longer-term production demands likely to be?

To what extent are there likely to be any constraints on capital equipment and in raw materials and supplies?

Can labour requirements be met and what is labour productivity likely to be?

What are the likely costs of production and what are the costs of alternative processes, raw materials and bought-in supplies?

Finance

What are the likely cash requirements over the short and intermediate terms and what are the likely sources of raising finance?

What are the likely credit terms demanded by creditors and debtors?

What are the likely movements in interest rates?

Are any radical changes in the methods of company financing expected and how will these affect the firm in its present structure and in its expected future structure?

What changes are expected in direct and indirect taxation, credit restrictions and price controls?

What are the long-term capital requirements of the business?

Corporate Planning

What are the likely risks and returns from the company's activities as they are now structured over the next 5, 10, 20, 50 years?

What are the expected longer-term returns from other operations to which the company can easily adapt itself?

What are the expected longer-term returns from completely new operations and what are the constraints to moving into these fields?

What longer-term strategies are being adopted by other companies?

What radical governmental, social and economic changes are likely to take place and what is the impact on the business expected to be?

Technological Forecasting

What major technological changes are expected to occur in both the company's business and other possible activities it could enter?

What effect is the impact of technological changes in other areas of activity likely to have on the company and its activities?

What are the constraints to successful research and development of technological breakthroughs?

What are the costs and the likely time scales of technological change and research and development?

Figure 1.4

transfer, the likely wage rates and many other factors. Skilled labour may take up to five years to train, so forecasts of the likely demand for these people, both for the industry as a whole and for the company, are needed. Other forecasts that are required include wage rates, trends in working hours and conditions, absenteeism, lateness, and retirement patterns and factors relating to any pension obligations of the firm.

The accountancy function of the business requires the forecasts that have been prepared for the other departments in order to forecast future profits and cash flows. It is usually the responsibility of the accountant to acquire the necessary funds to enable the company to undertake profitable projects, so forecasts of the cash requirements are needed. The accountant then has to choose the correct balance of funds with a view to future liquidity requirements and retaining the confidence of creditors. This involves decisions concerning long- and short-term funding, financial gearing ratios, raising loan and equity capital, stock market sentiment and leasing versus buying. Specific forecasts that the accountant requires include those relating to the availability of long- and short-term borrowing, the movement of interest rates, taxation, hire purchase and credit restrictions, price controls and foreign exchange conditions.

The compilation of *pro forma* financial statements allows the top management to examine the impact that the various possible decisions will have on the organization and the optimum set of decisions can then be taken. The accountant is very often the executive in charge of budgeting and variance analysis and must prepare a set of budgets for various revenues and costs over say a period of a year, compare the actual results with the budgets and attempt to obtain explanations for the differences. These budgets are based on short term forecasts which will have been prepared by the various responsible officials along with the planning department and the accountant.

Many companies have set up separate planning departments which deal with the longer-term aspects of the business and these have a very obvious need for accurate forecasts. Indeed the forecasting personnel of many companies are actually situated within the planning department. Typical responsibilities of a planning department include technological forecasting, research and development forecasting, and corporate planning, where even the nature of the business activities the company is engaged in are assessed to see if more profitable opportunities exist. Examples of technological forecasting might include, for example aircraft companies estimating what the future forms of public transport will be. This could very well be rocket propelled transport and some broad ideas of when this might be practical, the likely development costs and the technological problems involved would need to be estimated. Technological forecasts are long term and a whole host of mainly qualitative techniques have been specially developed for them. The forecasts of technological change provide data for research and development decisions and these items are often so interwoven that they are looked after by the same personnel. Research and development expenditure is undertaken when management considers that the potential returns outweigh the uncertainty involved. As the time between the initiation of the research and development and the marketing of the resultant product is often as much as ten years, it is obvious that significant losses can be incurred if the forecasts are substantially wrong. Forecasts are required all the way through the research and development process to monitor such things as competitor reaction or changes in consumer taste so that adaptations can be made to the project. The continuous appraisal may also, of course, discover that the project is no longer commercially viable, so the losses can be cut straightaway at that point.

Corporate or strategic planning is concerned with the long-term objectives of the company and especially the industries and markets within which it operates. The planning is conducted by assessing the long-term potentials of different activities and examining whether the company has, or could acquire, the resources to operate within these activities. Typical forecasts that are required include long-term industry sales prospects, market share forecasts which in themselves require a forecast of competition, and possible technological or production constraints. For example, some petroleum companies are diversifying into other energy resources as there are growing fears of the world's oil reserves running out by the end of the century. Although this seems a distant prospect, a period of as much as twenty-five years may be needed in order to achieve the requisite technological breakthrough (one major oil company is looking at solar energy sources, while a number of others are looking at the large-scale utilization of nuclear energy) or to increase the capacity of other known fuels (yet another oil company has decided to diversify into coal as an energy source. However, the vast amounts of coal that will be needed to make up for the current production of oil will require a lot of time for the finding of the necessary deposits, the building of extraction plants and the sinking of mines.) Thus corporate planning requires forecasts of the major parameters to growth; it is not concerned with short-term operational management. Clearly forecasting has an important role to play in corporate planning as the strategies based thereon commit the firm heavily to certain technologies and formats which, if they prove commercially unviable, may lead to bankruptcy.

Apart from basic forecasts required for the various functional divisions of the firm, forecasts are also required as inputs into many of the recently adopted 'sophisticated' management techniques. For example, linear programming, which is used to optimize the use of scarce resources, requires forecasts of sales demand, prices and production constraints. Again capital expenditure appraisal techniques require forecasts of future cash flows, indeed it is these to which the greatest effort is normally given. The actual appraisal methods can be conducted very quickly on a computer. Thus forecasting forms an integral part of most operational research and other decision-making techniques that are available to management.

Clearly many of the forecasts made for the specific functional areas overlap to a considerable extent; for example, the estimates of sales have ramifications throughout most of a firm's operations. As mentioned earlier in the chapter, it is important both to build a model of the business which shows the interaction of the separate decision-making centres and to use consistent assumptions throughout the forecasting process. For this reason the forecasting personnel are often situated in a planning department and not in, say, the marketing or accounting functions; this often allows a greater overall view of the business to be gained.

Summary

The purpose of this chapter has been to introduce forecasting and explain its role in business. The central theme is that forecasting provides information on which plans can be made and decisions taken. It is not an isolated function existing independently of the rest of the business. This theme will be extended in the next chapter to describe how forecasting techniques can be applied to business situations so as to aid the decision-taker. A brief description has been given of the value of future forecasts to the various functional departments and importance has also been laid on adopting an overall corporate approach. Forecasting is an integral part of the planning process and the monitoring of performance is a vital feedback in management control.

Suggested reading

The references below relate to general readings on planning and the role of forecasting in the firm.

1. Ansoff, H. I., *Corporate Strategy*, Pelican, 1968.
2. Argenti, J., *Corporate Planning, A Practical Guide*, Allen and Unwin, 1968.
3. Grinyer, P., and Wooller, J., *Corporate Models Today: A New Tool for Financial Management*, Institute of Chartered Accountants in England and Wales, 1975.
4. Hussey, D. E., *Introducing Corporate Planning*, Pergamon, 1971.
5. National Industrial Conference Board, *Forecasting Sales*, Business Policy Study No. 106, 1964.
6. Robinson, C., 'Some Principles of Forecasting in Business', *Journal of Industrial Economics,* **1,** 14, 1965.
7. Robinson, C., 'The forecasting system and techniques', *Management Decision,* Winter, 1968.
8. Steiner, G. A., *Top Management Planning*, Macmillan, 1969.
9. Zinkin, M. A., 'A child's guide to planning', *Applied Economics,* May, 1969.

2

Forecasting situations and the characteristics of forecasting techniques

The purpose of this chapter is to identify the major common elements that are desired in a forecast and to establish the major characteristics of forecasting techniques. This type of analysis is a necessary prerequisite to the selection of an appropriate forecasting technique for a particular problem. It also helps focus management's attention on the importance of forecasts and the building of an adequate management information system.

Requirements of a forecast

The major aim of forecasting is to aid the decision-making processes of management, thus the elements of a forecast which contribute to this end need to be highlighted. At first sight it might appear that accuracy is the major requirement, but this is not necessarily so and indeed is very rarely so in an unqualified sense. A number of considerations figure large in forecasting requirements and these can be classified into the following characteristics: accuracy; time horizon; speed and regularity; detail; relevance.

Accuracy

For some decisions a high degree of accuracy in forecasting is vital. For example, a project which involves very heavy fixed costs and whose profits are earned on its, say, top two per cent of sales would be very vulnerable to a shortfall in those sales. Figure 2.1 shows a breakeven chart for a product which has heavy fixed costs. If the forecast sales were £105 000 then the company would be making a reasonable return on the capital investment of £10 000. If, however, the sales were only £95 000, then the company would be incurring significant losses. This discrepancy of 9·5% of the actual sales from the forecast has led to a serious decision error which could easily bankrupt many firms.

For other decisions a high degree of accuracy is not so vital and errors of $\pm 10\%$ could be easily manageable (indeed for long-term forecasts $\pm 10\%$

errors may represent an exceptionally high degree of accuracy and in many cases much bigger discrepancies would have to be accepted). Thus for some decisions a lower level of accuracy has to be accepted, while for others a lower level of accuracy may be traded off against the advantage of another attribute (for example, speed of forecast or the cheapness of the technique).

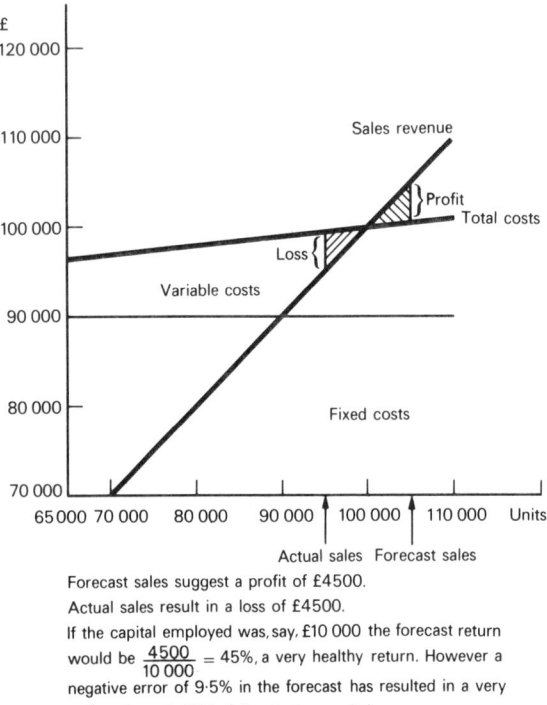

Forecast sales suggest a profit of £4500.
Actual sales result in a loss of £4500.
If the capital employed was, say, £10 000 the forecast return would be $\frac{4500}{10\,000} = 45\%$, a very healthy return. However a negative error of 9·5% in the forecast has resulted in a very serious loss of 45% of the starting capital.

Figure 2.1 A breakeven chart for a product with heavy fixed costs

Time horizon

This is the time span over which the decision will have an impact; it has a good deal of significance in the preparation of the data, the selection of appropriate techniques and the analysis of the forecast result. Divisions such as immediate term, short term, medium term and long term can be made, however to attach any precise meanings or dates to these will not be particularly fruitful. Immediate- and short-term forecasts are often made for control purposes where only operating or tactical decisions can be made, i.e. allocation of raw materials to different products and production processes. Short- and medium-term forecasts cover areas where major policy variables can be embarked upon; they typically take the date range from around 3 months to two or three years. Longer-term situations range from, say, two years upwards and allow for major strategic alterations to be made to the company's objectives. The longer the time scale the greater is the opportunity to rearrange and collect data so that the selection of the appropriate forecasting technique is not constrained by data requirements. In

Time period	Approximate duration	Types of decisions	Examples
Immediate	0–3 months	Operating decisions, budgetry control	Physical distribution management, i.e. the allocation of stocks to specific retail outlets
Short-term	1–6 months	Operating decisions, budgetry control, purchasing decisions	Purchasing fashion goods for retailing
Medium-term	3–24 months	Strategic decisions	Leasing plant and equipment; training employees for new processes
Long-term	2–10 years	Strategic decisions including major expansion	Research and development; purchase of properties; acquisitions and mergers
Very long-term	10 years	Strategic decisions including those changing a company's major characteristics	Technological forecasting aiding research and development and strategic planning.

Figure 2.2

analyzing the forecasts of long-term situations, greater emphasis has to be laid on the assumptions involved; the sensitivity of the results must be tested, in recognition of the larger error element that exists. Figure 2.2 gives some brief examples of the type of time horizon that can be attributed to different decision areas.

Speed and regularity
In some situations very quick forecasts are required, in order to control operations or identify turning points at an early stage. For business data which follows a very volatile pattern and where there is a short-term decision situation it is often important for forecasts to be adapted continuously to the latest data so that the decisions can be modified very quickly. This

close monitoring of business data to spot turning points in patterns often requires different data and different techniques to those employed in longer-term situations where major patterns are identified and extrapolated. Thus many situations need regular forecasting outputs which have a quick response rate to major changes in patterns; a common example is in production control, where detailed forecasts of the sales of the various product lines need to be made at, say, weekly intervals. In some cases reduced accuracy in forecasting the absolute value of the variables may be accepted in exchange for an increase in the speed of determining changes in the direction of the variable.

Detail
Different decision or control situations require different levels of detailed forecasts as information inputs. For example, the corporate planning function would only require forecasts of overall sales or sales by the major groupings, while the production department would require a detailed breakdown of the sales forecasts by product types in order to determine future stock requirements and schedule production. The differences in the level of decision detail required usually involve different qualities and amounts of data inputs and may influence the choice of forecasting technique.

Relevance
This requirement relates to the need for the forecast to be appropriate to the decision situation: for example, it can be all too easy for a highly mathematical-orientated forecaster to become immersed in forecasting sophistication at the expense of producing a relevant forecast.

Summary of the requirements of a forecast
The above constitute the major elements to consider in a decision situation and represent a general guideline in deciding between various forecasting techniques. In certain situations other requirements may be demanded of the forecast, but these will have to be dealt with individually. The desired characteristics in many cases are in conflict (for example, speed and accuracy), so management will have to balance these requirements in the light of the techniques available. The next two sections of the chapter introduce the various forecasting techniques and their characteristics.

Forecasting techniques

There are a multitude of forecasting techniques, ranging from quite simple mechanical routines to very sophisticated statistical models and subjective

Forecasting situations and the characteristics of forecasting techniques 21

human judgement methods. These techniques can, however, be grouped into broad categories by their underlying concepts. The major types of techniques are time series analysis, causal models and qualitative forecasting.

Time series models
These consist of establishing patterns and trends in a historical series of data and extrapolating them into the future. The model is based on the assumption that the pattern will recur over time, an assumption which is obviously more likely to be valid in the short term and for relatively stable business data. Thus time series analysis is likely to be most appropriate in short-term forecasting and where there is a relatively stable variable being forecast, such as the sales of an old established product or some efficiency ratio such as labour productivity. Time series techniques are not so applicable in longer-term decision areas, situations where there is little data, or for measuring the impact of a major policy decision by the firm. In the longer term, major socio-economic and customer taste changes can take place which render historical patterns useless; likewise, a major policy decision of the company such as a heavy promotional campaign on an existing product often renders historical patterns useless (where this pattern had never been regularly influenced by a heavy promotional campaign).

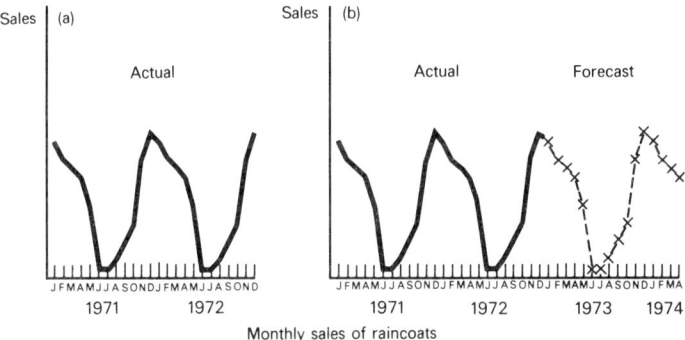

Figure 2.3

Time series models are constructed by taking sequential historical recordings of the factor being forecast and establishing a pattern over time. Examples of typical patterns are shown in Figures 2.4 to 2.9. Having established the pattern, it is then projected into the future in relation to time. Thus the data in Figure 2.3 (a) is extrapolated as in Figure 2.3 (b). The data requirements for time series analysis are often available in the form of traditional accounting information. The accountant generally records and classifies data in a sequential manner for various types of transactions and this information is therefore in a very useful form for time series methods. Chapters 3, 4 and 5 discuss the situations in which the individual techniques are particularly relevant.

Causal models

These are equations which express the relationship of the item being forecast (the dependent variable) to a number of independent variables which have some determining influence on the dependent variable; thus the model expresses mathematically the inherent causal relationships. For example, a causal model for brand sales might include as influencing variables advertising expenditure, prices, the number of salesmen and the discounts available (all as relatives to competitors). This can be described notationally as

Brand sales $= aAD + bRP + cSA + dDI$
where $AD =$ Relative advertising
$RP =$ Relative price
$SA =$ Relative number of salesmen
$DI =$ Relative discounts
$a, b, c, d =$ the weights attached to the factors

By using past data the above relationships can be quantified and the significance of the complete model as a prediction device can be ascertained. The model is derived by determining and testing the likely causal relationships until a statistically satisfactory 'fit' has been found. Many executives may be involved in helping build the model although the statistical testing is left to the expert personnel. It should be recognized that the model is likely to be revised across time as experience is gained and relationships change. The forecasts are made by substituting in values for the independent variables in the equation and then computing the dependent variable. Chapters 7, 8 and 9 discuss the methods and problems in obtaining values for the independent variables.

Causal models allow various statistical measures to be calculated which considerably improve the quality of the information available to decision-takers. These measures include forecasts being given as a range of outcomes with a certain level of probability (likelihood of occurrence). Thus a typical forecast produced from a causal model might be, for example, the prediction of a 95% chance (i.e. likely to happen in 95 out of 100 cases) that sales of product X will be in the range 20 000 to 21 000 units. Chapters 7 and 8 explain these statistical measures in detail and discuss their interpretation. Another useful function of causal models is that changes in the value of the independent variables can easily be incorporated in the model and the impact of these on the dependent variable measured.

Causal models are suitable techniques for longer-term forecasting, for the ascertaining of major turning points and for giving forecasts of the likely impact of a major policy or operational decision that is being contemplated by management. However, they are also the most costly to construct and operate, often requiring considerable human effort in data collection. An additional constraint on these models is that they are quite sophisticated and some managers and decision-takers may require training in interpreting the forecasts; it is hoped that this book will help in this respect.

Qualitative forecasts

These are made when there is little or no relevant quantitative data on which to work. For example, the introduction of a completely new product which has no competitor cannot be forecast by quantitative means as there is no data from which to construct models or derive patterns. Likewise, long-term forecasts, for example future technological developments, are incapable of being forecast by quantitative methods. In these cases of little or no data, human judgement of the various factors which might have an impact is required. These qualitative forecasts can, however, be systematized and various formal techniques have been derived to help remove personal bias and force the forecaster to consider various aspects and ramifications of the forecast. The major methods are summarized in Chapter 12.

Qualitative forecasts are possibly amongst the simplest to understand and they are generally cheap. The main cost is usually that of the time given up by senior management to help make these forecasts. In some cases computer time is required and this, of course, adds to the expense.

In many situations a combination of the broad category of techniques can be used, providing both a check on the forecasts and an improvement in the overall efficiency of the prediction. Similarly, at different stages of a forecasting situation different techniques can be used; for example sales for the short term may be forecast by time series methods, while at the slightly longer-term stage some qualitative adjustment may be made to the time series results. Another example of using several techniques is, say, the deseasonalizing of data by decomposition methods and then using a causal model to extrapolate into the future. To this causal model forecast could then be added seasonal variations as given by the decomposition model.

The attributes of forecasting techniques

The elements of a forecasting technique that must be examined by a manager when evaluating its suitability for a particular decision situation are closely linked to the characteristics of decision-making mentioned previously: accuracy, forecasting periods, speed, detail, data requirements, costs, acceptability and interactiveness. Each of the elements will now be considered in turn although the first four have already been dealt with to some extent.

Accuracy
Some techniques give more accurate results than others for various business situations. However, a high level of accuracy often involves some trade off in other characteristics and management must decide whether this is acceptable, in the light of all the various considerations. For instance causal models have been found to give the greatest accuracy in medium- and longer-term forecasts, but of course they are the most expensive to build. An additional accuracy factor that management will desire is the knowledge of the variability of the outcomes. Statistical causal model forecasting techniques can compute various probabilities of occurrence and in this respect provide greater data than, say, time series methods. Causal models can also include various different values for a variable and thus give a range of forecasts based on different environmental assumptions.

Forecasting periods (Time horizon)
Certain techniques are more appropriate than others for forecasting over various time periods. For example, the extrapolation of past data is probably the best guide for the short term, for medium/long term regression models are often the most appropriate, while for the very long term various qualitative methods should be considered.

Speed
Some techniques are better suited than others to identifying turning points in data at an early stage and thus they are more appropriate for certain business situations. Although the characteristic of speed in recognizing major changes in a pattern is an obvious advantage, this must generally be traded off against a greater inability to isolate the randomness in the data. Thus although some techniques can spot changes at an earlier stage, they also make more errors in determining the major changes; because of their sensitivity to small changes in data the forecasts adapt very quickly, but this also means they adapt to very temporary random-type changes in data

that do not represent major pattern formations. For situations where very quick reactions are required, a forecasting technique also needs to be used very regularly. Again, some techniques are more efficient than others in this regard: obviously other factors such as costs and data requirements also come into play.

Detail
Some techniques are more adaptable than others for forecasting at different levels of detailed information. Examples of some situations were discussed previously in the section on the requirements of a forecast.

Data requirements
An important factor in considering both the feasibility and the cost of a technique is the amount and type of data input required. For short-term decisions there is rarely enough time for the company to significantly rearrange its management information or to collect new data. Thus the technique chosen would be the one which could make best use of the existing information. For medium-term decisions management does have the choice of collecting the necessary data for even the most sophisticated forecasting methods, although this must be weighed against the costs involved.

In causal models estimates and assumptions are often required in placing values on the independent variables. Management must have regard to the reliability of these estimates in evaluating the causal model as an appropriate technique: if it appears that it is difficult to arrive at an accurate value for any of the independent variables, then that model may have to be ignored on the grounds of inadequate data (the forecasts of independent variables being input data).

Other factors in the selection of a forecasting technique are the nature and patterns of historical data. For example, some forecasting methods require longer series of data for them to give accurate results. The section below on time series patterns describes typical patterns in time series business data and several major types become evident; some techniques are more appropriate than others in extrapolating these types of patterns. It is therefore important to examine historical data to identify any strong patterns, since this will help in the selection of the optimum technique.

Costs
A major consideration in examining forecasting techniques is of course the costs involved and these can vary enormously. The major expenses of forecasting systems are the costs of developing models and systems, the costs of data acquisition and storage and the operating costs.

Development costs can be very expensive in the case of causal models, as these involve the time of many skilled personnel in establishing possible relationships, as well as the computer cost of quantifying and testing these relationships. Time series models involve the costs of determining the patterns and trends in data and again these can be fairly substantial, although generally nowhere near as expensive as the causal models. Procedures for initiating the forecasting systems and establishing monitoring facilities can also represent a significant cost.

Data costs can be especially high when the existing accounting and management information systems have to be rearranged or extended to provide the inputs for the various techniques. An additional expense is that of keeping the information required up to date, although a carefully built system should enable these expenses to be kept within reason. Some techniques and decision situations may require long series of data and this may mean the further expense of storage costs.

Operating costs relate very much to the computer time involved. Some decision situations require frequent repetitive forecasts and these incur significant computer usage. In qualitative forecasting significant labour costs may be incurred, since experts are usually involved in the examination of the problem in hand.

In general, causal models cost more than the sophisticated time series models and these in turn are significantly more expensive than the simple time series techniques. This is because of higher development costs and the longer computing time required. Chapter 14 discusses more specifically the benefits and costs of forecasting techniques and gives some guidelines as to the trade off. This trade off is fairly difficult to establish in many cases, for while the costs are ascertainable, the measurement of the benefits can be both complex and subjective.

Acceptability

The acceptability of the work involved in a forecasting technique and the capacity for understanding its output may impose some restrictions on the method chosen for a particular situation. The restrictions of data availability have already been referred to and in a like manner the human element may impose constraints. For example, labour is required for the often very boring and repetitive data collection and this may strain employee satisfaction, especially when large backloads of information are needed. Likewise, consideration must be given to whether management can understand the forecast output: for example, some statistical output may simply be beyond the abilities of the existing management. It is important to have management's confidence in the techniques and methods used, for, as emphasized in Chapter 1, the value of forecasting is as an aid

Forecasting situations and the characteristics of forecasting techniques 27

to planning and control. If management just place the forecast to one side and continue using their own judgement, then the resources utilized in making it will have been wasted and the people who have prepared it will become discouraged. While new concepts and techniques must be brought to the attention of management, care must be taken not to overwhelm them or to force excessive authority upon them by compelling them to use forecasts they do not understand. Thus to some extent the more sophisticated methods may take longer to introduce, because of the greater time needed to train personnel in the use of them.

Interactiveness
This relates to the ease with which the forecaster can interact with the forecasting technique. For example, the forecaster may wish to know the change in the forecast if different economic conditions are assumed, or if a different business decision is taken. Statistical techniques such as causal models provide a good interactive method which is easy to apply. Time series methods, however, cannot directly incorporate interaction with the forecaster. The characteristic of interaction is especially relevant for medium- and longer-term forecasts and thus it becomes an important consideration in selecting a technique.

Summary of the attributes of forecasting techniques
It is the above elements of a technique that the manager will be appraising when deciding between various forecasting methods for the situation at hand. In virtually all cases requiring a quick forecast, the technique will have to fit the data already in existence. In the longer term, however, the manager has the opportunity to reorganize the management information system so that adequate data banks can be built up and thus facilitate more sophisticated forecasting techniques. Chapter 13 deals at some length with data requirements and the design of an information system.

The various elements discussed above will have to be evaluated in some subjective manner by managers in deciding between techniques to adopt. Unfortunately there is no wholly objective way of determining the exact forecasting method for each decision situation. However, the careful application of the analyses presented so far in the chapter should cut down human bias and error. After a discussion of the various techniques in the intervening chapters, Chapter 14 examines again, but in more detail, the selection of forecasting techniques.

Time series patterns
The quantitative forecasting methods met later in the book are all based upon the premise that there is some pattern in the historical time series of

28 *Forecasting methods in business and management*

the variable under consideration or that the variable has some relationship with another factor(s). These patterns or relationships are then extrapolated according to the specific rules of the technique and forecasts of the future are thus obtained. A major element in selecting a forecasting

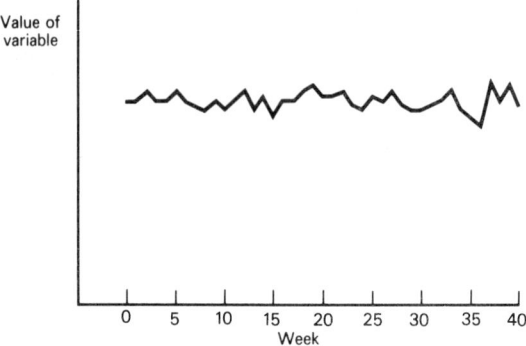

Figure 2.4 A horizontal pattern

technique is therefore the underlying time series nature of the variable being forecast. Qualitative and subjective forecasts also rely to some extent on past data, since the human judgement which goes into their preparation is almost certainly influenced by past patterns, trends and relationships. Although there are many types of patterns which occur in time series of business data, there are four broad classifications which occur fairly frequently: horizontal, seasonal, cyclical and trend. These patterns occur

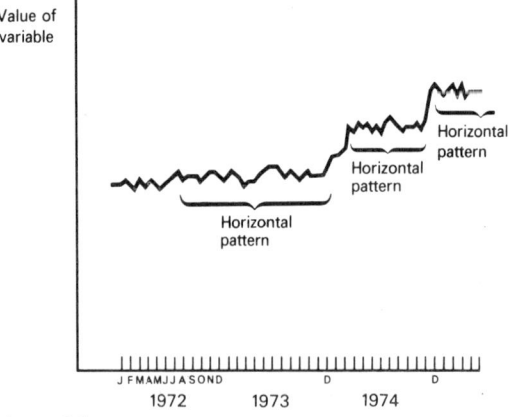

Figure 2.5

Forecasting situations and the characteristics of forecasting techniques 29

frequently in graphs of historical data, so should be examined more closely.

A *horizontal* pattern exists when the time series is said to be stationary. This is when there is no systematic increase or decrease in the data and the probability of changes in the data being an increase or a decrease is fifty-fifty. Figure 2.4 shows an example of a horizontal pattern. It should be recognized that a horizontal pattern can exist in a subset of longer-term upwards or downwards trends or seasonal and cyclical patterns; this is graphically shown in Figure 2.5. This variable can be forecast for short periods ahead by using horizontal pattern analysis, but the forecaster will also be attempting to ascertain at the earliest possible time the breakout of the variable into a new area (e.g. the early months of 1974 in Figure 2.5). Typical business situations where a horizontal pattern may be found include sales of well established food products, labour absenteeism, and the replacement rate of small machine tools in an engineering factory. Horizontal patterns are amenable to the simplest of forecasting techniques; that is, the best estimate of tomorrow's value is today's value. Although this forecast is naive it does recur frequently in short-term forecasts: the manager may make use of seasonal and cyclical patterns for longer periods but in planning, say, the production runs for the following week, the last week's totals may provide (with perhaps some adjustment) the best practical guideline.

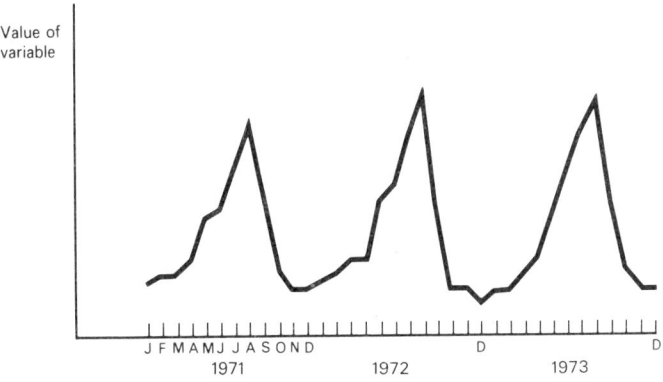

Figure 2.6 A typical seasonal pattern

A *seasonal* pattern is created when the time series is significantly and consistently influenced by a seasonal factor. This 'season' usually relates to the four seasons of the year, but it is also used as a description of other regular daily, weekly and monthly fluctuations, in a time series. Figure 2.6 shows a typical seasonal pattern. It should be quite clear from this that the following period's value will not be the same as that of the present period. Thus some more sophisticated (than that used in horizontal data) forecasting method is required. Examples of seasonal time series data include

1. Daily—sales at a supermarket. This enables part-time staff to be employed at the peak customer periods.
2. Weekly, monthly—cash and bank balances. Certain weekly and monthly expenses may be paid at specified dates and likewise the credit policy of the company will determine when cash is received.
3. Yearly—sales of overcoats and raincoats. These variations are often caused by weather conditions and social customs (Christmas, etc.).

Some 'seasonal' factors are the result of the firm's policies (such as credit policy and dates for paying bills), some are external (such as weather conditions) and some are external although they can be influenced by the firm (such as cheap off-peak travel encouraging passengers to travel at less popular times).

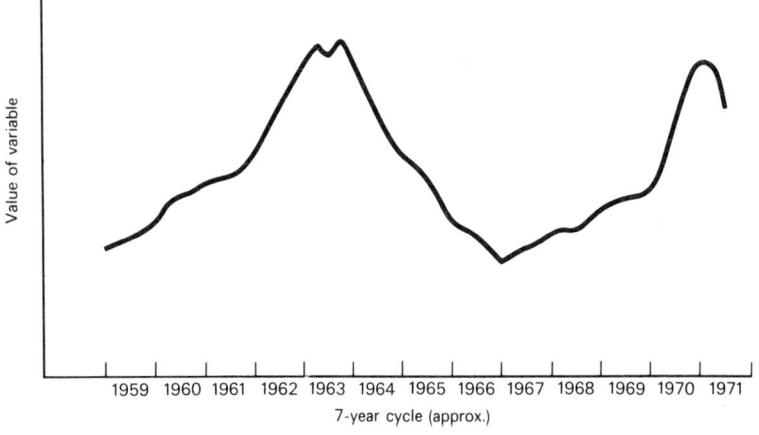

Figure 2.7 A cyclical pattern

Cyclical patterns are similar to seasonal patterns, the main difference being that the term 'cyclical' is given to regular fluctuations in time series data over longer periods (usually a number of years). An example is shown in Figure 2.7 and as can be seen the pattern is similar to Figure 2.6. Typical business fluctuations which are termed cyclical include the sales and profits of capital goods producers, inventory levels, mineral and commodity prices and housing starts.

Trend patterns exist when there is some general growth or decline in the variable over time. Most variables have some sort of trend over the longer time period and the seasonal and cyclical patterns are often subsets of longer-term trends. Figure 2.8 gives an example of an upward trend in the yearly recordings of a variable. Most business variables show an upward

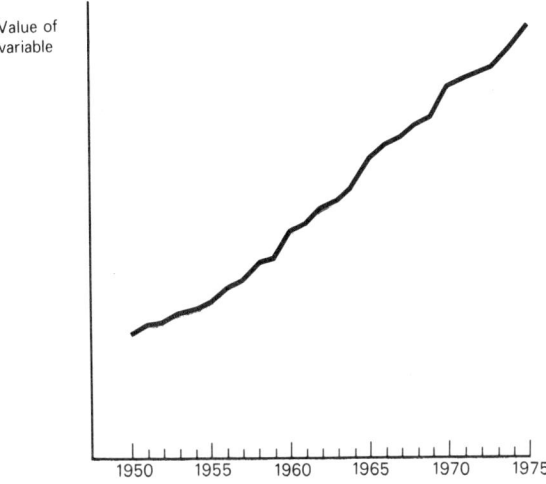

Figure 2.8 An upward trend

trend over time if only because of inflation in money values: if the inflation element is omitted, many time series still show trend patterns which are capable of fairly accurate extrapolation.

Although the above represent the major classification of patterns, others do exist and some will be met in later chapters. It should also be recognized that business time series may often consist of within-year seasonal factors, longer period cyclical patterns and an overall trend element. Figures 2.9 (a) and (b) show examples of this intermingling of patterns. This complex structure needs fairly sophisticated forecasting methodologies if a long-term, period by period forecast is required. Some skill is required in looking at the basic data, since many patterns are not visually obvious, unlike the examples illustrated in the figures here. Because of this 'blurred' data, arithmetical and computational exercises are often carried out so as to determine underlying patterns.

Quite apart from looking at past data in order to establish patterns, the forecaster can also use it to help determine the influencing variables. This is in fact one of the first steps usually undertaken in causal model building, the forecaster attempting to find the causes for the patterns shown in the graph of the historical data. The forecaster will also probably attempt to

32 *Forecasting methods in business and management*

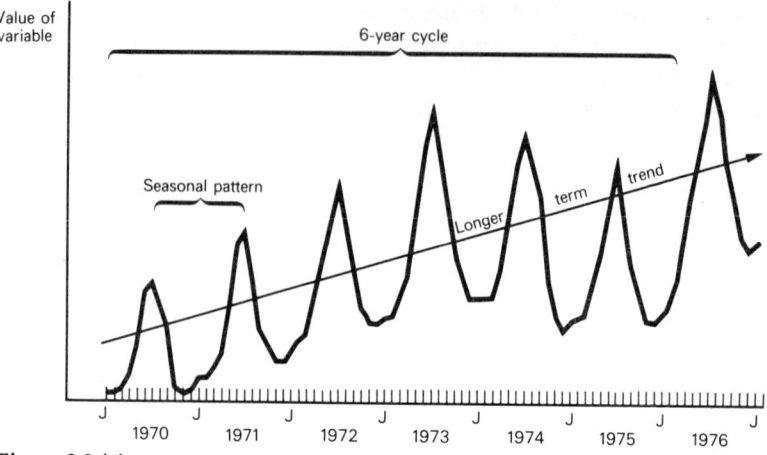

Figure 2.9 (a)

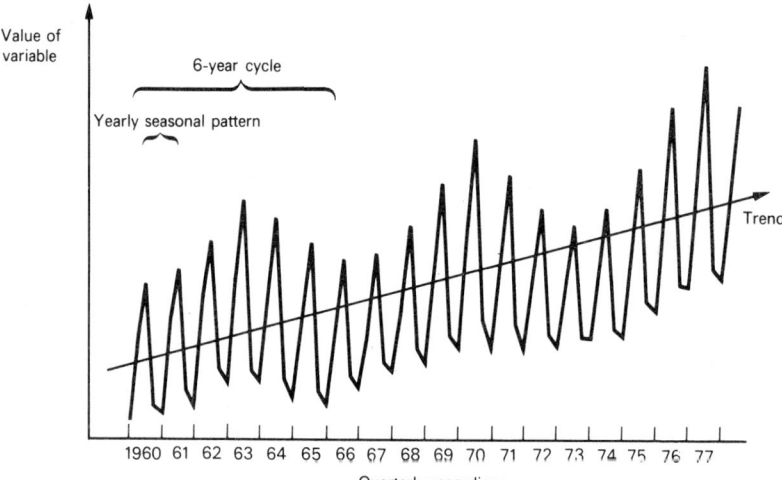

Figure 2.9 (b)

measure the relationship between the past recordings of the variable and the past recordings of some other influencing or associated variable(s). This may throw up variables which are highly associated with the variable to be forecast and which, if found, can considerably aid the forecaster. Thus graphing the historical values of the variable to be forecast is one of the first things the forecaster does: the analysis of this graph will probably indicate a possible suitable forecasting technique.

Measurements of forecasting error

One of the major characteristics of a forecast which is of interest to management is its degree of accuracy. Some mention has already been made of the degree of accuracy acceptable to management and the trade off of accuracy against other desired features of a forecast. When management select the technique to be used, they should have some idea of the degree of inaccuracy expected; the performance of the forecasts against actual results will give valuable feedback as to the efficacy of the technique. This section briefly introduces the general methods of measuring accuracy in a forecast; whether the level of accuracy that is found is acceptable is a separate consideration which will not be dealt with here.

The error of a forecast is given by

Error = Forecast value − Actual value

or notationally

$$E_i = F_i - X_i$$

where the subscript i relates to the particular time period forecast being considered. Of course management will need more than just one period's error in order to evaluate the efficiency of the forecasting system, so data

Table 2.1

1	2	3	4	5	6
Month	Actual sales	Forecast sales	Error	Absolute error	Squared error
	£'000	£'000	£'000	£'000	£'000
1	85	80	−5	5	25
2	91	89	−2	2	4
3	87	92	+5	5	25
4	94	96	+2	2	4
5	96	100	+4	4	16
6	102	108	+6	6	36
7	112	110	−2	2	4
8	98	100	+2	2	4
9	94	94	0	0	0
10	87	88	+1	1	1
11	84	78	−6	6	36
12	80	76	−4	4	16
Total	1110	1111	+1	39	171
Mean error			+0·083		
Mean absolute deviation				3·25	
Mean squared error					14·25

over some longer period is required. Columns 2 and 3 in Table 2.1 show the actual sales and the forecast sales figures for an engineering company. The difference between columns 2 and 3 represents the error and this is shown in Column 4. Although these errors are significant, they are both positive and negative, so when they are summed the average error is found to be very small. To the uninitiated this shows that the forecasting technique produces an 'accurate' forecast over the longer run, however it in fact hides the individual errors and these may prove to be very costly. For example, in the table the average error is small and management may think the forecasts are helping them optimize their business operations (such as their stock holding policy). However, the significant individual errors involve substantial costs in having too high a level of stocks (when the errors are positive) and in being out of stock (when the errors are negative). Thus although the forecast of yearly sales (£1 111 000) is very near to the actual yearly sales (£1 110 000) the forecasting accuracy month by month has been poor and has resulted in significant excess costs.

In order to gain a better picture of the errors in a forecasting system, the mean absolute deviation (sometimes known as the mean absolute error, since deviation is synonymous with error) and the mean squared error are usually computed. These are shown at the bottom of columns 5 and 6.

The mean absolute deviation is calculated by adding together the error terms of column 4 and dividing by the number of observations. However, the minus signs of column 4 are ignored in the addition, i.e. all items are treated as being positive. As can be seen, the mean absolute deviation is considerably higher than the mean error and management's attention can be quickly drawn to it. This error measurement places equal weight on the level of the error, i.e. an error of 2 counts for twice that of an error of 1 in computing the mean absolute deviation. In some cases, however, management may not be worried about small forecasting errors but very worried about larger errors. In this case some weighting is required in order to show the importance of the level of error. The mean squared error is one statistic that is commonly utilized in this situation. Column 6 shows the square of the error and the mean of this gives the mean squared error (the minus terms automatically drop out). This statistic has weighted the errors by their squares (i.e. an error of 2 counts 4 (2^2) times that of an error of 1); of course, other weighting factors could be used, but this is rarely found. The weighting allows the bigger deviations from the mean to influence more (in proportion to their squares) the total result.

The mean absolute deviation and the mean squared error both give adequate error measurements of the forecasting of time series patterns. In general the mean squared error is the measure used, although if no weighting is required, then resort should be made to the absolute error. It may well be that, while one technique has lower forecasting errors over the short term, it may have higher errors when forecasting a long way ahead.

Forecasting situations and the characteristics of forecasting techniques 35

In these cases management has to reconcile advantages of accuracy and the lead time with which to make decisions. In addition, some techniques may have lower forecasting errors when the data is fairly steady but far higher errors when it comes to major turning points or major jumps in the same time series. Again, management has to trade off the accuracy of one technique (which gives superior forecasts on most occasions, i.e. stable periods) against that of another which gives superior results on the few occasions when major turning points occur. So, while this section has described the standard methods of measuring forecasting errors, there is still the significant task facing management of interpreting the statistics in the light of the decision situation at hand. Later chapters will investigate this task.

There are also various other methods which can be used to measure accuracy; some of these analyze the errors into systematic overestimation and systematic underestimation, the rate of change and the ability to predict turning points in a series. One specific test is Theil's inequality coefficient statistic, U, which is based on a comparison of the actual change in the variable with the predicted change.

The statistic is as follows:

$$U = \frac{\sqrt{\frac{1}{n}\sum_{i}^{n}(F_i - A_i)^2}}{\sqrt{\frac{1}{n}\sum_{i}^{n}F_i^2} + \sqrt{\frac{1}{n}\sum_{i}^{n}A_i^2}}$$

where F_i are the forecasts for each period
A_i are the actual values for each period
n is the number of periods being compared.

The U statistic takes a value of 0 to 1 (unless $F_i = 0$ and $A_i = 0$ in which case U is undefined). If the value of U is 0 then the forecasts are perfect and if the value of U is 1 then the forecasts are all incorrect. The nearer the value of U is to 0 the more accurate the forecasting. For a description of this and other more complex error measurements, see the reference to Theil (2) at the end of the chapter. One problem with these more complex methods is that they require a fair amount of data which, especially in the case of continuously monitoring forecasting accuracy, leads to delays that are often unacceptable for managers.

Difficulty is met when appraising the errors of long-term forecasting, since it maybe 20 or 30 years before the 'actual' event occurs. One method of measuring 'error' is to re-evaluate the long-term forecast at various periods and examine the extent of the change in the forecast over the period; if this is substantial, reasons should be established for the changes. For example, an oil company in 1970 postulates that the type of energy being used in the year 2000 will be nuclear power. In 1975 the oil company revises its forecasts and predicts the main energy source in 2000 will be solar energy. The reasons for the change in a forecast should be examined and any ramifications for the forecasting system should be recognized. In general, however, it has to be accepted that the errors of longer time period forecasts are very difficult to evaluate.

Summary

Decision situations and forecasting techniques have various characteristics which can be ascribed to them and which form a useful guideline in the selection of an appropriate technique. This chapter has looked at these various characteristics and described their usefulness in matching a forecasting method to a problem situation; further discussions of the selection of a technique are now left to Chapter 14.

Quantitative forecasting techniques rely upon establishing some relationship or pattern in historical data and using this to predict the future. The set of historical data is therefore very important in the selection of an appropriate technique and in estimating the degree of accuracy likely from it. This chapter has briefly reviewed the major time series patterns; few patterns in real life are as clear cut as those shown in the figures, but with experience they should be discernible and should aid the forecaster's analysis.

Finally, the chapter described various measurements of forecasting accuracy. The monitoring of performance is extremely important for two reasons. Firstly, it gives management feedback on the efficacy of the forecasting process (both the technique itself and the input which it uses). Secondly, major changes in forecasting error may imply that there has been some substantial intrinsic change in the factors influencing the variable being forecast. In this case management is warned about the situation and new decisions can be made or new forecasting methods introduced.

The first two chapters have given a general introduction to the role of forecasting in business management and described major common elements in decision situations and forecasting techniques. The next few chapters describe specific forecasting techniques and analyze their usefulness in business situations.

Suggested reading

The following books can be added to the readings suggested at the end of Chapter 1:

1. Chisholm, R. K., and Whitaker, G. R., *Forecasting Methods*, Irwin, 1971.
2. Theil, H., *Economic Forecasts and Policy,* North Holland Publishing, 1965.
    Theil's book is a fairly mathematical text on a wide range of economic forecasting methods. It is included here because of its reference to the inequality coefficient statistic.
3. Wolfe, H. D., *Business Forecasting Methods,* Holt, Rinehart and Winston, 1966.

3

Time series forecasting: smoothing techniques

Time series forecasts are those which are the result of extrapolating past data into the future. Basically this involves arranging past recordings of a variable into datal order (a time series) and applying some mathematical function to this to obtain the forecast. Notationally, time series forecasting can be described thus

forecast of $V = f$ (time series of V)

where V = variable being forecast

f = function

time series of V = historical observations of V arranged in time order

The mathematical function used can vary from extremely simple to quite complex forms. The major functions are described in this and the next 2 chapters. The amount of historical data required for forecasting varies, depending on the method used.

The actual time series method used can be influenced by the following:

1. Ability and skills of the forecaster. This book intends, however, to help show management that even the more complex methods are within their understanding.

2. The availability of data. The forecaster should take care to see that the data is adequate for use in the analyses. All too often data is used which is spurious or biased in some way, which in turn means spurious forecasts, no matter how sophisticated the technique. The availability and adequacy of data are discussed in Chapter 13; for the following chapters we assume the data is adequate. It is, however, worth noting one consideration here: we must make sure the variable we are using in the time series is the variable we are forecasting. The major example here is that past sales may have been constrained by production capacity (and not demand). Thus if we are forecasting future demand (to see whether to expand or not), we cannot use past sales data without any, albeit subjective, adjustment, since this did not represent past demand but past production capacity. Similarly,

if one of our competitors has been on strike for a period then our sales will be higher than usual; to extrapolate this sales data will be spurious if our competitor's strike ends.

3. The underlying nature of the variable being forecast. Some time series forecasting methods are very unsuitable for certain types of time series data.

4. Expense. As usual a trade off between accuracy and cost has to be made. One element of cost has been mentioned previously, namely the availability of data. If the technique chosen requires collecting new data heavy costs may be incurred.

5. Accuracy. The accuracy of the various forecasting methods for individual variables needs to be assessed. The accuracy is usually measured by computing the mean absolute deviation (error) and the mean squared deviation (error).

Time series models rely solely on past recordings of the variable to be forecast and on the functional relationship linking these. This is contrasted with causal models where the actual influencing factors are identified and where forecasts are made based on these variables. Although causal models are more sophisticated, they usually require more data, time, effort and cost than time series models. Thus in the many situations where there is little difference in the accuracy of causal and time series models, management will turn to the time series methods because of the cheapness.

Time series methods are particularly appropriate in the following situations:

1. Where short-term forecasts are required. In the longer term various outside influences and changes in internal policies can render historical patterns useless.

2. Where the variable is following a horizontal pattern or where there is a fairly constant trend. If the variable is fairly erratic, possibly being highly subject to outside influences, then time series methods may give very poor results.

3. Where the variable is not subject to many violent policy changes (such as advertising campaigns) or external influences (such as credit controls). If this is not so then time series methods will give poor results, since they do not take account of these factors.

Examples of typical instances in which time series methods are used include short-term forecasts of sales of a multi-product business and various short-term national economic forecasts such as unemployment statistics. For the multi-product business it may be economically infeasible to build a separate causal model for each product line and so time series forecasts are used instead.

40 *Forecasting methods in business and management*

This chapter deals with the simpler time series methods, those generally known as *smoothing techniques*. Chapter 4 deals with forecasting models especially suited to seasonal data and Chapter 5 deals with more complex time series models.

The basic premise behind smoothing techniques is that there is some underlying pattern in the values of the variable being forecast. The actual values of the variable will, however, incorporate both the underlying pattern and random fluctuations. The smoothing techniques set out to average or smooth the values so that the extreme values in a historical sequence are eliminated (these are assumed to be generated randomly). In this way the forecaster aims to establish the underlying pattern. Smoothing techniques are often classified into two groups, one being where there is a broadly horizontal pattern (often known as a stationary pattern) in which the variable does not grow or decline significantly over time, the second being where there is a trend or fluctuation in the pattern.

The first step—data examination

The first thing the manager does is to examine the time series to see what sort of pattern and trend is evident. This gives a good idea of the type of time series function that might fit the data. In addition, of course, the forecaster should always examine past data to ascertain the economic and business reasons for the performance of the variable (this was covered in Chapter 2). Examples of typical patterns and the simplest techniques which can handle them are as follows (Figure 3.1 shows them graphically):

1. Horizontal pattern. This is the simplest time series of all; examples include the unit sales of a well established product. Moving average and exponential smoothing are the simplest of the appropriate techniques.

2. Trend data when there is little variation about the trend. This covers the case of unit sales where there has been a steady growth due, for example, to increases in consumer numbers or consumer spending power. Double exponential smoothing, linear growth models (e.g. Holt) and time series regression form the major techniques utilized.

3. Trend data which is non-linear. This can take several forms and be due to varying reasons; the most common example is that of the sales of a new product which often follows an S-shaped curve (see Figure 3.1). The reason for this type of trend is that customer adoption of the product is often slow at the start due to lack of awareness. There then follows an explosive growth (assuming the product is successful) followed by a maturity stage. The major technique here is to use a specific mathematical relationship to fit the non-linear data. It must be noted, however, that in many cases no specific mathematical relationship will fit the data.

4. **Seasonal and cyclical data.** This covers situations where sales are strongly affected by the time of the year. Classical decomposition offers the simplest technique, although both adaptive models and regression models can handle such time series.

5. **Strongly fluctuating data.** This occurs frequently in business situations, the fluctuations being such that the trend or seasonal pattern in the data is difficult to discern. The appropriate time series method here is one of the adaptive type which fit themselves to the changes in the data.

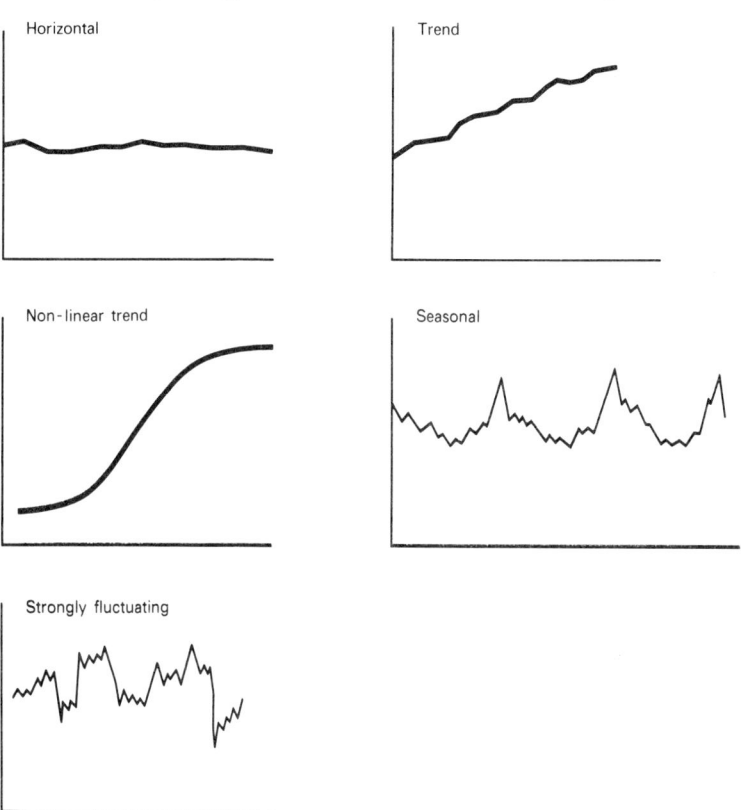

Figure 3.1

We deal first with horizontal or stationary patterns and the two main techniques used here are moving averages and exponential smoothing.

Moving averages

The simplest type of time series forecast is to use the last value as the forecast for the next period. Thus if last month's (May's) sales of a type of

42 *Forecasting methods in business and management*

chair amounted to 3500 units, then the simple naive forecast for June would be 3500 units. However May's figure may have been heavily influenced by random fluctuations, making the naive forecast very inaccurate. One way of reducing the impact of random fluctuations is to compute a moving average, by taking an average of several month's values. The premise here is that the random element in a month's results can be either positive or negative. By taking a number of month's results the positive and negative random elements will tend to cancel themselves out. Table 3.1 shows the monthly sales figures of the chair manufacturer along with the forecasts produced by the moving average technique. In the table three moving averages have been computed, these being three, four and five-monthly.

Table 3.1 Forecasting by moving averages

1	2	3	4	5	6
Month 1975	Month number	Actual unit sales	Forecast with three month moving average	Forecast with four month moving average	Forecast with five month moving average
January	1	4200			
February	2	4100			
March	3	4300			
April	4	3800	4200		
May	5	3500	4066	4100	
June	6	3700	3866	3925	3980
July	7	3400	3666	3825	3880
August	8	3300	3533	3600	3740
September	9	3800	3466	3475	3540
October	10	4200	3500	3550	3540
November	11	4400	3766	3675	3680
December	12		4133	3925	3820

Columns 1 and 2 of Table 3.1 give the month and month number for which sales are recorded. Column 3 gives the actual units of sales (number of chairs) sold in each month. The final three columns give the monthly forecasts given by the three moving averages. The three month moving average forecast for April is 4200. This is derived from the average of the actual sales figures for the three prior months, i.e.

$$\frac{4200 \text{ (January)} + 4100 \text{ (February)} + 4300 \text{ (March)}}{3}$$

The forecast for May is:

$$\frac{4100 \text{ (February)} + 4300 \text{ (March)} + 3800 \text{ (April)}}{3} = 4066$$

and so on. Note that no forecast was made for January, February or March as the technique requires the actual observations of the three prior periods.

The computations for four-monthly and five-monthly moving averages follow in the same way; for example, the four month moving average forecast for May is:

$$\frac{4200 \text{ (January)} + 4100 \text{ (February)} + 4300 \text{ (March)} + 3800 \text{ (April)}}{4} = 4100$$

and the five month moving average forecast for June is:

$$\frac{4200 \text{ (Jan.)} + 4100 \text{ (Feb.)} + 4300 \text{ (Mar.)} + 3800 \text{ (Apr.)} + 3500 \text{ (May)}}{5} = 3980$$

Again the first forecasts cannot be made until four months and five months respective data has been collected.

The moving average technique is described notationally as

$$F_{t+1} = \frac{V_t + V_{t-1} + V_{t-2} + \ldots + V_{t-N+1}}{N} \qquad 3.1$$

$$= \frac{1}{N} \sum_{i=t-N+1}^{t} V_i \qquad 3.2$$

where F_{t+1} = forecast for the next period, $t + 1$

$V_{t, t-1, t-2} \ldots$ = the actual value of the variable at time $t, t-1, t-2. \ldots$
N = the number of observations used in the average

Thus the three month moving average forecast for May given above can be described notationally as

$$F_{\text{May}} = \frac{V_{\text{April}} + V_{\text{March}} + V_{\text{February}}}{3}$$

$$4066 = \frac{3800 + 4300 + 4100}{3}$$

There are two major characteristics of the above formula which will be referred to later on as limitations to the technique: firstly, equal weighting is given to each of the N observations and secondly, any observations prior to period $t-N+1$ are ignored altogether in the forecast.

As can readily be seen, the different moving averages give different forecasts. Thus at the end of November we have the following three different forecasts for December:

	Forecast unit sales
3 month moving average	4133
4 month moving average	3925
5 month moving average	3820

The difference in the forecasts given in Table 3.1 are shown in Figure 3.2, where it is shown that the greater the number of recordings used in computing a forecast the greater the smoothing effect. In the case of stationary situations, the longer the moving average period the nearer the forecast comes to a horizontal line. In Figure 3.2 the difference between the highest

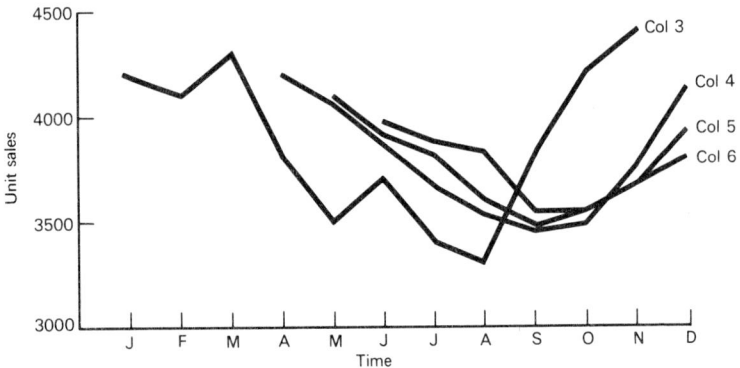

Figure 3.2

and lowest forecasts (from June to December) given by the three moving averages are as follows:

	High		Low	Difference
3 month moving average	4133	—	3466	= 667
4 month moving average	3925	—	3475	= 450
5 month moving average	3980	—	3540	= 440

The 5 month moving average gives the smallest difference, confirming the smoothing impact of lengthening the number of observations in the moving average.

The forecaster will of course want to know which moving average to adopt and there are a number of guidelines that can help when making this decision. The first is the forecaster's opinion of the underlying trend of the variable: if this is thought to be fairly stationary, with a lot of randomness in the historical values, then a greater number of observations in the

Table 3.2 Forecasting errors for moving averages

Month	Month number	Actual unit sales	3 month moving average				4 month moving average				5 month moving average			
			Forecast	Error	Absolute error	Squared error	Forecast	Error	Absolute error	Squared error	Forecast	Error	Absolute error	Squared error
January	1	4200												
February	2	4100												
March	3	4300												
April	4	3800												
May	5	3500												
June	6	3700	3866	166	166	27 556								
July	7	3400	3666	266	266	70 756	3925	225	225	50 625				
August	8	3300	3533	233	233	54 289	3825	425	425	180 625	3980	280	280	78 400
September	9	3800	3466	−334	334	111 556	3600	300	300	90 000	3880	480	480	230 400
October	10	4200	3500	−700	700	490 000	3475	−325	325	105 625	3740	440	440	193 600
November	11	4400	3766	−634	634	401 956	3550	−650	650	422 500	3540	−360	360	129 600
December	12						3675	−725	725	525 625	3540	−660	660	435 600
											3680	−720	720	518 400
		Total		1003	2333	1 156 113		750	2650	1 375 000		540	2940	1 586 000
		Mean		200·6	466·6	231 222·6		150·0	530·0	275 000		108	588	317 200

moving average may be warranted. If, however, there is felt to be some change in the underlying state of the data, then a smaller number of observations in the moving average will be required. The smaller the number of observations, the greater is the response of the moving average to any changes in the data. If the data is highly influenced by random elements, then the forecast (based on a small number of observations) may well be very poor. If the data is changing because of fundamental factors, then the moving average based on a small number of observations gives the best forecast. (However, as described earlier, if there is a strong rising or declining trend in the data, then any form of simple smoothing technique is likely to give poor forecasts.)

Apart from the above judgemental method, the forecaster can also compute the accuracy of the forecasts produced by the different moving averages. The one with the smallest inaccuracy will then be chosen. The forecasting errors of the forecasts for June to November given in columns 4, 5 and 6 in Table 3.1 are shown in Table 3.2. These months were used as they had forecasts from all three moving averages. Firstly the error is shown, then the absolute error (i.e. ignoring the plus (+) or minus (−) sign of the error) and then the squared error. (These methods of forecasting errors were discussed on pages 33 to 36.) The mean absolute and the mean squared errors were smallest for the three month moving average for the data, so this is the one to be used (other moving average periods can also be checked, the one with the smallest errors being the appropriate one). The forecaster should continue to check the accuracy of the various moving averages in case there is any change in their 'accuracy ranking'.

One factor influencing the choice of forecasting methods is cheapness. Within the moving average technique, the number of observations required can affect the cost, since the greater the number of observations required, the greater the computational workload and the greater the cost. The cost of storing data may also have to be considered, which can amount to a significant sum if regular forecasts are required of say 100 items each with their own moving average. If in the above example the most accurate forecasts had been given by the five month moving average, the forecaster would still have to appraise the cost factor before making a firm decision.

The major limitations in the simple moving average technique are:

1. That equal weighting is given to the various observations included in the moving average. This is often held to be strictly wrong, since one would expect the very last observation (t) to carry greater information than the furthest away observation ($t-N+1$), because it was influenced by currently prevailing or near currently prevailing factors.

2. That it disregards data prior to the period $t-N+1$. There is no real rationale behind giving equal weighting to all observations down to period

$t-N+1$ and then no weighting at all to observations prior to this date.

3. If the variable being forecast does not follow a broadly horizontal pattern or if it jumps to new horizontal pattern areas, then the technique is not really suitable.

The first two limitations can be met by using weighted moving averages, which are described below. The third limitation requires either new models or higher forms of smoothing models, which are described later.

Weighted moving averages

One of the limitations of the simple moving average technique is that it gives equal weight to all the observations, even though the more recent data should be considered more important (this is especially significant if the observations stretch back several months or even longer). By attaching weights to the data an improvement in the forecasting accuracy can often be achieved. Amongst the possible weighting systems are the decimal method and the fractional method. These are described notationally as

Decimal $F_{t+1} = 0 \cdot 4 V_t + 0 \cdot 3 V_{t-1} + 0.2 V_{t-2} + 0 \cdot 1 V_{t-3}$ 3.3

Fractional $F_{t+1} = \frac{1}{2} V_t + \frac{1}{4} V_{t-1} + \frac{1}{8} V_{t-2} + \frac{3}{32} V_{t-3} + \frac{1}{32} V_{t-4}$ 3.4

The actual decimal or fractional weightings can be adjusted to various values. The particular weighting system to be used is decided largely by the level of accuracy of the technique on prior data.

Exponential smoothing

There is also another weighting technique, known as exponential weighting, which has achieved a wide level of acceptance in many forecasting situations. It involves weighting past data with weights that decrease exponentially (i.e. decreasing geometrically with age) with time. The weights attached to each observation are thus

$$a V_t + a(1-a) V_{t-1} + a(1-a)^2 V_{t-2} + a(1-a)^3 V_{t-3}$$
$$\ldots + a(1-a)^n V_{t-n} \qquad 3.5$$

where V = individual observations for each period t to $t-n$
a = a value which lies between zero and one.

With a taking a value between zero and one means the sum of the weights adds up to one* and also that the weights decrease with age. The series is summed and this gives the exponential smoothed forecast for period $t+1$.

* If $a = \cdot 3$ then the weights are
$0 \cdot 3 + \cdot 3 (1 - \cdot 3) + \cdot 3 (1 - \cdot 3)^2 + \cdot 3 (1 - \cdot 3)^3 + \ldots$
$= 0 \cdot 3 + 0 \cdot 21 + 0 \cdot 147 + 0 \cdot 1029 + \ldots$
This series can be seen to approach a total value of 1.

Expression 3.5 could be written alternatively as

$$F_{t+1} = aV_t + (1-a)[aV_{t-1} + a(1-a)V_{t-2} + a(1-a)^2 V_{t-3} \ldots] \qquad 3.6$$

and F_t can be written as

$$F_t = aV_{t-1} + a(1-a)V_{t-2} + a(1-a)^2 V_{t-3} + \ldots \qquad 3.7$$

F_t is therefore the same as the expression appearing in the squared brackets of equation 3.6, so by substitution we have

$$F_{t+1} = aV_t + (1-a)F_t \qquad 3.8$$

Thus the exponentially smoothed forecast for period $t + 1$ (say June) is a times the actual value for May plus $(1-a)$ times the exponentially smoothed weighted average for May. Alternatively, the expression can be written as

$$F_{t+1} = F_t + a(V_t - F_t) \qquad 3.9$$

Thus the new forecast (F_{t+1}) is equal to the old forecast (F_t) plus a times the error in the old forecast. The closer a is to 1, the greater the new forecast will incorporate an adjustment for the error in the immediately prior forecast; the nearer a is to 0 the less sensitive the new forecast will be to the error in the immediately prior forecast.

Table 3.3 Forecasting by exponential smoothing

1	2	3	4	5	6
			Exponentially smoothed forecast		
Month	Month number	Actual unit sales	$a = \cdot 2$	$a = \cdot 5$	$a = \cdot 8$
January	1	4200			
February	2	4100	4200	4200	4200
March	3	4300	4180	4150	4120
April	4	3800	4204	4225	4264
May	5	3500	4123	4013	3893
June	6	3700	3998	3757	3579
July	7	3400	3938	3729	3676
August	8	3300	3830	3564	3455
September	9	3800	3724	3432	3331
October	10	4200	3739	3616	3706
November	11	4400	3831	3908	4101
December	12		3945	4154	4340

Table 3.3 shows the forecasts produced by exponential smoothing for the unit sales of chairs. The results from this can be compared with Table 3.1 which used moving average forecasts on the same data: column 3 of Table 3.3 gives the actual unit sales of chairs, this being identical with the figures

shown in column 3 of Table 3.1. Three values of α have been chosen, ·2, ·5 and ·8: this has been done to emphasize the differences in the results which could be obtained by using different αs. For the first period, February, there is no prior forecast available, so the observed value of 4200 for January is used as the forecast for February. The value for March when α is taken as ·2 is

$$F_{t,\text{March}} = F_{t,\text{February}} + \alpha(\text{Actual value for February} - F_t)$$
$$= 4200 + \cdot 2(4100 - 4200)$$
$$\text{Column 4}\quad \text{Column 3}\quad \text{Column 4}$$
$$= 4200 + \cdot 2(-100)$$
$$= 4180$$

This is used as the forecast for March and is shown in column 4. The forecasts for other periods and for using different levels of α are computed

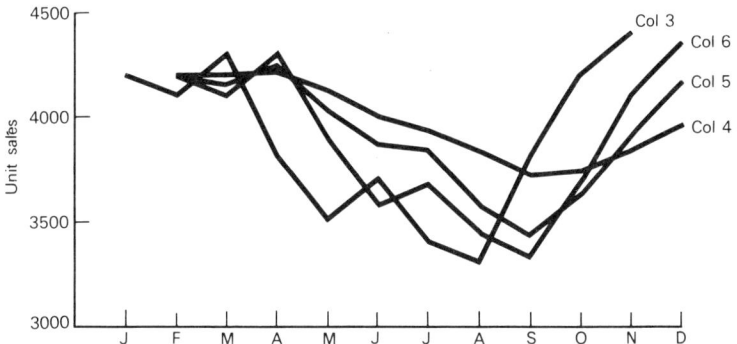

Figure 3.3

similarly. The forecasts are graphed in Figure 3.3 which shows clearly that an α of ·8 gives little smoothing, while an α of ·2 gives a good deal of smoothing.

As with moving averages, the method the forecaster uses to decide which level of α to use is to measure the errors. This is done in Table 3.4, which gives the absolute error and the squared error of the three levels of α. In this example α of ·8 gives the smallest errors and thus the best results. This shows that the benefits of a quick response to changing values outweighs the benefits of smoothing. The forecasting accuracy of the exponential smoothing technique can be compared against the forecasting accuracy of the moving average technique. The mean of the absolute errors and the mean of the squared errors are far less for the exponential smoothing technique than for moving averages (this is so even if the means for exponential smoothing are calculated on the June to November

Table 3.4 Forecasting errors for exponential smoothing

Month	Month number	Actual unit sales	$\alpha = .2$				$\alpha = .5$				$\alpha = .8$			
			Forecast	Error	Absolute error	Squared error	Forecast	Error	Absolute error	Squared error	Forecast	Error	Absolute error	Squared error
January	1	4200	4200	100	100	10 000	4200	100	100	10 000	4200	100	100	10 000
February	2	4100	4180	−120	120	14 400	4150	−150	150	22 500	4120	−180	180	32 400
March	3	4300	4204	404	404	163 216	4225	425	425	180 625	4264	464	464	215 296
April	4	3800	4123	623	623	388 129	4013	513	513	263 169	3893	393	393	154 449
May	5	3500	3998	298	298	88 804	3757	57	57	3 249	3579	−121	121	114 641
June	6	3700	3938	538	538	289 444	3729	329	329	108 241	3676	276	276	76 176
July	7	3400	3830	530	530	280 900	3564	264	264	69 696	3455	155	155	24 025
August	8	3300	3724	−76	76	5 776	3432	−368	368	135 424	3331	−469	469	219 961
September	9	3800	3739	−461	461	212 521	3616	−584	584	341 056	3706	−494	494	244 036
October	10	4200	3931	−569	569	323 761	3908	−492	492	242 064	4101	−299	299	89 401
November	11	4400	3945				4154				4340			
December	12													
	Total			1267	3719	1 776 951		94	3282	1 376 024		−175	2951	1 080 385
	Mean			126.7	371.9	177 695.1		9.4	328.2	137 602.4		−17.5	295.1	108 038.5

forecasts only). In this situation exponential smoothing appears to offer far more accurate forecasts. In addition, exponential smoothing is also usually cheaper to run because only two values have to be stored, the current actual value of the variable (V_t) and the last forecast made (F_t). For moving average computations, however, many more variables may be required.

The level of α is generally set by experimenting with several values until the one with the lowest error term is found. However, if the α found by this method comes to more than ·3 it implies that there is probably a trend present and the forecaster should look for other more appropriate techniques to use. Some of these are discussed below. In Table 3.3 an α of ·8 was found to give a better forecast than αs of ·2 and ·5. This indicates that there is possibly some trend present in the data.

In summary, exponential smoothing is often considered a superior forecasting technique than moving averages because

1. It gives greater weight to more recent data.
2. It incorporates all past data, so there is no cut-off point as happens with moving averages.
3. It requires less data to be held in storage than the longer period moving average methods.
4. Adaptations of the model can easily be made to account for changing conditions. This is facilitated by altering the value of α. Altering moving average methods is generally more costly.

Smoothing techniques for trend analysis

When there is a trend evident in the historical data, the simple moving average and the simple exponential smoothing techniques become much less useful. Instead, resort can be made to a number of other methods, some of which are briefly described below. The first step the forecaster needs to make is to identify the type of trend present in the data, since this will be of help in the selection of an appropriate technique.

Amongst the common groupings of trends are the following:

1. Additive trends. This is when a roughly similar amount is added to or deducted from the previous value of the variable. For example, the demand for chairs may increase by approximately 100 units each month. An example of an additive trend is shown in Figure 3.4.

2. Ratio or exponential trend. This covers situations where the increase or decrease in each succeeding period is some approximately constant percentage. For example, the demand for a particular product could be increasing at a rate of 1% per month (note this will only occur for a limited period). An example of this type of trend is shown in Figure 3.5.

3. **Seasonal trends.** This is where the value of the variable depends partially upon the period in the year (periods other than a year can be used if there is some established cycle). However, discussion of this situation is

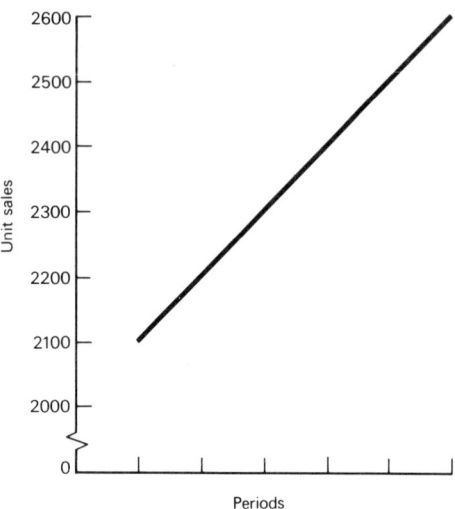

Figure 3.4 An additive trend

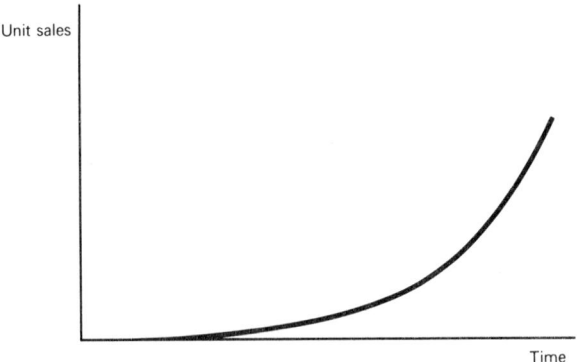

Figure 3.5 A ratio or exponential trend

left until Chapter 4, since there are a number of techniques especially suited to the analysis of seasonal and cyclical trends.

4. There are of course more complex trends than those detailed above, however in practice the forecaster may not always find it very useful to exactly determine their form. This is because of the difficulty in establishing

Time series forecasting: smoothing techniques 53

the pattern and because it is unlikely that there are any forecasting techniques specially suited to that pattern.

The above three simple patterns should be discernible to the forecaster from looking at past data. The major techniques for handling the above techniques are outlined in the next five subsections.

Double exponential smoothing (reference 2)

This method starts by computing the exponentially smoothed value as in Table 3.3. Another exponentially smoothed value using the first exponentially smoothed values as data is then computed. Adjustments are made to this latter figure in order to obtain the forecast.

Table 3.5 Forecasting by double exponential smoothing

1	2	3	4	5	6	7
Period	Actual unit sales	Single exponential smoothing	Double exponential smoothing	Value of a	Value of b	Value of a+b
1	87					
2	92	87	87			
3	93	88	87·2	88·8	0·2	89·0
4	98	89	87·56	90·44	0·36	90·8
5	102	90·8	88·208	93·392	0·648	94·040
6	101	93·04	89·174	96·906	0·966	97·872
7	108	94·632	90·265	98·999	1·091	100·090
8	107	97·305	91·673	102·937	1·408	104·345
9	111	99·244	93·186	105·302	1·514	106·816
10	113	101·595	94·867	108·323	1·682	110·005
11	116	103·876	96·668	111·084	1·802	112·886
12	114	106·300	98·594	114·006	1·926	115·932
13	116	107·840	100·443	115·237	1·849	117·086
14	124	109·472	102·248	116·696	1·806	118·502
15	131	112·377	104·273	120·481	2·026	122·507
16	134	116·101	106·638	125·564	2·365	127·929
17	130	119·680	109·246	130·114	2·608	132·722
18	132	121·744	111·744	131·744	2·500	134·244
19	138	123·795	114·154	133·436	2·410	135·846
20	140	126·636	116·650	136·622	2·496	139·118
		129·308	119·181	139·435	2·531	141·966

Table 3.5 shows an example of double exponential smoothing. Column 2 lists the data and column 3 gives the exponentially smoothed values using an α of ·2 (again the appropriate value for α is found by criterion of minimizing the forecasting errors). Column 4 gives the exponentially smoothed value of the data appearing in column 3. In plotting the data from columns 2, 3 and 4 in Figure 3.6 we see that the exponential value

(column 3) is below the actual values and that the double exponential values (column 4) are below the single exponential values (column 3). (This assumes that the trend is rising. If it is a falling trend, then the exponential values will be above the actual values, and the double exponential values will be higher than the single exponential values.) In fact, the degree of difference between the actual value and the single exponential value is approximately the same as the difference between the single and double exponential values. This is shown in the latter part of Figure 3.6; in the

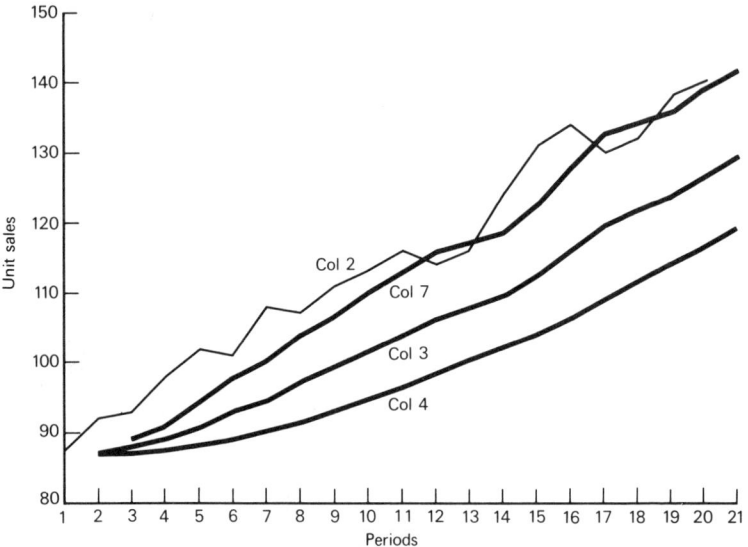

Figure 3.6

earlier part the values had not been properly established. This relationship suggests that if we add the difference between the single and double exponential values (i.e. the difference between the figures in columns 3 and 4) to the single exponential value, we obtain a value very near to the actual value. (If the trend is declining we would deduct the difference from the single exponential value.) The addition of the difference between the figures in columns 3 and 4 to the figure in column 3 is given in column 5; for example

$$88 \cdot 0 \text{ (column 3)} - 87 \cdot 2 \text{ (column 4)} = 0 \cdot 8$$

which is added to column 3 (88·0) to give a figure of 88·8 in column 5. However, a further refinement has been made which enables even more accurate forecasts to be made. The refinement, called b, is of the form

$$b = \frac{a}{1-a}(EF_{t+1} - EF_{t+1}^{\star}) \quad 3.10$$

where EF_{t+1} = single exponential value (column 3)
$EF_{t+1}^{\star}$ = double exponential value (column 4). This is the exponential value of the data appearing in column 3.

The entries for b are shown in column 6 of Table 3.5. The adjusted forecast for the next period is found by adding a (column 5) and b (column 6) together (which results in the figures shown in column 7).

Figure 3.6 shows the accuracy of the forecasts in graphical form. As the forecasting system became established, the adjusted double exponential smoothing forecast becomes very accurate.

The formulae for the computations are summarized below:

Column 3 $EF_{t+1} = aV_t + (1-a)EF_t$ single exponential value 3.11

Column 4 $EF_{t+1}^{\star} = aEF_{t+1} + (1-a)EF_t^{\star}$ double exponential value 3.12

Column 5 $a = 2EF_{t+1} - EF_{t+1}^{\star}$ difference between column 3 and column 4 added to column 3 3.13

Column 6 $b = \frac{a}{1-a}(EF_{t+1} - EF_{t+1}^{\star})$ adjustment factor 3.14

Column 7 $F_{t+1} = a + b$ forecast 3.15

If we wish to forecast more than one period ahead, we multiply the adjustment factor b by the number of periods and add this to a. The formula for column 7 is therefore of the general form

$$F_t + x = a + bx \quad 3.16$$

If we want to forecast the unit sales in period 22, we use the above expression as follows:

$$F_{t+2} = a + b\,(2)$$
$$= 139.435 + 2.531 \times 2$$
$$= 139.435 + 5.062$$
$$= 144.497$$

Similarly, the forecast for period 26 is

$$F_{t+6} = a + b\,(6)$$
$$= 139.435 + 2.531 \times 6$$
$$= 139.435 + 15.186$$
$$= 154.621$$

The further ahead the forecast is required, the greater is the inaccuracy that can be expected. The reader can use the above formula to assess the accuracy of the forecasting technique on the data in Table 3.5. Thus at the end of period 15 we may want to forecast the outcome for period 20:

$$F_{t+5} = a + b(5)$$
$$= 125 \cdot 564 + 2 \cdot 365 \times 5$$
$$= 125 \cdot 564 + 11 \cdot 825$$
$$= 137 \cdot 389$$

This compares with an actual outcome of 140 and is clearly a fairly accurate forecast.

The forecaster will want to calculate the absolute errors and the squared errors from using double exponential smoothing in order to obtain the best smoothing constant for a (in Table 3.5, for example, the accuracy of a higher value of a could be assessed) and to test the accuracy in general. Double exponential smoothing is a superior technique to single exponential smoothing, since it is a better method if there is a trend present in the data and it can equally well forecast horizontal pattern data.

Double moving average (references 1 and 2)
It is also possible to compute a double moving average which follows roughly the same methodology as that for double exponential smoothing. The procedure is as follows:

calculate the moving average

$$F_{t+1} = \frac{V_t + V_{t-1} + V_{t-2} \ldots V_{t-N+1}}{N} \qquad 3.17$$

Then compute the moving average of the above computed F_t values

$$F_{t+1}{}^\star = \frac{F_{t+1} + F_t + F_{t-1} + \ldots F_{t-N+2}}{N} \qquad 3.18$$

Then compute the difference between F_{t+1} and $F_{t+1}{}^\star$ and add this to F_{t+1} (again, assuming an upward trend)

$$a = 2F_{t+1} - F_{t+1}{}^\star \qquad 3.19$$

There then follows an adjustment factor, computed thus

$$b = \frac{2}{N-1}(F_{t+1} - F_{t+1}{}^\star) \qquad 3.20$$

The forecast is now

$$DMAF_{t+1} = a + b \qquad 3.21$$

where *DMAF* stands for double moving average formula.

If a forecast is required for several periods (x) ahead, this becomes

$$DMAF_{t+x} = a + bx \qquad 3.22$$

Again experimentation should be used to find the best number of observations to use in the moving average (that which gives the most accurate forecasts).

Double moving averages give superior forecasts to single moving averages when there is a trend in the data. However, they do not match the accuracy of double exponential smoothing and hence are not in very great use. An additional disadvantage of double moving averages is that they require a lot of data, in fact twice that of single moving averages, hence the method generally has a higher computational cost than double exponential smoothing.

Holt's method (reference 3)
This takes the exponentially smoothed average for a period and adds a growth factor (g_{t+1}) to achieve the forecast. The calculation of the exponentially smoothed average includes the value of the immediately past growth factor (g) and so revises the old value in line with the trend. Thus

$$E F_{t+1} = aV_t + (1-a)(EF_t + g_t) \qquad 3.23$$

and

$$g_{t+1} = B(EF_{t+1} - EF_t) + (1-B)g_t \qquad 3.24$$

where EF = exponentially smoothed forecast
a = smoothing constant
B = constant for growth rate. B lies between zero and one.

The forecast for the next period F_{t+1} becomes

$$F_{t+1} = EF_{t+1} + g_{t+1} \qquad 3.25$$

If the forecast is made for more than one period ahead, then g_{t+1} must be multiplied by the number of periods (note g_{t+1} is the growth for one period). In this particular method arbitrary values for both a and B must be found.

Muir's method (reference 6)
This represents a modification to Holt's method. Muir showed that if forecasts have been made for a fairly long period of time, then the forecast for x periods ahead becomes

$$F_{t+x} = F_{t+1} + g_{t+1}\left(\frac{1}{a} + x - 1\right) \qquad 3.26$$

where F_{t+1} = the exponentially smoothed forecast as given by equation 3.8
g_{t+1} = the growth rate as computed in equation 3.24.

Adaptive smoothing technique (reference 2)

Brown suggested a forecasting technique for additive trend analysis which uses regression methods. This method assumes there is some underlying pattern to the data and in order to quantify this a regression analysis is carried out; this regression is weighted, however, so that the greater emphasis is given to more recent data. Thus past data is discounted by some factor, d (equivalent to $(1-\alpha)$ in exponential smoothing). For a given level of d, the regression coefficients are computed and these are used in the forecasting process. The regression is run such that the sum of squared errors is a minimum, i.e.

$$\sum_{i}^{n} d^{i}(V_{t} - F_{t})^{2} \text{ is a minimum} \qquad 3.27$$

For a fuller treatment of the method and of short cut estimation procedures see reference 2.

Ratio trend

Muir has suggested the following form of model for forecasting when there is a ratio or exponential trend in the data (6). It is of the form

$$F_{t+x} = (EF_{t+1}) \times (r_{t+1}^{x}) \qquad 3.28$$

where F_{t+x} is the forecast for x periods ahead

$$EF_{t+1} = \alpha V_{t} + (1 - \alpha) r_{t} EF_{t} \qquad 3.29$$

and

$$r_{t+1} = \frac{\alpha V_{t}}{EF_{t}} + (1 - \alpha) r_{t} \qquad 3.30$$

where r_{t} represents the ratio trend factor

Ratio trends can also be used by transforming the data into logarithmic form.

Deseasonalizing methods

Holt (3), and Brown (2) have both modified their time series forecasting techniques to take account of seasonal factors. This is a necessary adjustment when the seasonal variations (i.e. periodic variations in the time series within a year) are great. The major time series technique used in seasonal forecasting is classical decomposition analysis which is dealt with in Chapter 4; this section deals solely with techniques which are based on prior mentioned time series techniques and in particular Holt's model. They are based on deseasonalizing the data (i.e. extracting the variations due to specific seasons or short-term periods) and then calculating the underlying trend.

Holt's exponential forecasting method described above is modified by incorporating a deseasonalizing factor. Thus equation 3.23 becomes

$$EF_{t+1} = \frac{aV_t}{S_{t-d}} + (1-a)(EF_t + g_t) \qquad 3.31$$

where S_{t-d} is the smoothed deseasonalizing factor. This is an estimate based on the seasonal index at the corresponding period of the last seasonal cycle (d is the number of periods in the seasonal cycle, e.g. quarterly periods). The smoothing constants for the seasonal factor are again calculated by exponential weights (this time designated C), i.e.

$$S_t = C \frac{V_t}{EF_{t+1}} + (1-C) S_{t-d} \qquad 3.32$$

The forecasting model of equation 3.25 becomes

$$F_{t+1} = (EF_{t+1} + g_{t+1}) S_{t-d} \qquad 3.33$$

where g_{t+1} has the same derivation as in equation 3.24

If the forecast is required for T periods ahead, this is described as

$$F_{t+T} = (EF_{t+1} + g_{tT}) S_{t-d+T} \qquad 3.34$$

Winters (8) has recommended the use of the following weights for the values of the exponential weights a, B, C of 0.2, 0.2 and 0.6. The above modification is often necessary if the time series is subject to significant seasonal variations, because the past trend becomes more difficult to establish and hence more difficult to forecast. Chapter 4 covers classical decomposition analysis which determines the seasonal factor so that the underlying trend can be estimated and so as to forecast for individual weeks or months ahead.

Mathematical trend curve fitting

In some time series it may be obvious that the data is non-linear but nevertheless following a specific pattern. In such cases the forecaster might attempt to fit a mathematical trend curve to it. If a satisfactory function can be found this will allow forecasts to be made by substituting the time factor into the formulae. Typical non-linear trends include the exponential curve, simple modified exponential curve, second, third and higher degree polynomials, sine-cosine curves, parabola, logarithmic parabola, logistic curve and the gompertz curve. For a description of mathematical trend curve fitting, see reference 4; Chapter 8 also has a brief section, under the heading curvilinear analysis, which covers regression approaches to fitting non-linear data. It must be appreciated, however, that few business variables are likely to fit a specific non-linear trend function.

Summary

This chapter has described the simpler time series forecasting techniques. There are also other forms of time series smoothing techniques, such as triple exponential smoothing techniques, but these become fairly complex and are difficult to use. One problem is that they are appropriate to particular patterns which have to be identified first by the forecaster; also they involve much greater computational costs. The interested reader should consult the references for a description of these methods. Chapter 4 discusses the breaking down of a time series into component parts and Chapter 5 discusses further time series methods which are of a more sophisticated type. For additional readings relating to simple time series techniques, see references 5 and 7.

References

1. Brown, R. G., *Statistical Forecasting for Inventory Control,* McGraw Hill, 1959.
2. Brown, R. G., *Smoothing, Forecasting and Prediction of Discrete Time Series,* Prentice Hall, 1962.
3. Holt, C. C., et al., *Planning Production, Inventories and Work Force,* Prentice Hall, 1960.
4. I.C.I Ltd., *Mathematical Trend Curves: an aid to forecasting,* I.C.I. Monograph No 1, Oliver & Boyd, 1964.
5. I.C.I. Ltd., *Short-Term Forecasting,* I.C.I. Monograph No 2, Oliver & Boyd, 1964.
6. Muir, A., 'Automatic Sales Forecasting', *Computer Journal,* **1.**
7. Ward, D. H., 'Comparison of different systems of exponentially weighted prediction', *The Statistician,* **3,** 13, 1963.
8. Winters, P. R., 'Forecasting Sales by Exponentially Weighted Moving Averages', *Management Science,* **6,** 1960.

4

Time series forecasting by classical decomposition analysis

The time series techniques discussed so far have sought to establish an underlying pattern in the data and to extrapolate the pattern into the future. This requires the technique to differentiate between the underlying pattern and the random elements. However, no attempt has yet been made to break down (decompose) the time series into constituent parts. In many time series it is possible to breakdown the pattern into a number of factors and the technique for doing this is known as classical decomposition; forecasts can then be made on the basis of this decomposition. The technique is in popular use in business and economic situations although there are other, more powerful, techniques which can be used in its place.

Traditional factors in a time series

Historically, the classical decomposition method has sought to identify three factors making up a time series; a trend factor, a seasonal factor and a cyclical factor. In some cases forecasters may only establish two factors, the most usual being trend and seasonal. The makeup of these factors are as follows.

The *trend* factor is the long-term underlying movement of the time series. This is usually computed as the linear growth or decline (or static movement) in the time series which, by measuring it over a long time period, eliminates seasonal and cyclical variations. The usual method of computing the trend is to use moving averages or a least squares regression line. In Figure 4.1 the trend factor is clearly upwards, thus the underlying pattern of the sales of sports goods is one of growth.

The *seasonal* factor is the periodic pattern in the data of a yearly time series. Quite a number of business variables are subject to seasonal variations:

1. Greeting cards retailers experience a boom sales period at Christmas and a mini-boom at Easter.

62 *Forecasting methods in business and management*

2. Rainwear retailers have boom sales in the late autumn and early winter.

3. Retailers of beachwear are likely to have a sales boom in the summer months and a slump during winter.

4. Retailers of motor cars may experience a small boom in sales during August of each year as new car registration numbers come out. Conversely, sales in July may be abnormally depressed.

Thus seasonal variations may arise because of weather, educational, institutional or other factors and the impact may be short term (e.g. lasting a

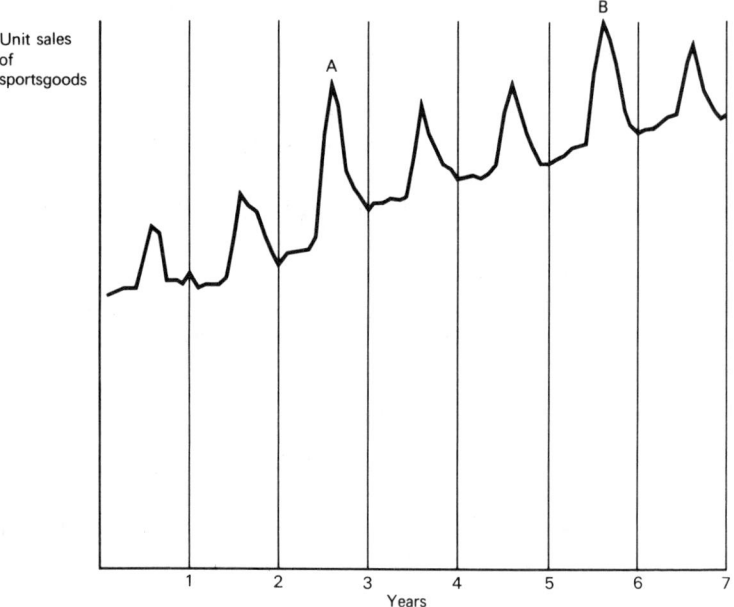

Figure 4.1

couple of weeks) or longer term (e.g. the winter). However, a seasonal variation must repeat itself in each year. In Figure 4.1 there is a fairly obvious seasonal peak in the sales of sports goods in the summer months of each year. During the remainder of the year sales of sports goods are at a much lower level.

The *cyclical* factor is a periodic pattern in time series data which takes a number of years before it repeats itself. The repetition of a cycle may vary in time, for example a cycle may consist of an eight year period, followed by a seven year period, followed by a nine year period. This should be borne in mind by the forecaster. In addition to the imprecise time duration of a cycle, the amplitude (the difference between the peaks and troughs) is also variable. Examples include economic trade cycles such as those evidenced by the housebuilding industry and the capital goods industry. There are also other cycles which affect the firm, such as the availability of funds, labour, etc., which may all restrict the growth of the firm. However, this chapter is mainly concerned with the cycles directly affecting demand since these are the most intractable of those affecting the firm. In Figure 4.1 there appears to be a cycle of three years duration (the peaks denoted A and B), this being the result, say, of economic prosperity followed by economic recession. It should be recognized that cyclical factors are usually the hardest to identify in any time series and in some situations where their impact is small they may be ignored altogether by the forecaster.

Apart from the difficulty in determining past cyclical patterns, the forecasting of their future occurrence can be very tenuous, i.e. the timing of the upturn-downturn of the cycle, the length of the cycle and the amplitude of cycle. In spite of the difficulty of forecasting, the importance of the business or trade cycle is so great for many medium-term decisions (e.g. up to 5 years) that any increase in the accuracy of its prediction will be worth paying for.

Classical decomposition models

The traditional form of classical decomposition can therefore be described notationally as

$$V_i = T_i \times S_i \times C_i + I_i$$

where V = value of the variable
T = trend factor
S = seasonal factor
C = cyclical factor
I = irregular factor, i.e. the random element in the time series
i = period i

The above model is in its multiplicative form and is the one usually used. Here the seasonal and cyclical factors are presented as indexes. The random element, I, is additive, although it is possible to use it in multiplicative form. (In practice this is rarely done.)

If $T = 500$, $S = 1 \cdot 40$ and $C = 1 \cdot 50$ then

$V = 500 \, (1 \cdot 40) \, (1 \cdot 50) + I$
$V = 1050 + I$

Unfortunately I is random and cannot be forecast. However, the model could be expressed in its additive form which is

$$V = T + S + C + I$$

In this case the absolute amounts have to be given. Thus if $T = 500$, $S = +400$, $C = +150$, then

$$V = 500 + 400 + 150 + I$$
$$V = 1050 + I$$

The additive model is more difficult to work with and also assumes that the individual factors are independent, e.g. that the trend has no impact on the seasonal factor no matter how high or low it becomes. This is generally untenable in all but the very short term, hence virtually all users of decomposition analysis use the multiplicative model.

Uses of decomposition analysis

The advantages of a decomposition analysis should be fairly obvious. Firstly, it allows the forecaster to determine the long-term trend of the variable under consideration. Thus if a company is examining the possibility of extending its plant and machinery, it will wish to know the sales potential over, say, the next twenty years. The projection of the trend factor will give an estimate of this. Secondly, it gives data on which the forecaster and management can make short-term plans. Thus although the firm's sales may be 12 000 units a year, it may be that the business is highly seasonal and that sales in the month prior to Christmas are in the order of 3000 units. By determining the seasonal impact management can make sure that there are sufficient stocks on hand and an adequate number of sales personnel. An assessment of the cyclical factor can also help in medium-term planning, for example recruitment of personnel could be speeded up or slowed down so as to have a more efficient labour force level.

Classical decomposition methods can be and are used in a wide variety of business situations. The technique is also in use at the macro-economic level; for example, the 'seasonally adjusted' figures for unemployment and exports are in fact the trend factor discussed above (i.e. after omitting seasonal variations).

The technique of decomposing a time series

In describing the technique of decomposition analysis we will utilize an example. This is based on the monthly unit sales of a university campus bookseller. The data is presented in Table 4.1 and illustrated in Figure 4.2.

Time series forecasting by classical decomposition analysis 65

It is important for the bookseller to decompose the time series so that

1. He can identify the longer-term trend. On this he can base plans for longer-term expansion, such as acquiring extra shop space.
2. He can identify medium-term cyclical factors. This gives him information on whether to recruit or replace staff and whether to preserve liquidity or expand.
3. He can identify seasonal peaks that occur during the year. This gives him information on the level of stocks to keep, information on planning his workload (such as the preparation of annual accounts which could be left until April-May when the business is relatively slack) and information on temporary staff assistance and the arrangement of holidays.

Table 4.1 Unit sales of a retail bookshop

Month	1969	1970	1971	1972	1973	1974
January	5452	6817	5236	6792	5480	6591
February	3897	4209	3913	4307	3786	4401
March	3621	3398	3720	3581	3726	3673
April	3802	3562	3783	3729	3787	3427
May	2970	3401	3006	3748	3089	3826
June	3067	3245	3121	3324	3108	3481
July	4896	5682	5016	5490	5003	5719
August	4002	4917	4123	4726	4217	4732
September	3679	3827	3502	4013	3513	4111
October	5826	6298	5761	6492	5700	6827
November	4093	4214	4129	4010	4016	3987
December	3527	3897	3681	3978	3583	3945

The forecaster should first of all look at the data to see if there are any obvious patterns; any initial opinions will be confirmed or denied in the calculations which follow. (If the opinion is denied then the data should be examined again, to check the calculations.) From Table 4.1 and Figure 4.2 there appears to be a strong seasonal component with high sales in the months of January, July and October. An 'economic' rationale should be established for this finding if possible. In the example the high sales for January and October are accounted for by the start of the two major teaching terms when new books are often recommended. In July the university runs a summer school for the local community and again set textbooks are recommended. Throughout the rest of the year book sales are lower, with troughs appearing in May, June, September and December. These correspond to the end of terms and the end of the summer school.

Apart from the seasonal trend there also appears to be a slight cyclical factor as well: sales in the years 1970, 1972 and 1974 were above those of the preceding year. These years in fact coincided with an increase in student numbers, this being a function of the government's expansionary/deflationary economic policies. Overall, however, there appears to be no long-term growth and the trend is hypothesized to be horizontal.

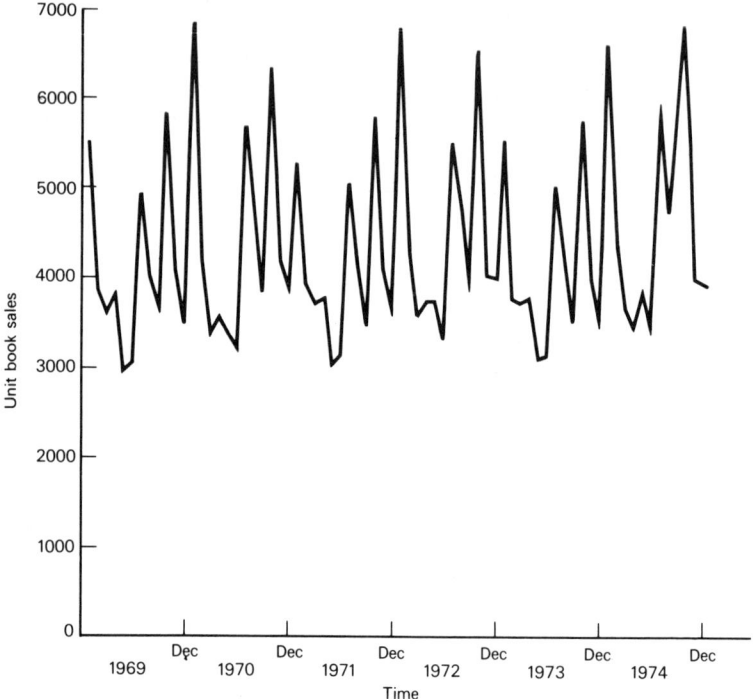

Figure 4.2

Seasonal index

Having obtained a rough idea of the possible components of the time series, the forecaster now has to quantify the relationships and confirm or deny these first impressions. The first step that has to be made in the analysis is to compute the seasonal index; thus we want to find

$$S \text{ index} = \frac{T \times S \times C}{T \times C} \text{ for the period}$$

or

$$S \text{ index} + I = \frac{T \times S \times C + I}{T \times C} \text{ if we include } I \text{ in the notation}$$

The method we use is to compute the moving average and divide this into the value for a particular period (monthly in this case), V, and this gives us the seasonal index for that month, thus

$$\frac{Vt}{\text{moving average centred on } Vt} = \text{seasonal index}$$

$t = \text{month } t$

The words 'centred on' mean that Vt is the middle month of the moving average.

Table 4.2 shows the computations for the bookseller example. Column 1 contains the actual monthly unit book sales (Vt). Column 2 gives the 12 monthly total (where Vt is the sixth month in the 12 monthly total). In some series quarterly data may be used, but this was inappropriate in the present situation as our initial glance at Table 4.1 and Figure 4.2 showed significant fluctuations in sales from one month to another. In choosing a moving average period it should be noted that the longer the period the greater the smoothing. This has the benefit of ironing out the impact of random elements but at the same time it can reduce the clarity of any cycle such that the cycle may not be recognized at all. The greater the smoothing, the greater is the influence the trend factor has on any forecast and the less the influence of turning points. Some textbooks advocate the use of weighting the data contained in a moving average; for example in a three month moving average we may give a weighting of ·25, ·5 and ·25 to the three months data, thereby giving greater importance to the month on which the forecast is centred. However, this weighting technique has gained very little acceptance in practice; see Croxton *et al.* (3) for a reference to this technique. The third column shows the twelve month moving total centred. This adjustment was calculated as follows:

12 month moving total centred on July 1969 = 12 month moving total (January 1969 to December 1969) + 12 month moving total (February 1969 to January 1970) ÷ 2

thus $\frac{48\,832 + 50\,197}{2} = 49\,514 \cdot 5$

This is only a slight adjustment in the case of the figures involved here but it is conceptually correct. Column 4 shows the monthly moving average; this is computed by dividing column 3 by 12. Column 5 gives the ratio of the actual value for a month to the moving average (column 1 ÷ column 4). This is the seasonal index, although if several years data are available, as in the example, then we average these to obtain an average seasonal index. The figure appearing in column 5 for July 1969 is 1·186, thus unit sales in July 1969 were 18·6% higher than the average annual value. The September 1969 index shows that unit sales were 12·5% less than the average annual value.

68 *Forecasting methods in business and management*

Table 4.2 Unit book sales: ratio of actual unit sales to 12 month moving average

	1 Actual	2 12 month total	3 12 month total, centred	4 12 month moving average	5 Ratio of actual to 12 month moving average
1969					
January	5452				
February	3897				
March	3621				
April	3802				
May	2970				
June	3067	48 832			
July	4896	50 197	49 514·5	4126·2	1·186
August	4002	50 509	50 353·0	4195·8	·953
September	3679	50 286	50 397·5	4199·8	·875
October	5826	50 046	50 166·0	4180·5	1·393
November	4093	50 477	50 261·5	4188·5	·977
December	3527	50 655	50 566·0	4213·8	·837
1970					
January	6817	51 441	51 048·0	4254·0	1·602
February	4209	52 356	51 898·5	4324·9	·973
March	3398	52 504	52 430·0	4369·2	·777
April	3562	52 976	52 740·0	4395·0	·810
May	3401	53 097	53 036·5	4419·7	·769
June	3245	53 467	53 282·0	4440·2	·730
July	5682	51 886	52 676·5	4389·7	1·294
August	4917	51 590	51 738·0	4311·5	1·140
September	3827	51 912	51 751·0	4312·6	·887
October	6298	53 133	52 022·5	4335·2	1·452
November	4214	51 738	51 935·5	4327·9	·973
December	3897	51 614	51 676·0	4306·3	·904
1971					
January	5236	50 948	51 281·0	4273·4	1·225
February	3913	50 154	50 551·0	4212·6	·928
March	3720	49 829	49 991·5	4165·9	·892
April	3783	49 292	49 560·5	4130·0	·915
May	3006	49 207	49 249·5	4104·1	·732
June	3121	48 991	49 099·0	4091·6	·762
July	5016	50 547	49 769·0	4147·4	1·209
August	4123	50 941	50 744·0	4228·7	·975
September	3502	50 802	50 871·5	4239·3	·826
October	5761	50 748	50 775·0	4231·2	1·361
November	4129	51 490	51 119·0	4259·9	·969
December	3681	51 693	51 591·5	4299·3	·856

The monthly seasonal indices also contain random elements and we can assume that it is these which account for the differences in monthly seasonal indices over several years (for example, the seasonal indices for July 1969, 1970, 1971, 1972, 1973, are 1·186, 1·294, 1·209, 1·230,

Time series forecasting by classical decomposition analysis   69

	1 Actual	2 12 month total	3 12 month total centred	4 12 month moving average	5 Ratio of actual to 12 month moving average
1972					
January	6792	52 167	51 930·0	4327·5	1·569
February	4307	52 770	52 468·5	4372·4	·985
March	3581	53 281	53 025·5	4418·8	·810
April	3729	54 012	53 646·5	4470·5	·834
May	3748	53 893	53 952·5	4496·0	·833
June	3324	54 190	54 041·5	4503·5	·738
July	5490	52 878	53 534·0	4461·2	1·230
August	4726	52 357	52 617·5	4384·8	1·077
September	4013	52 502	52 429·5	4369·1	·918
October	6492	52 560	52 531·0	4377·6	1·483
November	4010	51 901	52 230·5	4352·5	·921
December	3978	51 685	51 793·0	4316·1	·921
1973					
January	5480	51 198	51 441·5	4286·8	1·278
February	3786	50 689	50 943·5	4245·3	·891
March	3726	50 189	50 439·0	4203·2	·886
April	3787	49 397	49 793·0	4149·4	·912
May	3089	49 403	49 400·0	4116·7	·750
June	3108	49 008	49 205·5	4100·5	·757
July	5003	50 119	49 563·5	4130·3	1·211
August	4217	50 734	50 426·5	4202·2	1·003
September	3513	50 681	50 707·5	4225·6	·831
October	5700	50 321	50 501·0	4208·4	1·354
November	4016	51 058	50 689·5	4224·1	·950
December	3583	51 431	51 244·5	4270·4	·839
1974					
January	6591	52 147	51 789·0	4315·7	1·527
February	4401	52 662	52 404·5	4367·0	1·007
March	3673	53 260	52 961·0	4413·4	·832
April	3427	54 387	53 823·5	4485·3	·764
May	3826	54 358	54 372·5	4531·0	·844
June	3481	54 720	54 539·0	4544·9	·765
July	5719				
August	4732				
September	4111				
October	6827				
November	3987				
December	3945				

1·211). By taking the average of these values we hope to free the data from the random elements. Table 4.3 shows the computation of the recomputed mean seasonal indices. Forecasters often omit the highest and lowest monthly index of the data so as to remove extreme values and this has been done in Table 4.3. Thus for January the highest value of 1·602 and the

70 *Forecasting methods in business and management*

lowest value of 1·225 have been omitted and the average of the three intermediate figures has been taken, i.e.

$$\frac{1\cdot 569 + 1\cdot 278 + 1\cdot 527}{3} = 1\cdot 458$$

Forecasters can of course ignore this last methodology or they can substitute some other modification to take account of extreme values.

As the total of the above mean indices amounts to 11·980 instead of 12·000 (because of rounding errors, etc.), the last column modifies them. The figures appearing in the final column are known as the seasonal indices. If the un-

Table 4.3 Computation of seasonal indices

	1969	1970	1971	1972	1973	1974	Mean*	Seasonal index†
January		1·602	1·225	1·569	1·278	1·527	1·458	1·460
February		·973	·928	·985	·891	1·007	·962	·964
March		·777	·892	·810	·886	·832	·842	·843
April		·810	·915	·834	·912	·764	·852	·853
May		·769	·732	·833	·750	·844	·784	·785
June		·730	·762	·738	·757	·765	·752	·753
July	1·186	1·294	1·209	1·230	1·211		1·216	1·218
August	·953	1·140	·975	1·077	1·003		1·018	1·020
September	·875	·887	·826	·918	·831		·864	·866
October	1·393	1·452	1·361	1·483	1·354		1·402	1·404
November	·977	·973	·969	·921	·950		·964	·966
December	·837	·904	·856	·921	·839		·866	·868
							11·980	12·000

* After omitting the highest value and the lowest value for each month.

† Adjusted by the factor $\frac{12\cdot 00}{\text{Mean}} = \frac{12\cdot 00}{11\cdot 98} = 1\cdot 0016$, i.e. the seasonal index for January $= 1\cdot 458 \times 1\cdot 0016 = 1\cdot 460$.

derlying trend (and cyclical nature) of a variable is required then the monthly figure of the variable is divided by its seasonal index; the figure so obtained is known as the deseasonalized data. If, for example, the actual unit book sales for January 1975 came to 6500, then the deseasonalized trend and cyclical figure is

$$\frac{6500}{1\cdot 460} = 4452 \text{ units}$$

This represents the underlying trend and cyclical factor of book sales after omitting the variations caused by seasonal influences.

Instead of computing the mean of seasonal indices for one month over several years, it is possible to compute a regression line (see Chapter 7) of the form

$$y = a + bx$$

where $y =$ indices, $x =$ time 1, 2, 3 . . .

Time series forecasting by classical decomposition analysis 71

This might be especially relevant if the index has grown or declined strongly over the period. The random elements will be the difference between the actual values and the appropriate value given by the regression equation. As there was no pattern evident in the indices in the example, the regression approach did not seem warranted, so the mean value (omitting the highest and lowest figures) was used.

Table 4.3 now gives the final seasonal factors. Thus January sales are 46% higher than the yearly average, February's sales are 3·6% lower than the yearly average, and so on. Management can use this data in their decision making as regards inventory levels, etc. and also in performance appraisal. For example if sales for October are 20% above the yearly average, management should not be pleased; they would expect sales to be up by 40·4% as the seasonal index was 1·404, so in this instance there has been a shortfall in sales of 14·5% over those expected

$$\left(\text{i.e. } 100\% - \left(100 \times \frac{120}{140 \cdot 4}\right)\%\right)$$

The trend factor

The next step in the procedure is to compute the trend factor. This is done by computing the simple linear regression equation for the moving average (column 4, Table 4.2) data. (This technique is covered in Chapter 8. Very occasionally trend lines may be other than linear, in which case non-linear regression has to be used; see page 134.) The equation is of the form

$Y = a + bX$

where Y = actual values of Vt (moving average data)
X = time period (1 to 60)

However, the trend factor given in the regression equation was not statistically significant (a term described in Chapter 8). Our best estimate of the trend is in fact a horizontal trend of 4292 units (computed as the mean of the 60 moving average recordings). Figure 4.3 also suggests that the trend factor is horizontal. There is therefore no growth or decline in the underlying trend of unit book sales. From this information, management would seem unwise to expand their premises or become involved in any other capital expenditure project.

If the trend has not been horizontal then we would use the values given by the simple regression equation $Y = a + bX$. If the parameters a and b has been estimated as 2400 and 206·1 respectively then the trend value (Y) for month 20 would be

$Y = 2400 + 206 \cdot 1 (20)$
$Y = 6522$

The trend value for month 28 would be

$Y = 2400 + 206 \cdot 1 (28)$
$Y = 8170 \cdot 8$

The cyclical factor

If the forecaster feels that there is no cyclical factor, and as we stated before the cyclical factor is often difficult to identify, then the forecast could be based on the seasonal and trend components solely. Thus the forecast becomes

forecast = trend factor × seasonal index

In our example we will take the trend factor to be 4292.

However, in our initial look at Table 4.1 and Figure 4.2 we discerned a cyclical factor of two years duration. This cyclical factor is again in evidence in Figure 4.3 which plots the monthly moving averages; the

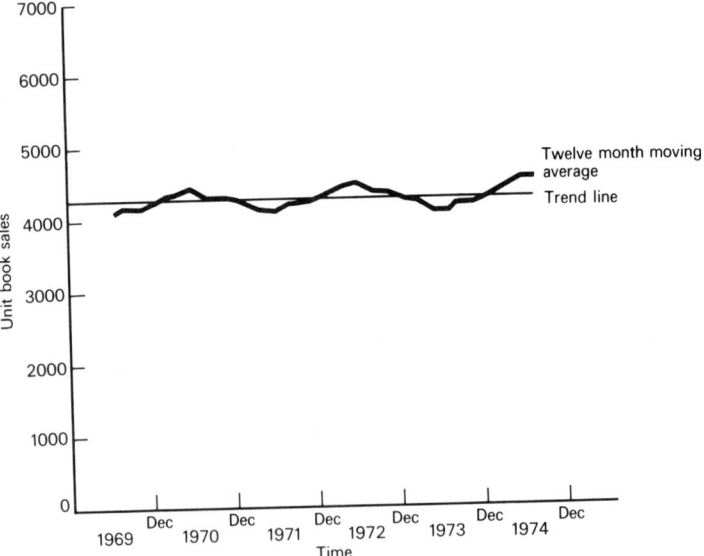

Figure 4.3

moving averages have removed the seasonal component and the trend is shown by the horizontal line drawn at 4292 units. The variations of the moving averages above and below the horizontal trend line therefore represent cyclical and random elements. However, they appear to follow a pattern, which indicates that a cyclical factor is present. If the variations had been scattered about the trend line in a random fashion, this would indicate that there was no cyclical factor. We now need to quantify the cyclical factor and assess its significance.

The cyclical factor is estimated by firstly removing the seasonal factor and then the trend factor. The seasonal factor is removed by taking the moving average of the data, as described above. Thus we now have

moving average = trend × cyclical × random element

and by dividing through by the trend we have

$$\text{cyclical} \times \text{random element} = \frac{\text{moving average}}{\text{trend}}$$

The figure for the trend for each value of unit sales (Vt) is obtained from the regression equation $Y = a + bX$ described above. In the example the trend was in fact approximately constant at 4292 units and this eases the computation of the cyclical factor which is shown in Table 4.4. The first column shows the actual values (taken from Table 4.1), the second column shows the twelve month moving average (taken from Table 4.2), the third column shows the trend figure (in this case a constant figure of 4292) and column 4 shows the cyclical factor (column 2 ÷ column 3). Figure 4.4

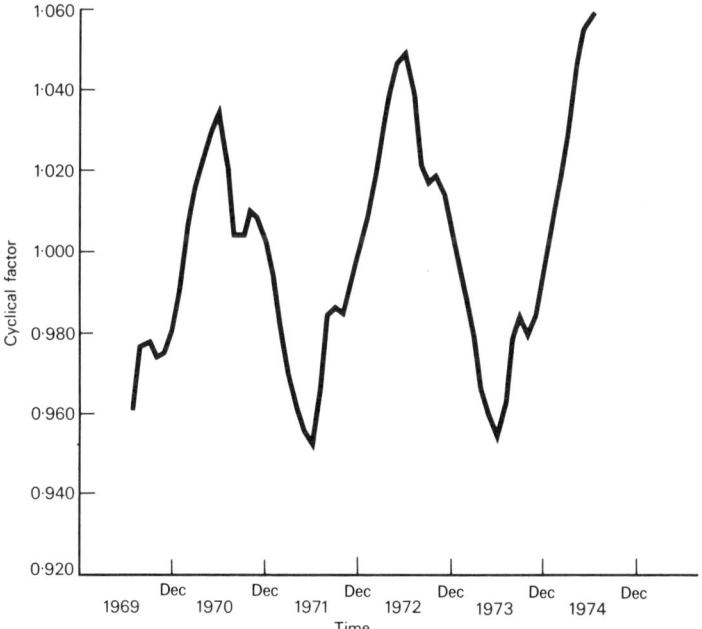

Figure 4.4

74 *Forecasting methods in business and management*

Table 4.4 Computation of the cyclical factor

	1 Actual	2 12 month moving average	3 Trend factor	4 Cyclical factor (column 2 ÷ column 3)
1969				
January	5452			
February	3897			
March	3621			
April	3802			
May	2970			
June	3067			
July	4896	4126.2	4292	·961
August	4002	4195.8	4292	·977
September	3679	4199.8	4292	·978
October	5826	4180.5	4292	·974
November	4093	4188.5	4292	·975
December	3527	4213.8	4292	·981
1970				
January	6817	4254.0	4292	·991
February	4209	4324.9	4292	1·007
March	3398	4369.2	4292	1·017
April	3562	4395.0	4292	1·023
May	3401	4419.7	4292	1·029
June	3245	4440.2	4292	1·034
July	5682	4389.7	4292	1·022
August	4917	4311.5	4292	1·004
September	3827	4312.6	4292	1·004
October	6298	4335.2	4292	1·010
November	4214	4327.9	4292	1·008
December	3897	4306.3	4292	1·003
1971				
January	5236	4273.4	4292	·995
February	3913	4212.6	4292	·981
March	3720	4165.9	4292	·970
April	3783	4130.0	4292	·962
May	3006	4104.1	4292	·956
June	3121	4091.6	4292	·953
July	5016	4147.4	4292	·966
August	4123	4228.7	4292	·985
September	3502	4239.3	4292	·987
October	5761	4231.2	4292	·985
November	4129	4259.9	4292	·992
December	3681	4299.3	4292	1·001
1972				
January	6792	4327.5	4292	1·008
February	4307	4372.4	4292	1·018
March	3581	4418.8	4292	1·029
April	3729	4470.5	4292	1·041
May	3748	4496.0	4292	1·047

Time series forecasting by classical decomposition analysis 75

	1 Actual	2 12 month moving average	3 Trend factor	4 Cyclical factor (column 2 ÷ column 3)
June	3324	4503.5	4292	1.049
July	5490	4461.2	4292	1.039
August	4726	4384.8	4292	1.021
September	4013	4369.1	4292	1.017
October	6492	4377.6	4292	1.019
November	4010	4352.5	4292	1.014
December	3978	4316.1	4292	1.005
1973				
January	5480	4286.8	4292	.998
February	3786	4245.3	4292	.989
March	3726	4203.2	4292	.979
April	3787	4149.4	4292	.966
May	3089	4116.7	4292	.959
June	3108	4100.5	4292	.955
July	5003	4130.3	4292	.962
August	4217	4202.2	4292	.979
September	3513	4225.6	4292	.984
October	5700	4208.4	4292	.980
November	4016	4224.1	4292	.984
December	3583	4270.4	4292	.994
1974				
January	6591	4315.7	4292	1.005
February	4401	4367.0	4292	1.017
March	3673	4413.4	4292	1.028
April	3427	4485.3	4292	1.045
May	3826	4531.0	4292	1.055
June	3481	4544.9	4292	1.058
July	5719			
August	4732			
September	4111			
October	6827			
November	3987			
December	3945			

shows the monthly cyclical factors in graphical form. Some forecasters may wish to compute a moving or yearly average of the figures appearing in column 4; a yearly average may be defended, since by looking at the results it appears the cycle is made up of a one year 'low' period and a one year 'high' period. Table 4.5 shows the mean annual cyclical factors; again the highest and the lowest observation have been omitted. The cyclical factor for the low years is around .977. For the high years the cyclical factor has grown. In the absence of any more data the forecaster should take the

Table 4.5 Computation of the average cyclical factor

Column 4, Table 4.4

	1969	1970	1971	1972	1973	1974
J		·991	·995	1·008	·998	1·005
F		1·007	·981	1·018	·989	1·017
M		1·017	·970	1·029	·979	1·028
A		1·023	·962	1·041	·966	1·045
M		1·029	·956	1·047	·959	1·055
J		1·034	·953	1·049	·955	1·058
J	·961	1·022	·966	1·039	·962	
A	·977	1·004	·985	1·021	·979	
S	·978	1·004	·987	1·017	·984	
O	·974	1·010	·985	1·019	·980	
N	·975	1·008	·992	1·014	·984	
D	·981	1·003	1·001	1·005	·994	
Mean*	·976	1·012	·977	1·025	·977	1·036

*after omitting the highest value and the lowest value.

cyclical factor for the next high year, 1976, to be about 1·035, this being the latest estimate.

An alternative method might have been to compute the cyclical factors for each month for low years and the cyclical factors for each month for high years. For example,

$$\text{cyclical factor (low years) for December} = \frac{·981 + 1·001 + ·994}{3} = ·992$$

$$\text{cyclical factor (high years) for December} = \frac{1·003 + 1·005}{2} = 1·004$$

The average cyclical factor for each month (in low years or other cyclical periods) are then added together and the average cyclical factors for each month (in high years or other cyclical periods) are added together. This gives the cyclical factor. For the example, however, we have kept to the prior aggregated values.

While seasonal and trend factors can be precisely calculated, the cyclical factor is more difficult to establish. From the above data, however, the forecaster may estimate it to be at about ·977 one year followed by a year at about 1·036. Clearly the cyclical component of a time series is the most difficult to identify and measure because of the different forces which create cycles, such as government economic policy not following a precise and consistent pattern.

In practice, some forecasters may calculate the seasonal and trend factors as above but estimate the future cyclical factor subjectively (possibly

Time series forecasting by classical decomposition analysis 77

also using the procedure described above). This is done because the cyclical factor is often so tenuous that computational techniques used alone may give authoritative but erroneous figures. The subjective methodology may involve a number of executives giving their opinions on the upturn-downturn, length and amplitude of cycles and the forecaster deriving probabilistic results (probabilistic forecasting is dealt with in Chapter 11).

Making a forecast using classical decomposition analysis

The forecaster is now in a position to prepare a forecast: for example, a forecast for January 1975 may be required. By using the expression

$$F_J = T_J \times S_J \times C_J$$

we can obtain a forecast (J standing for January); the random element has been dropped as this is incapable of being forecast. The trend factor we have established as 4292 for every month; the seasonal factor for January is taken from Table 4.3 which gives us a value of 1·460; the cyclical factor for 1975 we estimate as ·977. The forecast for January 1975 is therefore

$$F_t = 4292 \times 1·460 \times ·977 = 6122 \text{ books}$$

and the forecast for September 1975 (F_S) is

$$F_S = T_S \times S_S \times C_S$$
$$F_S = 4292 \times ·865 \times ·977$$
$$F_S = 3631 \text{ books}$$

Like many time series techniques, it is not possible to compute statistical confidence limits for the forecasts.

Review of the methodology

Classical decomposition forecasting can be summarized as follows:

1. Calculate the seasonal factor. This involves the ratio of the actual to the moving average method.
2. Calculate the trend factor. This is computed from a simple linear regression analysis of moving averages on time.
3. Calculate the cyclical factor. This is found by dividing the moving average by the trend factor. The cyclical factor is invariably the most tenuous as regards its use in forecasting.
4. The forecast is made by substituting in the values of the trend factor, the seasonal factor and the cyclical factor for the time period into the equation

$$F_t = T_t \times S_t \times C_t$$

where the subscript t stands for month t. Note the values of T and S normally change for each month. In the example the value of T just happened to be the same each month. The value of C may be taken as varying each month or may be regarded as changing over some other time period (for example a year, as in the example above).

5. The accuracy of the forecasts are again computed by measuring the mean absolute error and the mean squared error. The forecaster may use this analysis to see how much accuracy the cyclical element adds to the forecast; often this may be very little.

Classical decomposition analysis in use

Classical decomposition analysis has gained some popularity for a number of reasons:

1. It is intuitively appealing to managers and well within their powers of understanding. At the macro-economic level official statistics compiled by classical decomposition analysis are understandable by large numbers of the public.

2. It gives short-term forecasts which are of help to managers in the areas of stock planning, labour recruitment, etc. in seasonal businesses.

3. It has been found to give relatively good forecasting accuracy in the short term (say up to 2 or 3 years ahead). Thereafter it starts to deteriorate and its usefulness in longer-term situations (say beyond 5 years) is usually small.

The major costs involved with classical decomposition come at the development stage where the various trend, seasonal and cyclical factors are quantified. Once these have been established the forecasting is relatively cheap. Various standard computer programs are available for the calculations. The forecaster will need to recompute the various factors from time to time (when the forecasting errors become fairly large) and this of course will be fairly expensive again. In summary the technique is relatively cheap if the factors do not change significantly across time; if not, then the costs can be quite high.

Various modifications have been made to the standard classical decomposition method and two of them, Census II and Foran, are briefly described below. These add a certain level of sophistication to the technique. For the better equipped forecasting department, however, classical decomposition analysis is becoming a technique of declining importance. In particular the causal model building techniques described in Chapters 7, 8 and 9 can handle trend, seasonal and cyclical factors as well as many other items which affect the variable being forecast.

Modifications to classical decomposition analysis: Census II

This is a sophisticated version of classical decomposition analysis which has been developed at the United States Census Bureau since the 1950s. It consists of a computer program which, besides performing the traditional analysis, also adjusts the data in various ways:

1. It makes corrections to the time periods so that working or trading days are used instead of calendar months. This is done because the number of working or trading days in a calendar month vary, which of course influences business and economic data.

2. Extreme values are omitted from the analysis by statistical means; for example, values which are more than $\pm$ some number of standard deviations from a certain level are modified or dropped. This is in contrast to the method used in compiling Tables 4.3 and 4.5 where the highest and lowest values were dropped.

3. The irregular movements are isolated and smoothed and then used in the forecasting process.

4. Various graphical printouts are automatically given by the program.

5. Various modifications can be made to the method to take account of the particular circumstances.

Hence Census II provides advances in classical decomposition techniques as well as an easy to use computer program. It has received a fair amount of adoption in the U.S.A. both at the macro level and at the business firm level.

Foran II

This is another modified computer-based version of classical decomposition analysis, Foran being termed from forecasting analysis. It is designed to utilize any form of independent variable (i.e. not just time) and this has made it relevant to business decisions. The Foran method produces a number of forecasts along with their historical accuracy, each relating to a slightly differing model. The forecaster can then choose which model or combination of models to use in the forecasting process. Again this method has gained a fair amount of adoption by business firms. For a description of the technique see reference 6.

Link relative models

This is another method for forecasting when there are variations in the data. The procedure is as follows. First calculate the ratio of month to month (or other period) changes for successive months, i.e. (V June)/(V May). This gives the percentage growth during June. This growth may then be extrapolated for July. Alternatively the growth extrapolated for

July could be an average of several prior months; one such method is to compute the geometric average, e.g.

$$\sqrt[3]{\frac{V\,\text{July}}{V\,\text{June}} \times \frac{V\,\text{June}}{V\,\text{May}} \times \frac{V\,\text{May}}{V\,\text{April}}}$$

Thus if the sales values for April, May, June and July are 2000, 2500, 2750 and 3000 respectively, then the geometric average growth is

$$\sqrt[3]{\frac{3000}{2750} \times \frac{2750}{2500} \times \frac{2500}{2000}} = 1 \cdot 144$$

The forecast for August is $1 \cdot 144 \times 3000 = 3432$.

The forecaster must experiment on historical data to find the most suitable average to use. The above method is only likely to be of any use if there is a consistent growth in the trend and not too much seasonal variation. The link relative method and its derivatives are relatively weak forecasting models and little use has been, or is likely to be, made of them. They have been included in the present text as the method has been occasionally advocated in other text books.

Summary

Classical decomposition analysis and its various modifications offer considerable advantages over the simpler time series forecasting techniques when the data has a regular seasonal or cyclical pattern. Specifically it enables the underlying trend to be established, thus aiding longer-term forecasting; it also measures seasonal and cyclical factors, which aids short-term forecasting. Causal models and the more sophisticated time series models can also capture seasonal and cyclical factors, but these are more complex methods. Classical decomposition is instinctively appealing to many managers and hence its considerable popularity.

Suggested reading

1. Bonini, C., and Spurr, W., *Statistical Analysis for Business Decisions*, Irwin, 1968.
2. Business Cycle Developments 'Summary Description of X9 and X10 versions of the Census Method II Seasonal Adjustment Program', September, 1963.
3. Croxton, F. E., and Cowden, D. J., *Practical Business Statistics*, Prentice Hall, 1960.
4. Freund, J. E., and Williams, F. J., *Modern Business Statistics*, Prentice Hall, 1969.

5. Hamburg, M., *Statistical Analysis for Decision Making,* Harcourt, Brace and World, 1970.
6. McLaughlin, R. L., and Boyle, J. J., *Short-Term Forecasting,* American Marketing Association, 1968.
7. Shiskin, J., and Eisenpress, H., 'Seasonal Adjustments by Electronic Computer Methods', *Journal of the American Statistical Association,* December 1957.
8. Shiskin, J., 'Electronic Computers and Business Indicators', National Bureau of Economic Research, Occasional Paper 57.
9. U.S. Bureau of Labour Statistics, 'The BLS Seasonal Factor Method: Its Application by Electronic Computer', June 1963.
10. Young, A., 'Linear Approximations to the Census and BLS Seasonal Adjustment Methods', *Journal of the American Statistical Association,* June, 1968.

5

Adaptive methods of time series forecasting

Adaptive forecasting is the description given to methods which adapt themselves to the pattern of the data with which they are dealing. The basis of the methods is that the weightings used in the particular technique adjust as new data accrues. This contrasts with the time series methods described in Chapter 3 where the weightings used are fixed (e.g. the exponential smoothing fixed constant, a); when these weightings are tested and changed depends purely on the forecaster. This chapter briefly describes the major adaptive forecasting techniques. As will be seen, they correspond closely in nature to the techniques covered in Chapter 3, with the important difference that they include an adjustment process which alters the weightings to fit more accurately the changing state of the data. Adaptive techniques are especially important when the variable is non-stationary (this includes trend, seasonal, cyclical and rapidly changing data), since their forecasts respond quickly to changes in the data.

Adaptive filtering

This is a forecasting method based on moving averages but in which the specific data points have their own individual weights. The method requires the initial weightings to be estimated and then these are adjusted by a factor which is sometimes known as a learning constant. The adjustment is expressed as

$$W^\star = W + 2Ke\,V \qquad 5.1$$

where $W^\star$ = revised set of weights
W = old set of weights
K = the learning constant
e = error of the forecast
V = the values of the variable

The revised set of weights therefore equals the old set of weights plus some adjustment for the error calculated using the old weights. The adjustment is based on the error of the forecast using the old weights, the actual values of the variable under consideration and the value of the learning constant K. The learning constant determines how fast the weights are adjusted to match the situation, this being analagous to the α term in exponential smoothing.

The actual process of forecasting by adaptive filtering can be broken down into the following stages:

1. The forecaster has to set the number of weights and observations to include in the model. For monthly data 12 observations may be used, thus taking account of seasonal trends. A sales forecast would therefore be based on the sales of the preceding twelve months, although as we shall later see, the weights are derived by using several years of data. If there is no obvious number of observations to use then the forecaster can experiment with several numbers, again using forecasting accuracy as the criterion.

2. The forecaster must set a level for K. This is arbitrarily set although various values of K can be tried and the forecasting accuracy assessed. In general K should not be set at a value greater than ·25 as the process will not converge to the set of optimum weights; a value for K of ·10 may well be appropriate in many instances. As will be described later, the value of K has an important impact on the speed at which the weights are adjusted to those optimum for the time series data.

3. The forecaster has to estimate a set of initial weights, one for each of the twelve observations (monthly sales figures for the past year). These are often set arbitrarily, for example a $1/N$ weight may be assigned to each observation, N being the number of observations included in the model. (Other values could be used such as those based on the autocorrelations of the data: autocorrelation is described in Chapter 8.) These weightings are adjusted as described in stage 4.

4. We can now make a forecast for month 13, this being described as

$$F_{t13} = \sum_{i=1}^{12} W_i V_i \qquad 5.2$$

The error of the forecast is computed as $V_{13} - F_{t13}$ and designated as e. The weights W_i can now be revised using the learning process formula described earlier, i.e.

$W^* = W + 2KeV$

where W^* = new set of twelve weights
  W = old set of twelve weights
  K = learning constant, say ·10
  e = error = $V_{13} - F_{t13}$
  V = set of twelve observations, V_1 to V_{12}

5. The forecast for month 14 is now made using the new set of weights and the observations from month 2 to month 13. The error for month 14 is calculated and a new set of weights computed using the procedure described in 4. The procedure is continued over several years data, say up to month 60, the length of the period being determined by the availability of data. If there has been any major change in the level of demand, due to exceptional outside influences or changes in quality, then data prior to this change should be omitted. The weights established at month 60 are then used to recompute the forecast of month 13.

$$F_{t13} = \sum_{i=1}^{12} W_i V_i \qquad 5.3$$

where W_i = set of twelve weights established at period 60
V_i = set of twelve observations V_1 to V_{12}

The procedure is then continued up to month 60 and the whole process is reiterated. The number of iterations (i.e. runs over 60 months) to be done depends upon how accurate the forecasts are and what the increase in accuracy is for each additional iteration. The accuracy is again measured by computing the mean squared error; the percentage decrease in the mean-squared error gives the measure of the increase in accuracy of each successive iteration. The number of iterations that are required in order to get a reasonable level of accuracy depends upon both the nature of the variable and on the learning constant, K. The lower the level of K the less the response rate to errors in the prior forecast, while the higher the level of K the greater the response rate. The level which is set will be largely the result of the forecaster's judgement. If an inappropriate rate is selected, this means the number of iterations required to reach a certain level of accuracy will be greater than some other more appropriate level of K. If the value of K is below the optimum K, then there will be a lower error reduction with each iteration and hence more iterations will be required to reach a given level of accuracy. If the value of K is above the optimum K then the weights will be adjusted too rapidly and will be reacting to the random fluctuations in the data. Again this will lead to a greater number of iterations to achieve a given level of accuracy. The forecaster can test for various values of K on the data to see which is the most appropriate, although this requires significant computational costs. As a rough guide we can say that

    (a) The greater the random element in the data the smaller the value of K should be.

    (b) The greater the number of observations used the smaller the value of K should be.

    (c) As a general yardstick a K of greater than $\cdot 25$ is unsuitable as it does not converge to a set of optimal weights.

6. The optimum set of weights are now used to forecast future sales from month 61 onwards. The updating of the weights should continue at the same time so as to monitor any underlying changes in the time series.

Although there are a lot of calculations involved with adaptive filtering these are easily handled by a computer. The method only involves one equation, the revision of the weights equation, and the calculating of the errors, so the computing costs are relatively low.

Adaptive filtering is a far more powerful and sophisticated forecasting tool than those described in Chapter 3. Its main benefits come when the time series under investigation is fairly volatile, since other forecasting methods react very slowly to the changing values of the data. Additionally it can handle a wide variety of patterns and hence is not very restricted in its usage. Apart from its forecasting accuracy, adaptive filtering is also fairly easy to implement given computing facilities. For these reasons adaptive filtering techniques are likely to gain a growing acceptance during the coming years: for a more detailed discussion of adaptive filtering methods see references 8 and 9.

There are also a number of other methods which use an adaptive forecasting process and the major ones are described below.

Trigg and Leach's method (reference 7)
This method is akin to exponential smoothing but instead of using α, the value of Trigg's tracking signal is used (reference 6). The value of the tracking signal (designated S_t) changes according to the volatility of the data. Specifically S_t rises when the variable becomes more volatile and falls when it becomes more stable. In a stationary pattern situation the Trigg and Leach forecasting method is expressed as

$$F_{t+x} = S_t V_t + (1 - S_t) F_t \qquad 5.4$$

where F_{t+x} = forecast x periods ahead
V_t = value of variable at time t
F_t = forecast at time t
S_t = tracking signal value. This always takes a positive value

The value of the tracking signal is given by the ratio of the exponentially smoothed error ($e_t^\star$) to the exponentially smoothed mean absolute deviation ($MAD_t^\star$). Thus

$$S_t = \frac{e_{t+1}^\star}{MAD_{t+1}^\star} \qquad 5.5$$

where

$$e_{t+1}^\star = \alpha e_t + (1 - \alpha) e_t^\star \qquad 5.6$$

and

$$MAD_{t+1}^\star = \alpha \bar{e}_t + (1 - \alpha) MAD_t^\star \qquad 5.7$$

where $\bar{e}_t$ always takes a positive value thus minus signs are ignored (i.e. the absolute error).

When the forecasting inaccuracy starts to increase because of a change in the values of the variable, the value of S_t automatically increases (i.e. the $e_{t+1}\star$ rises proportionately faster than $MAD_{t+1}\star$) and therefore gives greater weight to the value of V_t (in equation 5.4). When the pattern becomes more stable the value of S_t falls and thus gives less weight to the last observed value, V_t. This prevents the model from over-reacting to small random fluctuations in the variable.

Trigg and Leach's method provides a model which is very responsive to sudden changes in data and represents a considerable improvement over exponential smoothing. The model can also be adapted for linear and seasonal trend data. Various modifications to the model have been proposed however; these have centred on the fact that even when the forecast accuracy becomes very good the value of the tracking signal still changes (i.e. the ratio given by equation 5.5 changes). One modification was that proposed by Shone who suggested lagging the value of S_t appearing in equation 5.4 (reference 4). Thus equation 5.4 now becomes

$$F_{t+x} = S_{t-1} V_t + (1 - S_{t-1}) F_t \qquad 5.8$$

Shone claimed that whilst this modification reduced the response of the forecast to changes in the individual values of V_t, it still rapidly captured the underlying changes in the value of the variable.

Chow's method (reference 2)
This is a somewhat cruder method than the two described earlier. It is based on forecasting by exponential smoothing but involves three equations which differ only by having a different smoothing constant. Methods can be devised which use more than three smoothing constants. The three values are the 'normal' value of a, a high value of a and a low value of a; for example, the three respective values could be 0·10, 0·15, 0·05. Forecasts are produced for the three constants. As soon as either the high or low constant gives a better forecast (using the minimization of error criterion), this a becomes the new normal constant. At this stage new high and low constants have to be derived. If the new normal a becomes 0·15 then the new high and low a terms might be taken as 0·20 and 0·10. In empirically testing the model Chow claimed the results were far better than those produced by exponential smoothing. However, as mentioned at the beginning of the paragraph, the method is cruder than many others and it also involves significant computational costs since a fair amount of data has to be stored.

Thamara's method (reference 5)

This method involves adjusting the value of the exponential smoothing constant, α, according to the degree of error in the prior forecast. Thamara especially advocated its use with seasonal data. Table 5.1 shows Thamara's estimates of the value of α required for various error sizes. Thus

Table 5.1

Exponential smoothing constant	Size of error %
0·20	10
0·22	11
0·30	15
0·34	17
0·38	19
0·40	20
0·50	25

if an error reaches say 15% of the value, V_t, then the smoothing constant to use is 0·30. If the error then rises to 20%, an α of 0·40 is required for the next forecast.

Thamara found this method significantly improved the accuracy of the forecasts over those given by exponential smoothing. Like Chow's method the model is somewhat crude, thus the adaptive filtering model and Trigg and Leach's model appear to be the best of the adaptive methods.

Box–Jenkins forecasting (reference 1)

The Box–Jenkins method is the most sophisticated and complex approach to analysing and forecasting time series data. Its main advantages lie in its ability to handle a wide variety of time series patterns and its usually greater forecasting accuracy. Against this must be weighed the increased costs of operating the technique which include computing time and the need for specialists to implement the model. The technique is complex and the forecaster has to interact with the model, hence experience of handling the Box–Jenkins approach is of considerable importance.

The Box–Jenkins approach is best described by referring to Figure 5.1 which gives a diagrammatic representation of the method. The Box–Jenkins approach postulates three general classes of model which can be used to describe any time series pattern. From one of these general models the forecaster makes an estimate of the specific type of model that might fit the data (Stage 1). At the next stage the parameters to the specific model are estimated and a check on the accuracy of the model is made. If the specific model is not adequate then the forecaster returns to stage 1 and identifies another specific model which may fit the data. This process is continued until a satisfactory model is found. When this occurs the forecaster passes on to stages 3 and 4 where the forecasts for future periods are made and where control systems are derived.

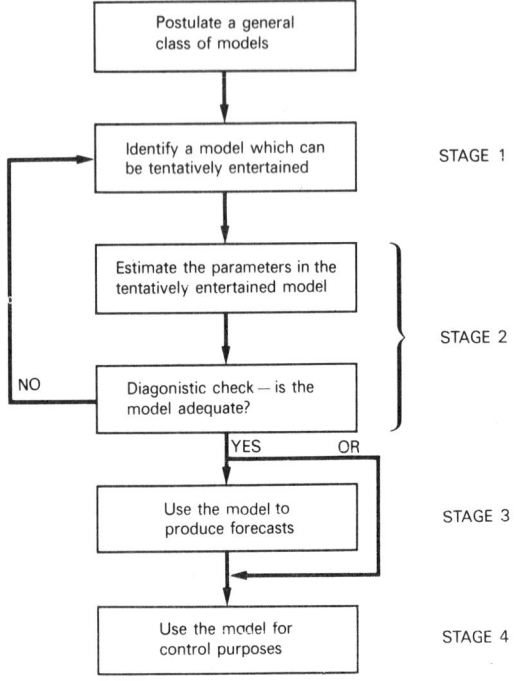

Figure 5.1
Source: *Time Series Analysis, Forecasting and Control* by Box and Jenkins, Holden-Day, 1970.

The Box–Jenkins approach postulates three general classes of model which can describe any time series pattern. These are autoregressive (AR), moving average (MA) and autoregressive integrated moving average (ARIMA) which is a combination of the first two.

The autoregressive model (AR) is of the type

$$X_t = \phi_1 X_{t-1} + \phi_2 X_{t-2} + \phi_3 X_{t-3} + \ldots \phi_p X_{t-p} + e_t \qquad 5.9$$

where X_t is the dependent variable, say unit sales,

$X_{t-1}, X_{t-2}, \ldots X_{t-p}$ are the independent variables representing past values of the dependent variable, i.e. past unit sales,

$\phi_1, \phi_2, \ldots \phi_p$ are the cofficients which are found by minimizing the sum of the squared errors (usually a non-linear regression routine is used),

e_t is the error term which represents the elements that cannot be explained by the equation. Various statistics on the forecast error, e_t, can be computed which give confidence limits for the forecasts of variable X.

Thus future values of sales are influenced by the past values of sales according to the relationship given in equation 5.9.

The moving average (MA) model is of the type

$$X_t = e_t - \theta_1 e_{t-1} - \theta_2 e_{t-2} - \theta_3 e_{t-3} \ldots - \theta_q e_{t-q} \qquad 5.10$$

where e_t is the error in period t and $e_{t-1}, e_{t-2}, \ldots e_{t-q}$ are prior values of the forecasting error. Equation 5.10 therefore says that the dependent variable X_t is influenced by the previous values of the forecasting errors. θ represent the weights of the dependent variables.

The autoregressive integrated moving average method (ARIMA) is a combination of the above two models (AR and MA) and is one which fits many time series data. It is of the form

$$\begin{aligned} X_t = &\phi_1 X_{t-1} + \phi_2 X_{t-2} + \ldots + \phi_p X_{t-p} + e_t \\ &- e_t - \theta_1 e_{t-1} - \theta_2 e_{t-2} - \ldots - \theta_q e_{t-q} \end{aligned} \qquad 5.11$$

Thus the forecast value of the dependent variable X (unit sales) is dependent upon both the past value of unit sales and the past values of forecasting accuracy.

The choice between these models has to be made by the forecaster. This choice and the deriving of a specific model (e.g. values for p and q) are conducted by examining the autocorrelations and the partial autocorrelations of the time series. Autocorrelation represents the correlation between the different values of one variable. Thus in a time series of say unit sales (X) autocorrelation is the correlation between $X_t, X_{t-1}, X_{t-2}, \ldots$. Autocorrelation can be measured over various lags, i.e. $X_t, X_{t-2}, X_{t-4} \ldots$; this is one factor that the forecaster will have to consider when deriving the specific model. The procedures involved with identifying suitable models from autocorrelations and partial autocorrelations are complex and require the help of a specialist; the interested reader should consult Box and Jenkins' book on time series analysis (reference 1). What can be said at this point however is that skill and judgement are required in formulating the models, hence experience in using the technique is an important attribute of the specialist.

The model is tested by computing the forecasting errors, that is the difference between the actual values of X_t and the forecast values of X_t. The autocorrelation of the errors is then measured. If the autocorrelations are very small and have no pattern, then the model fits the data and we can proceed to step 3 in Figure 5.1. If, on the other hand, the autocorrelations differ from zero and follow some sort of pattern, this indicates that our specific model is unsuitable and we must go back to stage 1 and identify a new specific model. The autocorrelations of the errors will be used to help in this identification, although again the exact procedures involved are beyond the realm of this text.

Once a correct model has been established we can then use it for forecasting purposes. In doing this, confidence limits can be attached to the forecast to give a range of likely outcomes. (As described on page 110 confidence limits are intervals within which we can be $X\%$ certain that the actual value will occur. Thus if the forecast is 11 150 units and the 95% confidence limits are 10 250 and 12 050 units, this means we can be 95% certain that the actual value of the variable will be between 10 250 and 12 050 units.) If there are any changes in the pattern of data then these will be highlighted by the method and the Box–Jenkins procedure can be repeated to find the new optimal model.

Summary

In summary, the Box–Jenkins method is the most powerful and sophisticated of the time series forecasting methods. Specifically it can handle a wide variety of data patterns and its forecasting accuracy is normally much better than other methods (see reference 3 for a recent comparison). However, these advantages have to be weighed against the increased costs of operating the system. As stated at the beginning of this section, significant computing and labour costs are required, the latter in the form of specialist staff who are vital if the method is to be successfully implemented. Whether the advantages outweigh the costs involved depends very much on the particular situation and here management has to exercise its judgement.

References

1. Box, G. E. P., and Jenkins, G. M., *Time Series Analysis, Forecasting and Control,* Holden-Day, 1970.
2. Chow, W. M., 'Adaptive control of the exponential smoothing constant', *Journal of Industrial Engineering,* **5,** 16, 1965.
3. Newbold, P., and Granger, C. W. J., 'Experience with forecasting univariate time series and the combination of forecasts', *Journal of the Royal Statistical Society,* A, 137, 1974.
4. Shone, M. L., 'Viewpoints', *Operational Research Quarterly,* **3,** 18, 1967.
5. Thamara, T., 'Exponential Smoothing With Automatic Weight Assignment', paper presented at the TIMS/ORSA Joint National Meeting, San Francisco, May, 1968.
6. Trigg, D. W., 'Monitoring a forecasting system', *Operational Research Quarterly,* 15, 1964.

7. Trigg, D. W., and Leach, A. G., 'Exponential smoothing with adaptive response rate', *Operational Research Quarterly*, **1,** 18, 1967.
8. Wheelwright, S. C., and Makridakis, S., 'An Examination of the Use of Adaptive Filtering in Forecasting', *Operational Research Quarterly*, **1,** 24, 1973.
9. Widrow, B., 'Adaptive Filter 1: Fundamentals', SU-SEL-66-126, Systems Theory Laboratory, Stanford University, Stanford, California, December 1966.

6

The monitoring of time series forecasting methods

It is obviously important to monitor the accuracy of any forecasting system as business and economic situations change over time. In the case of very regular, short-term forecasts a formal monitoring system is required, whereas in the case of longer-term forecasting, such as say econometric modelling, the monitoring process is likely to be less systematized. This chapter describes two techniques which have been used to monitor short-term, regularly-made time series forecasts. These are quantitative methods and as such they give consistent and unbiased results. Many forecasters still use either judgement or the visual inspection of a graph of the forecasts and the actual values as their sole monitoring process. While visual inspection and judgement will highlight major forecasting inaccuracies, they do not catch these at an early stage, so the forecasting system is usually well out of control (i.e. inappropriate to the changed circumstances and giving fairly large errors) by the time the forecaster recognizes that there has been a change. Additionally, if there are many forecasts to monitor (say 100) then human judgement and visual methods become quite arduous and time-consuming and can lead to poor performance.

Given that the monitoring process indicates a change in the underlying situation, the forecaster now has to try and explain why this is so and to remedy the forecasting procedures. Among the possible courses of action that can be taken are the following:

1. To see if there have been any substantial changes in the underlying economic factors which influence the value of the variable. This is especially necessary in regression and econometric modelling where these influencing variables are explicitly included in the model. Examples of changes in underlying economic factors are substantial relative price changes, substantial relative advertising changes and say changes in credit facilities allowed by the government.

2. To see if there have been any step rises in the time series of the data. This is particularly necessary when time series forecasts are required. An example of a step jump in the value of a variable is shown in Figure 6.1. The

sudden rise could be the result of say a reduction in a tax on sales (such as value added tax). Before the jump and after the jump the data follows a horizontal pattern, hence simple or double exponential smoothing provides a suitable forecasting technique. However at the time of the jump the techniques break down. This breakdown will be highlighted by the monitoring system and on realizing that it was caused by a step jump the forecaster can change the system, such that the forecast for month 4 will be the same as that of month 3, and build up a new set of exponential smoothing averages from there.

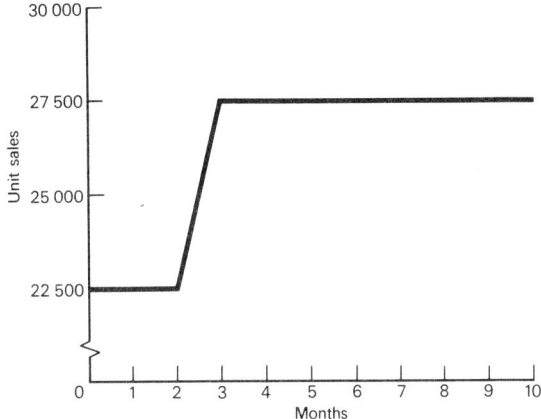

Figure 6.1 A step jump

3. To see if the variable has become more volatile or less volatile. If so, then new values of weightings can be established such as determining a new set of αs for the various techniques using some sort of exponential smoothing. Thus although the actual forecasting method has not been changed, its parameters have.

It is important that the forecaster makes the fullest use of the results of the monitoring process to improve forecasting accuracy and efficiency. The techniques described below represent two of the major formal monitoring measurements.

Cumulative sum technique (cusum) (reference 4)
This method involves calculating the cumulative sum of the forecasting errors and seeing if these break through predetermined control limits. If so, this indicates substantial inaccuracy by the forecasting method and the forecaster should investigate and take any necessary remedial action. A graphical form of the model is shown in Figure 6.2. The cumulative sum of

the errors is calculated and plotted on the graph. The control limits are shown in the figure in the shape of a V. In Figure 6.2 the forecasting system is under control, while in Figure 6.3 the cumulative sum of the errors

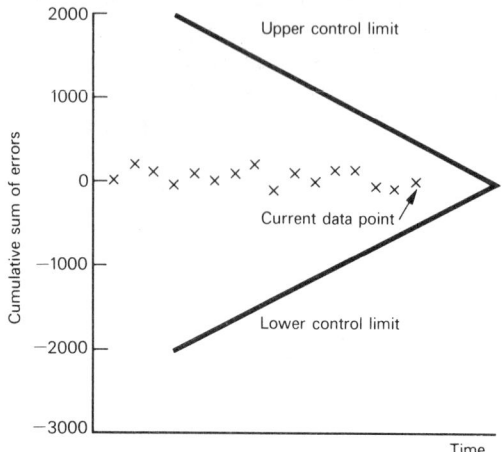

Figure 6.2

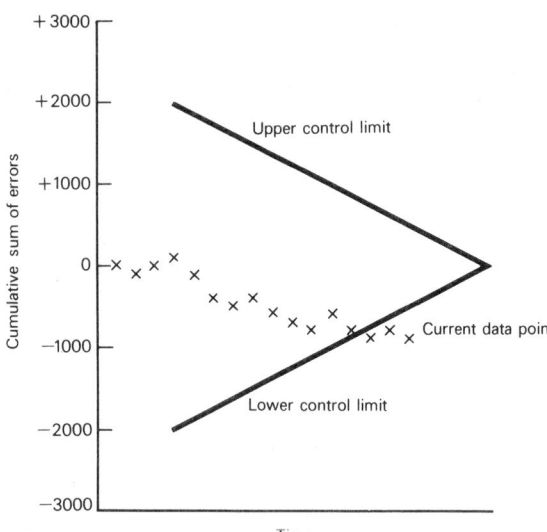

Figure 6.3

breaks through the lower control limit, suggesting significant inaccuracy in the forecasts.

The main problem facing the forecaster is to compute the values of the control limits: for a description of the methods that can be employed in determining these see reference 3. In practice, however, the control limits are often derived subjectively.

The cusum method can be used for

1. Identifying even small changes in the average of a variable and the time at which they occurred.
2. Determining an estimate of the new average level of a variable after a change.
3. Making short-term forecasts of this new average level of the variable.

The technique is especially suited to quality control situations where specified levels are set for the variable (for example, the weight of a foodstuff) and where tolerance levels are set. In such cases regular monitoring is needed and the control limits can perhaps be more easily set (i.e. having reference to any tolerance levels). Unfortunately the method is more difficult to apply in other situations and has therefore received little attention outside of quality control. (See reference 2 for a recent application of the technique.)

Trigg's method (reference 5)
This method is based on calculating what Trigg called the tracking signal (as used in Trigg and Leach's adaptive forecasting method, page 85), whose value suggests whether or not the forecasting system has become inappropriate for the situation. Further estimates of the statistical confidence intervals for the tracking signals have been made and these add to the sophistication of the method. The tracking signal (S_t) is given by the ratio of the exponentially smoothed error ($e_{t+1}{}^\star$) to the exponentially smoothed mean absolute deviation ($MAD_{t-1}{}^\star$). This is expressed as

$$S_t = \frac{e_{t+1}{}^\star}{MAD_{t+1}{}^\star} \qquad 6.1$$

where $e_{t+1}{}^\star = \alpha e_t + (1-\alpha) e_t{}^\star$ $\qquad$ 6.2
$\qquad e_t = V_t - F_t$ i.e. the difference between the actual value and the forecast including the $+$ and $-$ sign

and
$\qquad MAD_{t+1}{}^\star = \alpha \bar{e}_t + (1-\alpha) MAD_t{}^\star$ $\qquad$ 6.3
$\qquad \bar{e}_t = V_t - F_t$ i.e. the difference between the actual value and the forecast but ignoring the $+$ and $-$ signs (the absolute error)

Normally the value of α is the same for both equations 6.2 and 6.3, although it is possible to differentiate the values if thought necessary. The tracking signal takes the value between ± 1 and estimates of statistical confidence limits have been made: Table 6.1 shows some values. This table was constructed by Batty (1) and differed somewhat from Trigg's original table, which was biased to some degree as autocorrelation (see Chapter 8) is present in the forecasting errors when exponential smoothing methods are used.

If, for example, the tracking signal amounted to ·59 when an α of 0·2 was being used in the forecasting situation, then from Table 6.1 we could be 95% certain that the forecasting system had gone out of control, i.e. substantial errors were being made (there being a 5% probability that the tracking signal had arisen from purely random factors). The sign of the

Table 6.1 Values for Trigg's tracking signal

Level of confidence %	Tracking signal (+ or −)				
	$\alpha = 0.1$	$\alpha = 0.2$	$\alpha = 0.3$	$\alpha = 0.4$	$\alpha = 0.5$
70	0·24	0·33	0·44	0·53	0·64
80	0·29	0·40	0·52	0·62	0·73
85	0·32	0·45	0·57	0·67	0·77
90	0·35	0·50	0·63	0·72	0·82
95	0·42	0·58	0·71	0·80	0·88
96	0·43	0·60	0·73	0·82	0·89
97	0·45	0·62	0·76	0·84	0·90
98	0·48	0·66	0·79	0·87	0·92
99	0·53	0·71	0·82	0·92	0·94
100	1·00	1·00	1·00	1·00	1·00

Source: *Operational Research Quarterly*, 20, 1969, Table 2.

tracking signal indicates whether the forecasts are giving lower values of the variable than those actually occurring (+ sign) or whether the forecasts are above the actual values (− sign).

Trigg's method has been found to give good results both for quality control and demand forecasting. It has already gained some acceptance in these particular areas.

Summary

Apart from the above techniques which are specifically applicable to time series data, the forecaster will also make use of the measurements of the mean absolute error, the mean squared error and Theil's inequality coefficient. These were described in Chapter 2 and have been referred to several times throughout the text when discussing accuracy. The forecaster has to use judgement when interpreting the error measurements as regards the reliability that can be placed on the forecasts.

References

1. Batty, M., 'Monitoring an exponential smoothing forecasting system', *Operational Research Quarterly,* 20, 1969.
2. Bestwick, P. F., 'A Forecast Monitoring and Revision System for Top Management', *Operational Research Quarterly,* **2,** 26, 1975.
3. Harrison, P. J., and Davies, O. L., 'The use of cumulative sum (cusum) techniques for the control of routine forecasts of product demand', *Operations Research,* 12, 1964.
4. I. C. I., *Cumulative Sum Techniques,* I.C.I. Monograph No. 3, Oliver & Boyd, 1964.
5. Trigg, D. W., 'Monitoring a forecasting system', *Operational Research Quarterly,* 15, 1964.

7

An introduction to simple regression and correlation

In Chapters 3, 4 and 5 we discussed forecasting methods which involved predicting values on the basis of time only. These methods made no attempt to identify the causes of the changes in the value of the variable being predicted but instead used patterns in historical data to forecast the variable. This and the next two chapters discuss the more sophisticated causal model type of forecasting. Specifically this chapter introduces the statistics of the approach, while Chapter 8 expands on the techniques and Chapter 9 discusses the building of causal or explanatory models.

Causal models

Causal models (also known as explanatory or relational models, or regression models when the descriptive causal models have been quantified) are those that relate the value of the variable being forecast (known as the dependent variable) to various independent variables which influence it. For example, the volume sales made by a raincoat manufacturer (S) may depend on a number of factors such as the price of the raincoat relative to competitors' products (P), the personal disposable income of the population (I), the amount spent on advertising relative to the industry average (A) and the level of rainfall (R). The volume of raincoat sales is the dependent variable (i.e. it depends upon the values of P, I, A, and R) and the variables P, I, A, and R are the independent variables. P, I, A and R influence or cause the value of S, hence the use of the terms causal and explanatory models. Of course there may be many more variables which influence raincoat sales and these should be incorporated into the model. This requires a detailed knowledge of the business and the markets in which it operates. The identification of the influencing variables is perhaps the most important part of the analysis and Chapter 9 discusses this aspect in some detail.

The above raincoat example can be expressed notationally in the

An introduction to simple regression and correlation 99

following equation:

$$S = f(P, I, A, R)$$

where f stands for function. This contrasts with time series methods, where forecasts of sales of raincoats would be a function of past sales, e.g.

forecast of $S = f$(time series of S)

The function would depend upon the particular time series technique being used. The causal model says raincoat sales depend upon the values of P, I, A and R.

The next thing that a manager will want to know is by how much do volume sales of raincoats vary with changes in relative prices, personal disposable income, relative advertising and relative rainfall. Thus having formed an economic model of the influencing variables, it is now necessary to quantify the relationships. This quantification of the economic model involves statistical procedures which are grouped under the headings of regression and correlation. These provide weightings for the various independent variables and give measures of association of the independent variables with the dependent variable, the reliability of the model and the uncertainty surrounding the forecast made from the model.

The raincoat sales model can be expressed in the form

$$S = aP + bI + cA + dR$$

once the statistical stage has been completed. The letters a, b, c and d stand for the regression coefficients or weightings attached to each independent variable. The impact of a change in any of the independent variables on the volume sales of raincoats can now be measured from the regression model. The model can be used as a forecasting device by inserting values of the independent variables in the equation and thus determining the dependent variable. In doing this the independent variables must either (a) be known in advance of the dependent variable (b) be forecast with a good deal of accuracy (c) be in a lagged relationship with the dependent variable; this means that the independent variable is known in advance. Apart from its usefulness in forecasting, the regression model can also tell management of the impact of its various policy decisions. Thus in the raincoat example the management has virtually no control over individuals' personal disposable income or over the amount of rainfall, but it does have some control over the prices it charges to customers (this is governed to some extent by competitors' pricing strategies) and its advertising expenditure. Management will want to know what changes it should make in its pricing and advertising policies in order to maximize its volume sales. (In fact management will probably want to maximize the present values of future cash flows.

Thus another model relating prices and advertising to cash flows is required. For convenience here we assume that maximizing sales volume is consistent with maximizing the present value of cash flows.) By experimenting with various possible strategies within the model format, management will be able to determine its optimum policy. Thus apart from forecasting the future under existing business strategies, causal models also allow us to forecast future outcomes after allowing for changes in various factors under management's control. This facility is not available with time series methods, giving a significant advantage to causal models.

Advantages of causal models in forecasting

The major advantages of causal models over time series methods can be summarized as follows:

1. Causal models search for the underlying factors affecting the value of a variable. If any of these influencing variables change dramatically from their prior values (e.g. a large increase in indirect taxation on the product) then time series models will be hopelessly inaccurate; causal models if specified adequately can capture this impact and take it into account in producing a forecast. If we cannot identify a cause and effect model but we know there is some degree of association between various variables we can still use this fact to forecast if we know the values of the associated variables ahead of the variable we are attempting to forecast.

2. The forecast produced from the model can be expressed as a range of outcomes and the reliability of the forecast can be expressed in objective probabilistic terms.

3. The impact of changing policies relating to controllable variables can be measured.

However, causal models are more expensive than time series methods, because of the cost of labour in building the model and collecting data to test it, and herein lies their main disadvantage.

The initial building of the causal model is discussed in Chapter 9 where various cases of the actual application of model building are described. The remainder of this chapter describes the basic statistical techniques used in quantifying the causal model. The emphasis however is on the interpretation of the statistics, the requirements of the method, and the uses and benefits from it. The theory of regression is not discussed, since this does not need to be known by the manager or indeed the forecaster. Regression analyses are available for virtually every make and system of computer, hence the forecaster need only concentrate on the inputs into the computer (the model format and quantitative data) and the outputs (interpreting the results and making forecasts). The reader who is interested in the theory of

An introduction to simple regression and correlation 101

regression should consult the references at the end of this chapter.

In this chapter we are considering simple regression and correlation; this is where there is only one independent variable, enabling the techniques to be clearly established without encumbering the text with large amounts of arithmetic. These basic techniques are also used in multiple regression analysis, which is dealt with in Chapter 8 along with a description of the various problems involved with regression.

Simple linear regression and correlation

Simple linear regression quantifies a causal model where there is just one independent variable. Thus $Y = f(X)$ where Y is the dependent variable and X is the independent variable. Further, the relationship (f) is linear, that is the relationship between Y and X can be explained by a straight line.

Table 7.1

Mail order sales in units	Replies (to whom a catalogue sent)
Y	X
4	30
10	54
8	40
40	140
64	173
15	59
32	86
87	210
26	92
51	150
80	147
53	137
48	130
22	64
11	55
69	150
87	251
37	102
72	191
44	120

As an example, take the case of a mail order firm, MOF Ltd, which is trying to forecast its future sales. Each month MOF circulates householders with a promotional brochure and asks them to return a postage paid card if they wish to receive a mail order catalogue. This catalogue relates to goods on offer that month, the catalogue being changed each month. In order to see if any relationship exists between the replies and sales volume, management investigates recent data. The data is shown in Table 7.1 and plotted in Figure 7.1. From Figure 7.1 it can be seen that the relationship between replies and sales can be approximated by a straight line. This straight line relationship can be then used to forecast future sales from replies. For example, if the replies came to 180 in the next month then volume sales for that period would be read off from Figure 7.1 as 69 units.

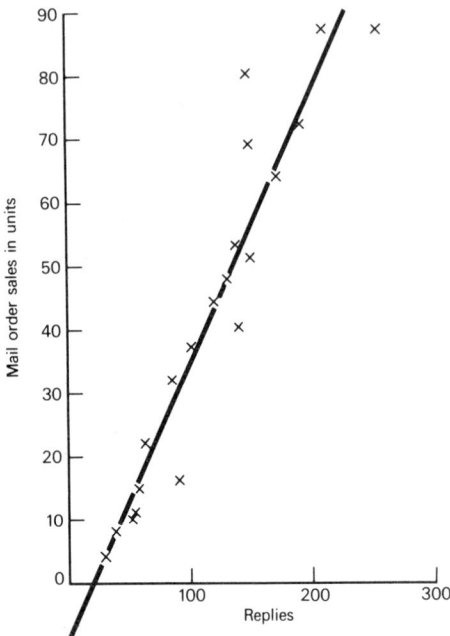

Figure 7.1

Management will, however, want to quantify the relationship shown in Table 7.1 and Figure 7.1. The reason for this is that economic data is usually scattered about the straight line and problems arise in

1. Determining the straight line.
2. Ascertaining the reliability that can be placed on the forecast.

Figure 7.2 (a) and (b) show relationships between two variables. In (a) the recordings lie very near to a straight line and in this case management could use the graph alone in forecasting. In (b), however, there are a number of straight lines which could plausibly fit the data and the recordings are some way from the straight line(s). A relationship such as Figure

An introduction to simple regression and correlation

7.2 (b) needs to be quantified and this figure is representative of most economic and business data.

3. When the causal model includes more than one independent variable it becomes impossible to plot the relationship on graph paper and fitting a straight line by eye also becomes impossible.

The relationship is quantified by simple regression analysis, which assumes that the relationship between the two variables can be expressed by a straight line. In practice we would first plot the recordings on graph

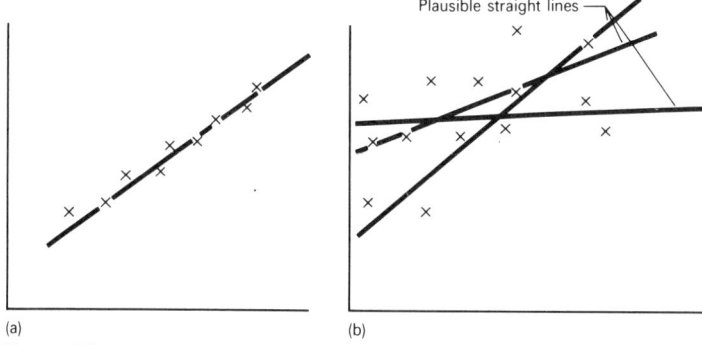

(a) (b)
Figure 7.2

paper to see if the linearity assumption holds before commencing with regression analysis. In notational terms simple regression is expressed as

$Y = a + bX$

where Y = volume sales and X = replies. The terms a and b are known as regression coefficients although a is often referred to as the constant, since its value and impact on Y never changes. The coefficient b represents the change in the value of Y for a one unit change in X. The figure for b represents the slope of the straight line.

Because the observations plotted in Figure 7.1 do not lie exactly along the straight line, the relationship is more properly described as

$Y = a + bX + U$

where U represents the error term. This indicates that Y is not precisely determined for given values of X, which may be due to other variables influencing Y quite apart from X and/or errors in the measurement of variables. The U term, however, is expected to have a mean of zero; that is, the addition of the Us (some being positive, some negative) adds up to zero. There are further requirements that the error term, U, has to meet and these are discussed on pages 120 to 122.

Least squares method

We need to determine the values of a and b in order to use the causal model as a forecasting device. These parameters are found by what is known as least squares regression. This method minimizes the sum of the squared deviations for all the observations. The deviations represent the differences between the actual observation and the corresponding value on the straight line. Figure 7.3 gives a simplified graphical example. The observed values

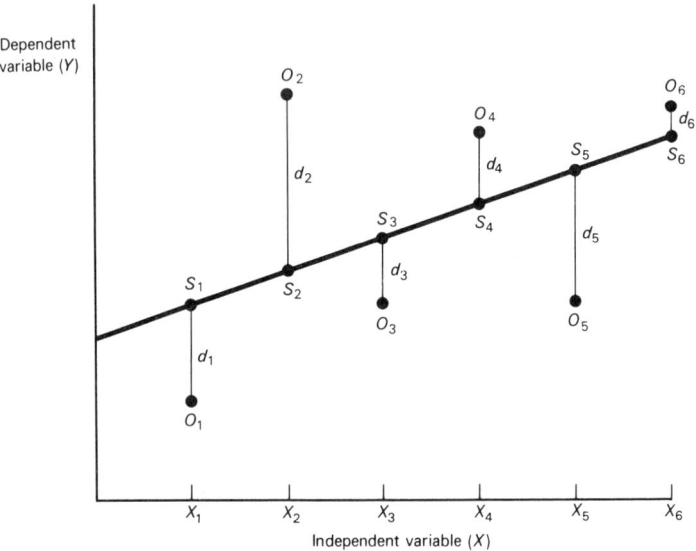

Figure 7.3

of the dependent variable are designated $O_1, O_2, O_3, O_4, O_5,$ and O_6. The corresponding values on the straight line are designated $S_1, S_2, S_3, S_4, S_5,$ and S_6. The deviations between the observed values and the values given by the regression line are designated $d_1, d_2, d_3, d_4, d_5, d_6$. (Thus $d_1 = O_1 - S_1$.) The values of $S_1, S_2, S_3, S_4, S_5,$ and S_6, are obtained by substituting the known values of X into the regression equation; for example, $S_1 = a + bX_1$, where X is the independent variable. The least squares regression line is the one which is produced by minimizing the sum of the squared deviations; that is, the sum of $d_1^2, d_2^2, d_3^2, d_4^2, d_5^2, d_6^2$ is a minimum, or alternatively, $\Sigma (O-S)^2$ is minimized (where $(O-S) = d$). In addition, the sum of the deviations $(O - S)$ equals zero, showing that the deviations are spread evenly above and below the regression line.

Using the criterion of minimizing the sum of the squares we can determine the values of b and a by the following expression:

$$b = \frac{n \Sigma XY - (\Sigma X)(\Sigma Y)}{n \Sigma X^2 - (\Sigma X)^2} \qquad 7.1$$

$$a = \frac{\Sigma Y}{n} - \frac{b \Sigma X}{n} \qquad 7.2$$

where n equals the number of observations. These expressions can be simplified by calling the mean value of the Ys and Xs as $\overline{Y}$ and $\overline{X}$. Hence

$$\overline{Y} = \frac{\Sigma Y}{n} \text{ and } \overline{X} = \frac{\Sigma X}{n}$$

Equations 7.1 and 7.2 now become

$$b = \frac{\Sigma (XY) - \overline{X} \Sigma Y}{\Sigma (X^2) - \overline{X} \Sigma X} \qquad 7.3$$

$$a = \overline{Y} - b\overline{X} \qquad 7.4$$

Table 7.2 shows the computations involved in calculating the regression coefficients for data relating to sales and the number of sales representatives employed by a firm. (Six observations is an unrealistically small

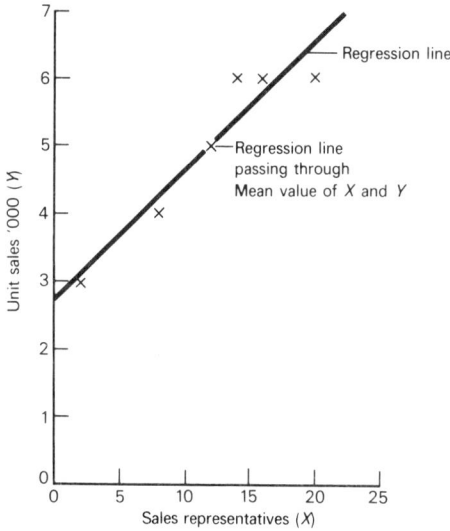

Figure 7.4

number used only for ease of computation.) Figure 7.4 plots the recordings graphically. The regression equation has been determined as

$$Y = 2 \cdot 72 + \cdot 19 X$$

Table 7.2

Sales representatives	Unit sales '000					
X	Y	X^2	Y^2	XY	Ye	$Y - Ye$	$Ye - \bar{Y}$
2	3	4	9	6	3.1	−0.10	−1.90
8	4	64	16	32	4.24	−0.24	−0.76
14	6	196	36	84	5.38	+0.62	+0.38
12	5	144	25	60	5.00	0.00	0.00
16	6	256	36	96	5.76	+0.24	+0.76
20	6	400	36	120	6.52	−0.52	+1.52
72	30	1064	158	398		$\Sigma(Y - Ye) = 0.00$	$\Sigma(Ye - \bar{Y}) = 0.00$

Note: Ye is the estimate of Y given by the regression equation ($Y = 2.72 + .19 X$)

$$\bar{X} = \frac{72}{6} = 12$$

$$\bar{Y} = \frac{30}{6} = 5$$

$$b = \frac{\Sigma(XY) - \bar{X}\Sigma Y}{\Sigma(X^2) - \bar{X}\Sigma X} \qquad a = \bar{Y} - b\bar{X}$$

$$= \frac{398 - 12(30)}{1064 - 12(72)} \qquad = 5 - .19(12)$$

$$= \frac{398 - 360}{1064 - 864} \qquad = 5 - 2.28$$

$$= \frac{38}{200} \qquad = 2.72$$

$$= .19$$

which is interpreted as follows:

1. Even if no salesmen were employed, unit sales would still be 2720 (2·72 thousand). Thus customer loyalty and lack of competition produces sales without the firm employing sales representatives.
2. For every sales representative employed unit sales will be increased by 190 units (·19 thousand).

It will be noted that the regression line passes through the mean value of X (12) and the mean value of Y (5). Further, the sum of the deviations of the observations from those given by the regression line is zero ($\Sigma(Y - Ye) = 0$).

Management can use the regression line in forecasting future sales. By knowing the number of sales representatives it is going to, or can, employ a forecast of sales can be made. For example if 24 salesmen are employed in the subsequent year, the sales will be

$Y = a + bX$
$Y = 2\cdot72 + \cdot19(24)$
$Y = 7\cdot28$ thousand
$Y = 7280$ units

(In practice this relationship may not be linear beyond a certain point; other factors come into play, such as market saturation. However, for the example the relationship is assumed to be linear.) Management will then examine the impact of this level of sales and the costs involved in relation to profits, and will take any action that it is required.

Table 7.3 shows the computation of the regression coefficients for the earlier example of the mail order sales. The equation is

$Y = -8\cdot159 + \cdot4297X$

This is interpreted as follows:

1. If no replies are received then volume sales will be minus 8·159 units! Clearly this is impossible and shows that management has to use judgement in certain instances in examining regression results. In this case the recording has arisen because the regression coefficients used in quantifying the model are only approximates of the true coefficients and because the linearity assumption may be true for only certain ranges.
2. For every reply received volume sales can be expected to increase by ·4297 units. This is represented by the b term. Thus b gives an average of the number of mail order unit sales generated by replies; some replies will result in sales of varying amounts of units, while others will generate no sales at all.

Management can now use the regression equation to forecast future sales; for example, if the replies received from the latest circulation come to 200 then unit sales for the forthcoming month will be

$Y = a + bX$
$Y = -8 \cdot 15 + \cdot 4297(200)$
$Y = 77 \cdot 79$
$Y = 78$ units

Table 7.3

Mail order sales units	Replies			
Y	X	Y^2	X^2	XY
4	30	16	900	120
10	54	100	2 916	540
8	40	64	1 600	320
40	140	1600	19 600	5 600
64	173	4096	29 929	11 072
15	59	225	3481	885
32	86	1024	7 396	2 752
87	210	7569	44 100	18 270
26	92	676	8 464	2 392
51	150	2601	22 500	7 650
80	147	6400	21 609	11 760
53	137	2809	18 769	7 261
48	130	2304	16 900	6 240
22	64	484	4 096	1 408
11	55	121	3 025	605
69	150	4761	22 500	10 350
87	251	7569	63 001	21 837
37	102	1369	10 404	3 774
72	191	5184	36 481	13 752
44	120	1936	14 400	5 280
860	2381	50 918	352 071	131 868

$\bar{Y} = \dfrac{860}{20} = 43$

$\bar{X} = \dfrac{2381}{20} = 119 \cdot 05$

$b = \dfrac{\Sigma XY - \bar{X} \Sigma Y}{\Sigma (X^2) - \bar{X} \Sigma X}$

$ = \dfrac{131\,868 - 119 \cdot 05\,(860)}{352\,071 - 119 \cdot 05\,(2381)}$

$ = \dfrac{131\,868 - 102\,383}{352\,071 - 283\,438 \cdot 05}$

$ = \dfrac{29\,485}{68\,612 \cdot 95}$

$ = \cdot 4297$

$a = \bar{Y} - b\bar{X}$
$ = 43 - \cdot 4297\,(119 \cdot 05)$
$ = 43 - 51 \cdot 159$
$ = 8 \cdot 159$

An introduction to simple regression and correlation 109

Accuracy of the regression model

The regression equation is subject to two types of error, both of which can seriously effect the accuracy of a forecast:

1. There may be other factors influencing the dependent variable, so that the model $Y = a + bX$ does not give a perfect fit.
2. In determining the coefficients a and b we only use a sample of observations, it usually being impractical or impossible to obtain recordings of all the population. Thus the figures found for a and b are only estimates of the true α and β of the population. The inaccuracies of these estimates are known as sampling errors. The greater the number of observations taken, the greater is the accuracy of the regression. Of course the collecting of data is expensive and time consuming and so there has to be a trade off with accuracy. Fortunately regression theory has evolved methods of quantifying the accuracy and significance of models and of the forecasts produced therefrom. The main measures of accuracy and significance that will concern management are discussed in the following paragraphs.

Typically management will want to know

1. How confident are we when we make a forecast of Y that the actual value of Y will be within a narrow range of the forecast?
2. What reliability can be placed in the regression coefficients? Are they significantly different from zero? Within what range of the true coefficients do the estimated coefficients lie (remembering a and b are calculated from sample data)?

There are two major methods of assessing how well a calculated regression coefficient fits the given observations. One method is to compute what is known as the standard error of the estimate, while the other is correlation. The standard error of the estimate (SEf) is given by the expression

$$SEf = \sqrt{\frac{\Sigma(Y - Ye)^2}{n - 2}} \qquad 7.5$$

where Ye represents the estimate of Y given by the regression equation and n equals the number of observations of Y.

The above formula for the standard error of the forecast is applicable if the number of observations is large and if the scatter of the actual observations around the regression line is narrow. If these conditions are not met then an adjustment has to be made to the formula to allow for the fairly high sampling error that will be present in estimating the coefficients a and b. This adjustment is

$$SEf = \sqrt{\frac{\Sigma(Y - Ye)^2}{n - 2}} \sqrt{1 + \frac{1}{n} + \frac{(X - \bar{X})^2}{\Sigma(X - \bar{X})^2}} \qquad 7.6$$

where $\bar{X}$ equals the mean of the recordings for X.

The standard error of the forecast is in fact the standard deviation of the differences between the actual values of Y and the values calculated from the regression line (Ye). Thus for the data in Table 7.3 the standard error of the estimate is

$$\sqrt{\frac{1257 \cdot 4}{20 - 2}} = 8 \cdot 35$$

The bigger the standard error of the estimate as a percentage of the actual value of Y, the less precise any forecast will be.

This standard error of the estimate can now be used to calculate confidence limits for our forecast of Y. Confidence limits are the range in which we can be $X\%$ certain that the actual value of Y will occur. Tables exist for normal distributions which show the probability of an actual event being within so many standard deviations of the forecast value of that event. Figure 7.5 shows a normal distribution and one, two and three standard deviations from the mean on either side of the mean. The statistical tables for normal distributions which are given in basic texts on statistics show that 68·27% of events come within 1 standard deviation of either side of the mean, 95·45% of events come within 2 standard deviations and 99·73% come within 3 standard deviations. These are usually referred to as the 68%, 95% and 99% confidence limits. The 95% confidence limit or interval is the usual significance level adopted. As described before, if we receive 200 replies in the next period the model gives a forecast of 77·79 unit sales. Having calculated the standard error of the estimate to be 8·35 we can now say that we are 95% certain that the actual

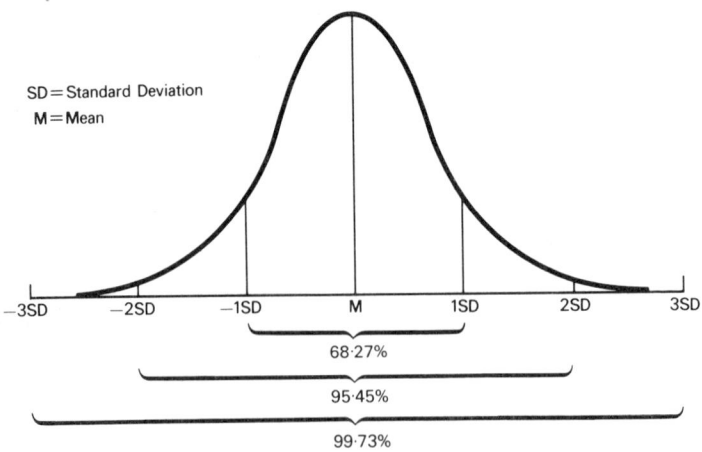

Figure 7.5 A normal distribution and one, two and three standard deviations

outcome for sales will be within ± 2 (8·35) units of the mean, i.e. between 94·49 units and 61·09 units.

This information greatly aids management since, quite apart from giving a central value forecast, the probability of sales of any other amount can be derived. Figure 7.6 shows a cumulative distribution of possible sales for a level of replies received. It can be seen that there is an 85% chance

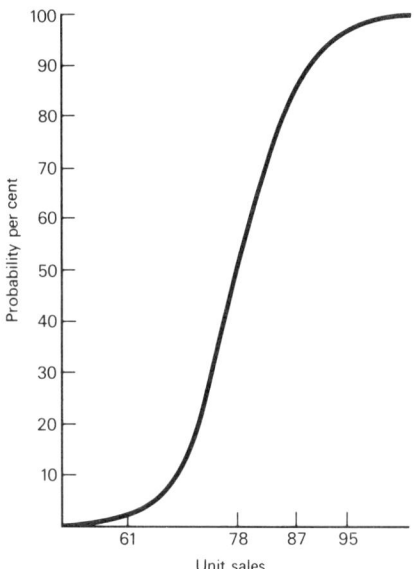

Figure 7.6 A cumulative distribution

that sales will be less than 87 units. The profits relating to each level of sales can be substituted and in this way a probabilistic picture of possible outcomes is given. (See page 194 for another example of the use of normal distribution tables in producing probabilistic forecasts.) Figure 7.7 gives a hypothetical profits profile relating to the sales. On this basis, management can take any action considered necessary given their attitudes to risk and the possible outcomes derived from the forecast. The confidence limits for a forecast depends on how far the forecast is from the mean of the replies ($\bar{X}$). Figure 7.8 shows the range of confidence limits for a regression line.

The coefficients a and b are obtained from sample data and are therefore only approximates of the true values of α and β. Here we shall only discuss significance tests for bs. There are tests for examining the significance of the constant coefficient a but because of the usual relative unimportance of

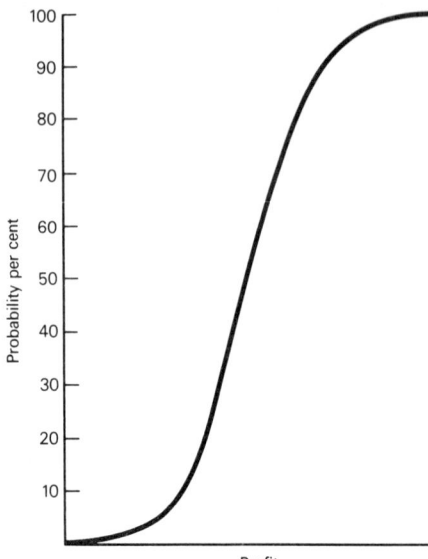

Figure 7.7

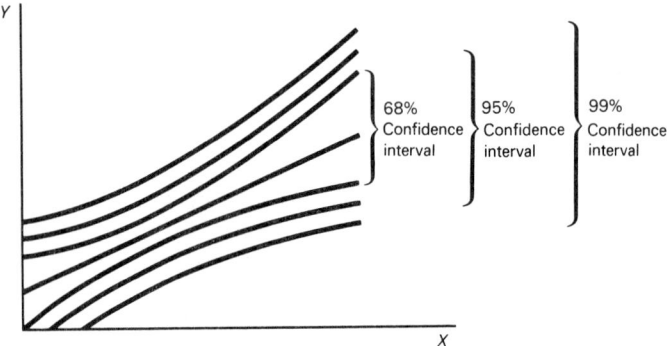

Figure 7.8

this coefficient we shall not discuss the tests here; the interested reader should consult the suggested reading at the end of the chapter. The measure of the sampling error of b is obtained by calculating the standard error of b from one sample to another; it is expressed as

$$SEb = \frac{\sqrt{\frac{\Sigma(Y-Ye)^2}{n-2}}}{\sqrt{\Sigma(X-\bar{X})^2}} \qquad 7.7$$

where Ye, $\bar{X}$, and n have the same meanings as before.

An introduction to simple regression and correlation 113

The standard error of the coefficient for the mail order example is computed as ·0319.

The t test is a statistical procedure to see if the value obtained for b is in fact significantly different from zero, i.e. the value for b could just have occurred through chance. The t statistic is obtained by dividing b by the standard error of b:

$$t = \frac{b}{SEb} \qquad 7.8$$

The value of t is then compared against the tables of t values to test for significance at certain significance levels (usually the 95% significance level). If the t value is higher than the figure appearing in the t tables, then the b coefficient is different from zero at that level of significance. In the example the t value is computed as follows:

$$t = \frac{b}{SEb}$$

$$= \frac{\cdot 4297}{\cdot 0319}$$

$$= 13 \cdot 46$$

In general a t value of 2 or more tells us that we can be very confident that the b value is not zero. If, however, the b coefficient was calculated from a small sample, say less than 15, then a high value of t is required. In the example the regression coefficient, b, is clearly significant.

The b coefficient is only an estimate of the true population β as it is based on sample data. Confidence limits can be constructed within which we can be X% certain that the true value of β lies. If the sample size is greater than 15 then we can be 95% certain that the true value of β lies within ± 2 standard deviations of the calculated b. If the sample size is say between 5 and 15 then we can be 99% certain that the true value of β lies within ± 3 standard deviations of the calculated b. In the mail order example we can be 95% certain that the true value of β will be within $\pm 2(\cdot 0319)$ of the value ·4297, i.e. between the values ·4935 and ·3659.

Simple correlation

Another measure of the closeness of the relationship between X and Y, apart from the standard error of the estimate, is to measure the correlation between these variables. This is especially helpful when it is difficult to establish which of the variables is dependent and which is independent, i.e. which variable 'causes' the other. In such cases the form of the regression model is difficult to derive. The coefficient of correlation is usually denoted by the term r and its value is obtained from the formula

$$r = \sqrt{\frac{\Sigma(Ye - \bar{Y})^2}{\Sigma(Y - \bar{Y})^2}} \qquad 7.9$$

where Ye is the estimate of Y given by the regression equation for each value of X.
$\bar{Y}$ is the mean of the recordings of Y. Y gives the actual values of the dependent variable.

The correlation coefficient, r, can be alternatively derived from the expression

$$r = \frac{n\Sigma XY - (\Sigma X)(\Sigma Y)}{\sqrt{(n\Sigma X^2 - (\Sigma X)^2)(n\Sigma Y^2 - (\Sigma Y)^2)}} \qquad 7.10$$

which is known as the product-moment formula.

The correlation coefficient for the mail order example is

$$r = \frac{20(131\,868) - (2381)(860)}{\sqrt{(20(352\,071) - (2381)^2)(20(50\,918) - (860)^2)}}$$

$$= +\cdot9537$$

This coefficient is very high, implying a near perfect correlation. The plus sign is as expected, i.e. high mail order sales associated with a high number of replies.

The correlation coefficient takes a value in the range $+1$ to 0 to -1. If the $r = 0$ then there is no relationship at all between the values of Y and X and hence no predictive ability could be expected from a regression model based on these variables only (the significance tests for the regression equation already described would have reached a similar conclusion). If a correlation coefficient is greater than 0 then there is said to be positive correlation, i.e. where increases in the value of Y are associated with increases in the value of X. If a correlation coefficient is less than 0 then it is described as negative correlation, i.e. one variable is increasing while another is decreasing. If r is exactly $+1$ or -1 then this is described as perfect positive correlation or perfect negative correlation. In such a case all the data points would lie on a straight line and the movements in X would give us the exact movements in Y, and vice versa (i.e. the actual values of Y are the same as the predicted values—the standard error of the estimate in such cases is zero).

The square of the correlation coefficient (r) is known as the coefficient of determination (r^2) and is expressed as

$$r^2 = \frac{\Sigma(Ye - \bar{Y})^2}{\Sigma(Y - \bar{Y})^2} \qquad 7.11$$

An introduction to simple regression and correlation

This statistic gives the ratio of the explained variation ($\Sigma(Ye - \bar{Y})^2$) to the total variation ($\Sigma(Y - \bar{Y})^2$); that is, of the total amount of variation in Y (i.e. the difference between the actual value of Y and the mean value of Y, $\bar{Y}$), the variation between the regression line and the mean ($Ye - \bar{Y}$) is explained (i.e. explained by the regression).

In the mail order example the coefficient of determination is ·9097 (i.e. ·9537^2). Thus 91% of the variation in the number units sold is represented by the variation in the number of replies received.

As with regression, there are a number of tests for significance concerning the correlation coefficient. The most common test is that of sampling error as r is an estimate of the true correlation coefficient, p, based on sample data. The usual test for sampling error concerns determining whether the true correlation p is significantly different from zero. This is tested by the expression

$$t = r\sqrt{\frac{n-2}{1-r^2}} \qquad 7.12$$

For the example the t statistic is

$$t = \cdot 9537 \sqrt{\frac{20-2}{1-\cdot 9097}}$$
$$= 13 \cdot 456$$

This result is then compared against the values appearing in tables of t values or specific tables prepared for testing the significance of correlation coefficients. In the example the correlation coefficient is significant.

As mentioned earlier, correlation analysis is especially useful if it proves impossible to identify a cause and effect relationship between variables. For example, if we know there is a high degree of association between two variables but we do not know which is the dependent variable (if indeed there is one), then the r^2 statistic can be used to make a forecast if the value of one of the variables is known in advance of the other.

Summary

This chapter has introduced the techniques of regression and correlation and has shown the mathematical calculations required. The following chapter describes multiple regression which is the technique used to quantify models which have more than one independent variable. These models are highly applicable in business and economic forecasting, since most dependent variables are influenced by a number of factors. The technique of multiple regression is an extension of the simple regression and correlation discussed in this chapter.

Suggested reading

For a simple treatment of regression and correlation see, for example, the following texts:
1. Clark, C. T., and Schkade, L. L., *Statistical Methods for Business Decisions*, South Western Publishing Co., 1969.
2. Croxten, F. E., Cowden, D. J., and Klein, S., *Applied General Statistics*, Pitman, 1968.
3. For a more advanced treatment see Ezekiel, M., and Fox, K., *Methods of Correlation and Regression Analysis*, Wiley, 1959, and Johnston, J., *Econometric Methods*, McGraw-Hill, 2nd edition, 1972.

8

Forecasting by multiple regression causal models

In the previous chapter we discussed simple regression and correlation which was defined as quantifying a linear relationship between just two variables. However, in order to obtain useful causal models we will almost certainly have to utilize more than one independent variable; there are very few economic models which can be adequately represented by a single independent variable. In the example described at the beginning of the last chapter we derived a model of raincoat sales which had four independent variables. Quantifying the weightings of these variables is again conducted by the method of least squares but the technique is known as multiple regression. The methodology is therefore exactly the same as in the simple regression case although the volume of arithmetic becomes large. Many computer programs have been built which enable the building and testing of models to be conducted rapidly.

As with simple regression and correlation, various tests can be applied to multivariable models which tell us of the significance of the factors and the levels of confidence we can attach to them. Recall that these tests are required as (a) there may in fact be no or a very poor linear relationship between the variables, and (b) the regression coefficients are based on sample data and thus sampling errors can arise. It is vital to check the significance of the model because the relationships might be poor and so lead to highly inaccurate forecasts. The main significance tests that need to be carried out on multiple regression are discussed below.

1. The standard error of the forecast. The formula is

$$SEf = \sqrt{\frac{\Sigma(Y - Ye)^2}{n - v - 1}} \qquad 8.1$$

where v is the number of independent variables in the regression. In the simple regression case there is only one independent variable, so the denominater in the formula is $n - 1 - 1 = n - 2$; this is the difference between the above formula and equation 7.5 (page 109).

The standard error represents the standard deviation of the regression line. Having established the standard deviation we can now express confidence limits around the forecast. If the forecast is based on forecasted independent variables then the confidence limits applied to the forecast will only be approximates. This is because the forecasts for the independent variables will probably differ somewhat from their mean values. An example of the construction of confidence intervals around a forecast is given on page 128.

2. The significance of the overall regression. Although a regression may have a fairly high R^2 this could possibly be due to chance. In order to test for this the F statistic test is applied, which tells us with $X\%$ confidence whether the complete set of regression coefficients are significantly different from zero.

The F statistic is computed as follows:

$$F = \frac{\frac{\Sigma(Ye - \bar{Y})^2}{v - 1}}{\frac{\Sigma(Y - Ye)^2}{n - v}} \qquad 8.2$$

where v = the number of variables
n = the number of observations
This can be equivalently expressed as

$$F = \frac{\frac{R^2}{(V - 1)}}{\frac{(1 - R^2)}{(n - v)}} \qquad 8.3$$

If the F value is above the value appearing in the appropriate F statistic tables, then the entire regression equation is significant and the R^2 value has not arisen by chance. The values appearing in the F statistic tables depend on the number of observations and the number of independent variables in the model. As a general rule, however, an F value of over 6 is significant at the 95% confidence level, where the number of observations exceed 6. If the number of observations are less than 6 then the required value for F rises dramatically; however it should be obvious that any regression based on so few observations will require very stringent significance levels. An example of the F statistic is given later in Tables 8.2 and 8.4 (pages 123 and 125).

3. The significance of the regression coefficients. The significance of these are derived by computing the t value as explained in equation 7.8 (page 113). If this value is above that appearing in the t tables then the independent variables have a statistically significant impact on the depen-

dent variable. In general a t value of over 2 is significant at the 95% confidence level unless the sample data is very small, say under 15 observations. Table 8.2 shows an example of the t values for an equation regressing four independent variables on volume sales of raincoats.

Requirements involved in using least squares regression

In using regression analysis there are a number of requirements that need to be met. The major items are referred to as linearity, multicollinearity, autocorrelation, homoscedasticity and the distribution of the error terms. If these terms do not meet certain criteria then the results of the regression may be spurious. It is therefore necessary to test for these items. This particularly applies when the model appears to be a good fit, as evidenced by R^2 and the F statistic, since this is when great reliance is placed on it.

Linearity
Linear regression assumes that the independent variables are linearly related with the dependent variable. If they are not then the R^2 value will be very low, showing that the independent variables explain very little of the movement in the dependent variable. Thus if management has constructed what appears to be a good descriptive causal model but the statistical significance is poor (low R^2, non-significant F value), then this may be due to the model being non-linear. Management can now take two steps: first the variables may be transformed into new variables which do have a linear relationship with the dependent variable. This commonly involves converting data into its logarithmic form or first difference form (see page 134). If the regression equation still has a poor statistical significance then management may attempt to fit a curvilinear relationship to the data. Curvilinear regression is discussed later: it should be recognized however that there will probably be few business and economic variables which can be approximated by a curvilinear expression. If the regression is still not significant then it would appear that there is no adequate causal explanation which can quantify the dependent variable (assuming all the various plausible models have been tested).

A graphical approach can also be adopted to examine for linearity. This involves graphing each independent variable against the dependent variable: managers can then see if the recordings lie approximately along a straight line. This type of analysis may be useful in determining whether a relationship is curvilinear: the particular pattern may indicate a specific mathematical function.

Multicollinearity
This term is applied when two or more of the independent variables are highly correlated. This can lead to one or more of the variables having a

statistically non-significant impact on the regression (i.e. low t value) even though from a commonsense point of view they have an obvious causal connection. The reason for the statistical non-significance of the variable is that its impact on the dependent variable has already been accounted for by another variable, with which it is highly correlated. Thus in Table 8.2 the t value for advertising is non-significant, showing that it does not contribute towards the explanation of the movement in raincoat sales. This, however, is against what is expected, so multicollinearity may be present. By looking at Table 8.3 we can see in fact that advertising is quite highly correlated with both relative price and rainfall, so it is likely that there is multicollinearity present. One way of testing whether multicollinearity is present is to re-run the regression equation by leaving out the variables relative to price and/or rainfall and seeing whether advertising becomes significant.

The important item as regards multicollinearity, however, is its impact on the accuracy of the forecast. In this respect multicollinearity is often of little importance. Technically slightly more significant results are obtained by running the regression with only the independent variables which have a significant t value. Thus in the raincoat example (page 125) the regression is re-run but omitting the advertising variable. The R^2 statistic improves slightly and the F value becomes more significant.

In practice many economic and business variables are likely to be correlated, especially when measured over time. Thus we can expect to find a certain amount of multicollinearity when building regression models which have economic and business time series as independent variables.

Homoscedasticity and heteroscedasticity

The three final requirements of a regression model have to do with the properties of the residuals or error terms. These residuals are the differences between the actual values of Y and the predicted values of Y given by the regression equation. Thus the residuals are denoted by U in the formula

$$Y = a + bX_1 + cX_2 + \ldots zX_{25} + U$$

The first requirement is that the errors should have a constant variance; this is technically known as homoscedasticity. This requirement is shown in Figure 8.1(a) where the scatter of the observations about the computed regression line is constant. In cases such as Figures 8.1(b) and (c) the error terms are not constant and hence the requirement of homoscedasticity is not met; in this case the variance is technically known as heteroscedasticity.

If the variance is heteroscedastic then the statistical significance of the regression equation is likely to be small even though the model appears to be sound from an economic viewpoint. Heteroscedasticity generally implies that one or more important independent variables are not in the model, so the model builder should seek to identify more causal variables. If the errors are still heteroscedastic, then the regression will probably still be non-significant.

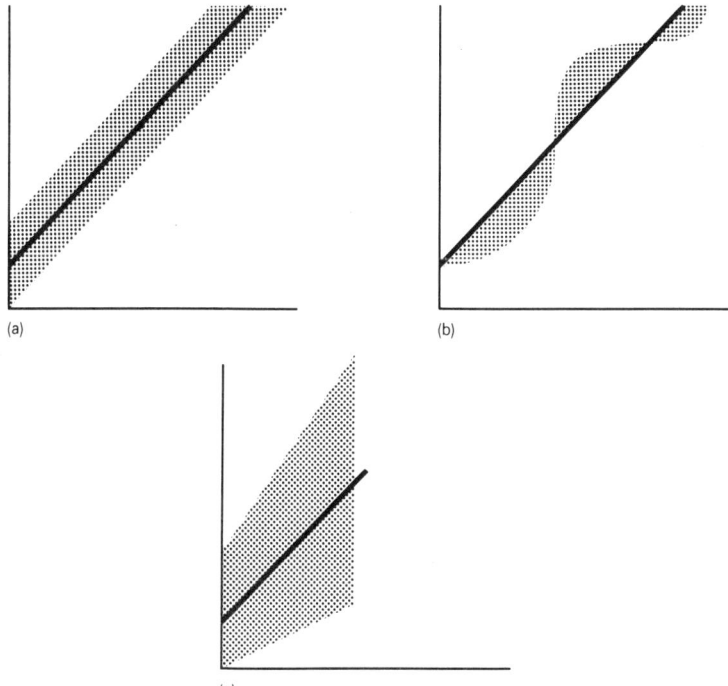

Figure 8.1

The presence of heteroscedasticity can be detected by the Durbin Watson statistic which is automatically produced in computer programs of regression analysis.

Autocorrelation
Another requirement of the residuals term in the regression equation is that they be independent of each other. For example the chance of the next recording of Y being above or below the computed regression value is 50–50. If the successive recordings of residuals are not independent then this is termed autocorrelation (sometimes referred to as serial correlation). Autocorrelation is often found when the data relating to the

122 *Forecasting methods in business and management*

variables consists of time series and so particular care should be taken in these cases. Figure 8.1 (b) shows an example of autocorrelation where there is a clear pattern in the residuals. Autocorrelation is tested for by the Durbin Watson test and/or the Von Neumann test (for all practical purposes these give identical results.) Tables 8.2 and 8.4 show these statistics for the raincoat example.

Autocorrelation tells us that there is some systematic pattern in the residuals, which suggests that an important independent variable has been left out of the regression. This means of course that the regression will not be so accurate and that its forecasting ability will be much poorer. In order to reduce the autocorrelation the model builder should first try to ascertain what this missing variable (or variables) is and then include it in the model. If it proves impossible to identify this variable then a change of the form of the variables (e.g. curvilinear relationship or logarithms of the variables) may be tried. Yet another technique, and one which is quite common, is to transform the data into first differences (see page 135).

Normal distribution

The final requirement is that the residuals should be normally distributed (this being a particular form of distribution). If this is not met then the tests of significance (e.g. F and t statistics) and the confidence limits applied to the variables and the forecast will not be strictly applicable. If the other requirements of the multiple regression model have been met and if a largish number of observations have been used, then it can be taken that the residuals are distributed normally.

An example of multiple regression

The first stage in multiple regression is to build a causal model relating to the dependent variable. In the case of the raincoat example (which we shall now call Rainco) the model was expressed as

$$S = aP + bI + cA + dR$$

Table 8.1 gives the data relating to the dependent and independent variables over the past 15 years. A least squares regression was applied to this data and the causal model is quantified as follows:

$$S = -610 \cdot 403 - 415 \cdot 118P + \cdot 0578I + 290 \cdot 052A + 14 \cdot 107R$$

The figure $-610 \cdot 403$ is a constant term.

The results were obtained from a computer program; it is no longer practical to give the arithmetical detail in the text.

Along with the coefficients, computer programs will also automatically produce the various significance tests associated with the regression equation. These statistics are shown in Table 8.2. In column 1 the regression

Table 8.1

Year	Volume sales of raincoats	Relative price	Personal disposable income	Relative advertising expenditure	Absolute level of rainfall inches
	S '000	P	I £million	A	R
1960	361	·92	10 291	1·04	30·6
1961	400	·90	10 463	1·05	32·4
1962	431	·90	10 674	1·03	34·1
1963	350	1·01	10 972	1·00	29·6
1964	614	·92	11 573	1·21	39·7
1965	453	·98	12 417	·97	32·0
1966	597	·89	13 001	1·20	37·8
1967	312	1·02	13 561	·87	29·1
1968	307	1·09	13 972	·79	26·8
1969	797	·89	14 635	1·32	38·2
1970	890	·80	15 239	1·37	40·2
1971	927	·79	16 008	1·43	39·6
1972	720	·92	16 541	1·01	31·7
1973	645	1·17	17 417	·82	32·1
1974	841	·80	17 908	1·00	31·7
1975	925	·85	18 246	1·16	32·3

Table 8.2 Regression equation for volume raincoat sales

Independent variables	1 Regression coefficient	2 Estimated standard error	3 t value
Constant	−610·403	289·107	−2·111
Relative price P	−415·118	205·962	−2·015
Personal disposable income I	0·057	0·004	12·943
Relative advertising A	290·052	201·144	1·442
Rainfall R	14·107	6·923	2·037

$R^2 = ·9577$
$F = 85·89$
Standard error of estimate $= 40\,400$
Durbin Watson $= ·838$
Von Neumann $= ·894$

coefficients for each variable are shown. The constant term a is $-610\cdot403$. The second column gives the estimated standard error of these coefficients and from these confidence limits can be constructed for the coefficients. The third column gives the t values for the coefficients. As described previously, this statistic tells us whether the true value of the coefficient is significantly different from zero. Recall also that the general rule for the significance of the t value is that it must have a value of 2 or greater (either positive or negative) if the coefficient is statistically different from zero at the 95% confidence level (i.e. we are 95% certain the coefficient is not zero). The t values therefore tell us that the coefficient of the variable, relative advertising expenditure, is not significantly different from zero and hence does not help explain the movements in sales. This lack of significance could be due to there being no linear causal relationship between advertising and sales or to there being multicollinearity between some of the independent variables.

The f value for the regression is $85\cdot89$ and this is clearly significant remembering that an F value of 6 or over is significant at the 95% confidence level with a sample size of over 6. Thus the independent variables as a whole provide a statistically significant causal relationship. The R^2 term shows a very close fit with $95\cdot77\%$ of the variation in the volume sales of raincoats being explained by the independent variables. The significance of the F statistic can be improved, however, by omitting the non-significant independent variable, relative advertising, from the regression equation. The results of this regression are shown in Table 8.4

Table 8.3 shows the correlation matrix of the variables: this expresses the simple correlation between each pair of variables. From the table we

Table 8.3 Simple correlation matrix

	Price (P)	Income (I)	Advertising (A)	Rainfall (R)	Volume sales (S)
Price	1·000000	−0·134170	−0·790602	−0·598642	−0·625624
Income(I)	−0·134170	1·000000	0·870692	0·683165	0·757965
Advertising(A)	−0·790602	0·870692	1·000000	0·890725	0·678213
Rainfall(R)	−0·598642	0·683165	0·890725	1·000000	0·630800
Volume Sales(S)	−0·625624	0·757965	0·678213	0·630800	1·000000

can see that the correlation between advertising and sales is quite high, with a coefficient of $\cdot678$ ($r^2 = 45\cdot99\%$). This therefore implies that there is some association between advertising and sales and that the non-significant t value for advertising may be the result of multicollinearity. Looking further at Table 8.3 we can see that there is a strong relationship between advertising and relative price ($r = -.79$) and between advertising and rainfall ($r = .89$). Relative advertising expenditure tends to rise when the relative price declines (i.e. a strengthened advertising campaign is put into action when the firm reduces its prices and/or when competitors put up their prices) and rise when rainfall rises! The latter may reflect the firm's ability to suddenly increase advertising at the time of a deterioration in the weather. These high correlations therefore suggest that the impact of advertising on sales is largely accounted for, statistically speaking, by the relative price and the rainfall. A re-interpretation of the t value for advertising is that this variable does have an impact on sales but that this, in the regression equation, has been accounted for by relative prices and rainfall.

Table 8.4 Revised regression equation for volume raincoat sales

Independent variables	1 Regression coefficient	2 Estimated standard error	3 t value
Constant	−385·178	253·992	−1·5165
Relative price P	−624·842	152·253	−4·104
Personal disposable income I	0·057	0·004	12·357
Rainfall R	22·604	3·794	5·956

$R^2 = .9538$
$F = 104·44$
Standard error of estimate = 49 200
Durbin Watson = 1·324
Von Neumann = 1·423

If the advertising variable is found to have little or no correlation with sales, then this implies that advertising is wasteful and should be abandoned, since it costs money and creates no benefits.

Table 8.4 shows the revised regression equation. The R^2 statistic hardly alters and the F statistic remains significant. The t coefficient for the constant term becomes non-significant, however, so strictly we should revise the equation yet again. For all practical forecasting purposes, however, any of the equations as represented by Tables 8.2 and 8.4 and the revised equation omitting the constant term could be used, since they are virtually identical in significance. The Durbin Watson and Von Neumann statistics are not significant in both Tables 8.2 and 8.4, hence there is no evidence of any autocorrelation in the error terms. The significance of these statistics is appraised by comparing the computed values with those appearing in tables. These tables, which are fairly straight forward to use, are given in most statistics textbooks.

Table 8.5 shows the accuracy of the results of the regression equation.

Column 3 gives the residuals or differences between the actual values of sales and those predicted by the model. Column 4 expresses these residuals as a percentage of the actual values.

Table 8.5 Comparison of actual and predicted values of volume sales

1 Actual volume sales	2 Predicted volume sales	3 Difference between 1 and 2	4 Percentage of error, $3 \div 1$
361 000	325 011	35 989	9.9
400 000	388 112	11 888	2.9
431 000	438 705	− 7 705	− 1.7
350 000	285 436	64 564	18.4
614 000	604 625	9 375	1.5
453 000	441 747	11 253	2.4
597 000	662 759	− 65 759	−11.0
312 000	417 163	−105 163	−33.7
307 000	345 132	− 38 132	−12.4
797 000	766 014	30 986	3.8
890 000	902 283	− 12 283	− 1.3
927 000	939 308	− 12 308	− 1.3
720 000	710 239	9 761	1.3
645 000	613 579	31 421	4.8
841 000	864 039	− 23 039	− 2.7
925 000	865 847	59 153	6.3

In examining the results of the regression we should see whether they are consistent with the basic intuitive causal model. If not, then further investigation should be made, because there may have been some misspecification of the input data into the model producing spurious regression results. For Rainco the regression coefficients are as expected. Specifically

1. The price variable is negatively correlated. As the price charged by the firm declines as a percentage of the industry average this increases the demand for the firm's products.

2. The personal disposable income variable is postively correlated. As consumer wealth grows, greater sales of raincoats can be expected.

3. The rainfall coefficient is positive. As the amount of rainfall increases we would expect the volume sales of raincoats to increase.

4. Although the t value for advertising is not significant, this was thought to be due to the presence of other factors (multicollinearity). If these other factors had been omitted then the t value for advertising would be significant. The positive sign of the coefficient is in the direction expected; that is, an increase in relative advertising expenditure is expected to increase volume sales.

The very high R^2 value along with the significant F statistic show that the independent variables explain virtually all of the changes in the sales of raincoats. With a result like this we would not normally search for any more explanatory variables. The regression should be re-run at regular intervals to re-assess the weightings attached to the coefficients and to assess the significance of the equation.

Rainco has established a very good causal model relating to the volume sales of raincoats. Thus when the relative price moves up by ·01 the number of raincoats sold falls by 6248; when personal disposable income rises by £1 million the number of raincoats sold rises by 57; when rainfall increases by 1 inch the number of raincoats sold rises by 22 604. Rainco's management now has to use this model as a forecasting technique whereby it predicts future sales. In order to forecast mangement has to incorporate values for relative prices, personal disposable income and rainfall. These values either have to be known in advance of the sales figure or have to be forecast with a substantial amount of certainty (the independent variables must be easier to forecast than the dependent variable itself). The length for which forecasts can be made depends upon the length of time for which accurate values of the independent variables can be made. Another factor to consider is the standard error of the estimate. If this is large then the coefficients of the regression may change over time.

In the example it is perhaps fairly obvious that the values for the independent variables for say 1976 will be difficult to ascertain; certainly forecasting any further ahead than 1976 is likely to be valueless. The relative price variable for 1976 may be estimated fairly accurately by using the figures appearing in the sales catalogues for each firm in the industry, assuming that there are catalogues specifying the prices for the forthcoming season. The value for personal disposable income may be derived from official forecasts prepared by government economists; these are likely to be fairly accurate for up to one year hence. The value for relative advertising (assuming for the moment that the variable is significant) could be estimated if any trade statistics are available, e.g. the percentage of the planned advertising budget for the year of Rainco against the total industry advertising. The likelihood of there being up-to-date and accurate industry data is small. The value for rainfall is likely to be a pure guess. The relative price and the relative advertising variables could be approximated by assuming that competitors' prices and advertising policies remain the same as in the previous year and then calculating the firm's current policies thereon. Testing this method on prior data will tell management how much reliance can be placed on it.

Unless reliable values can be obtained for the independent variables in the regression equation, its use as a forecasting technique is worthless. It should therefore be recognized that an 'excellent fit' causal model does not mean that it will be in any way useful in forecasting. This is emphasized in the case of Rainco where, although the R^2 was ·9538, the estimating of the independent variables beyond a year is so tenuous that forecasting beyond one year is likely to be highly inaccurate. It may be that a regression model can be built which, while having a lower R^2, still gives superior forecasts; for example, Rainco might well experiment with a model which excludes rainfall as a variable. While the R^2 will be much smaller, the forecasting may be superior as no forecast of rainfall is required to be put into the model.

Assuming for the moment that the independent variables are known or can be forecast with a high degree of certainty for the next few years, then forecasts of volume raincoat sales can be made. Table 8.6 shows data

Table 8.6

	Relative price	Personal disposable income (£ million)	Absolute rainfall	Forecast of volume sales
1976	·90	19 065	32·6	876 060
1977	·90	19 800	34·0	949 601
1978	·95	20 550	34·5	972 410

Sales '000
1976 — 385·178 − 624·842(·90) + 0·057(19 065) + 22·604(32·6) = 876·060
1977 — 385·178 − 624·842(·90) + 0·057(19 800) + 22·604(34·0) = 949·601
1978 — 385·178 − 624·842(·95) + 0·057(20 550) + 22·604(34·5) = 972·410

relating to the independent variables for the next three years and the resultant forecasts. To these figures can be attached approximate confidence intervals using the standard error of the forecast. For example, we can be 95% certain that the sales figure for 1976 will be 876 060 ± 2 standard deviations (49 200 from Table 8.4), i.e. sales will be between 777 660 and 974 460 units.

Simultaneous equations

This method is sometimes referred to as econometric modelling, although the term econometric is also often applied as a general description of quantitative economic models, including the regression analyses discussed so far. Up to now we have discussed regression models where the dependent variable is related to a number of independent variables and where the values of these independent variables do not rely upon the dependent variable. In practice, however, many economic variables are interdependent and thus causal relationships are two way. For instance, in the Rainco example we had a model which expressed sales as a function of price, income, advertising and rainfall; however, the values of the variables price and advertising are likely to be a function of sales expectations. Thus management sets prices in the light of what they think sales will be, i.e.

price (dependent variable) = f (volume sales)

In many economic models we will find variables which are determined within the system, known as endogenous variables. Variables determined outside the system, such as rainfall in this example, are known as exogenous. Instead of making an arbitrary division into dependent and independent variables the problem should strictly be handled by deriving and solving a number of simultaneous equations.

Although a simultaneous equation approach should be used in an interrelated model it is often found that a single equation regression model will and has to suffice, on the grounds that:

1. For many business variables the forecasting accuracy of single equation models is very nearly as good as simultaneous equation models.

2. The cost of building simultaneous equation models is considerably more expensive than for building single equation models.

Because of the costs involved most firms rely on using single equation regression models and for many problems they are found to give satisfactory forecasts. In the case of Rainco the independent variables of relative price and relative advertising were considered to be largely determined outside the model (i.e. through cost functions and competitive pressures). For very large firms, trade associations and government economists, the use of simultaneous equation models becomes tenable and they are often the only reliable forecasting method. The subject of simultaneous equation models is fairly technical and so only a very brief outline is given here; the references at the end of the chapter provide a comprehensive coverage of the topic.

In using the simultaneous equation approach we have to specify the various inter-relationships. For example, in determining the relationship between quantities and prices we have two endogenous variables, i.e. quantities (bought or sold) depend upon price and the setting of the price depends upon quantities (bought, sold)*. Figure 8.2 shows various price-quantity combinations and while it is possible to fit a regression line to these observations it would not be clear that either a demand or a supply

---

* In practice it may be that supply-demand quantities are dependent upon prices charged in the immediately prior period or prices specified in advance (i.e. price tags). In such cases the model is no longer simultaneous as price is a known, exogenous, variable. As long as the data shows sufficient detail a single equation regression model will be valid in quantifying the relationships.

equation would result. In order to solve this type of problem we have to find variables which affect demand but not supply, and vice versa. Thus the demand function may be specified as

$$Q_D = a + bP + cZ \qquad 8.4$$

where Z is some variable which affects demand but not supply. An example might be personal disposable income, for while this influences the demand

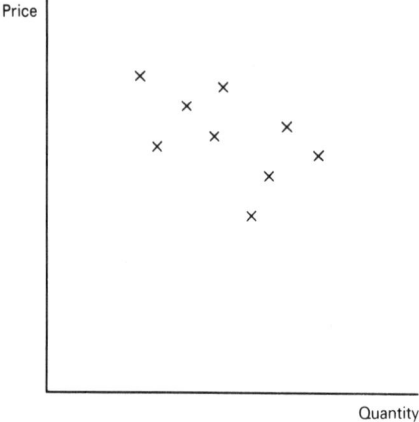

Figure 8.2

for a product, it is unlikely that demand will significantly affect it (Z is therefore an exogenous variable). Further, personal disposable income does not affect the quantities supplied.

We now have to do the same for the supply function. Again we have to build an equation which has an exogenous variable(s), which while influencing supply does not influence demand:

$$Q_S = d + eP + fY \qquad 8.5$$

where Y is an exogenous variable.* In the case of the supply of farm products this could be the weather (rainfall, sunshine, etc.), since this variable influences the supply of goods but not the demand for them, and is also not itself determined by the supply of goods. The search for suitable exogenous variables is one of the most important aspects of simultaneous equation analysis. Care is needed in distinguishing between exogenous and

---

* Both the demand and the supply equations would have error terms in them denoting that various influencing variables had been left out of the equation and/or the presence of sampling errors in determining the coefficients.

endogenous variables; one can postulate that nearly all economic variables are inter-related in at least a small way. The exogenous variables should be those which are, for all practical purposes, completely determined outside the model.

In the above example there are two endogenous variables, price and quantity ($Q_D = Q_S = Q$), and these must be expressed in two equations (which are known as structural equations). If there are more than two endogenous variables there must still be an equivalent number of equations. The above equations are said to be exactly or just identified; it is possible for equations to be over-identified and under-identified.

The necessary condition (i.e. minimum condition) for an equation to be exactly identified is that the number of variables (exogenous and endogenous) absent from that equation must equal the number of endogenous (dependent) variables in the system minus one. As an example of this test take the demand-supply equation example described above where

$$Q_D = a + bP + cZ \qquad 8.4$$
$$Q_S = d + eP + fY \qquad 8.5$$

Here there are two endogenous or dependent variables, Q_D (or Q_S) and P. Using the identification rule it must be possible to find one variable excluded from each equation but included elsewhere in the model. Thus in the demand equation Y does not appear, but it does appear elsewhere. Of the four variables (Q, P, Z and Y) only one (i.e. the number of exogenous variables (2) minus one) does not appear in the demand equation. The demand equation is now said to be identified. The supply equation is also identified, since Z is excluded but it does appear elsewhere in the model.

Consider the case where there are two exogenous variables which taken together influence the movement in the demand equation but have no impact on the supply equation. The demand equation becomes

$$Q_D = a + bP + cZ + gX \qquad 8.6$$

The supply function (equation 8.5) is now over-identified, since there are two variables which are excluded from it but present elsewhere. In these cases we will obtain a number of answers for the coefficients c and g if we use least squares regression.

For an example of under-identification, suppose the demand-supply equations are

$$Q_D = a + bP \qquad 8.7$$
$$Q_S = c + dP + eZ \qquad 8.8$$

The demand equation is identified, as Z is excluded but appears elsewhere. The supply equation is not identified, however, as it does not meet this criterion. In this case the coefficient d will not be capable of solution. Every effort should be made to make a model at least 'just identified' otherwise no solution is possible unless arbitrary values or assumptions are used.

The method by which the coefficients of the just identified model are derived is known as indirect least squares. The structural equations 8.4 and 8.5 are transformed into what are known as reduced form equations in which P and Q are expressed in terms of the exogenous variables Z and Y. The process is as follows:

1. Subtract equation 8.4 from equation 8.5 which gives

$$Q = (d-a) + (e-b)P - cZ + fY$$

2. To solve for P transpose P to the left-hand side of the equation and divide the right-hand side terms by $(b-e)$. This gives

$$P = \frac{(d-a)}{(b-e)} - \frac{cZ}{(b-e)} + \frac{fY}{(b-e)} \qquad 8.9$$

3. To solve for Q multiply each term in equation 8.4 by e and each term in equation 8.5 by b. This gives

$$eQ = ea + ebP + ecZ$$
$$bQ = bd + beP + bfY$$

Subtracting the first equation above from the second gives

$$(b-e)Q = (bd-ea) - ecZ + bfY$$

and by dividing through by $(b-e)$ we obtain Q:

$$Q = \frac{(bd-ea)}{(b-e)} - \left(\frac{ec}{b-e}\right)Z + \left(\frac{bf}{b-e}\right)Y \qquad 8.10$$

The reduced form equations are therefore equations 8.9 and 8.10.

Thus we have expressed the two endogenous variables in terms of the exogenous variables. Note we also have two reduced form equations, one for each endogenous variable. We can now find the coefficients of the reduced form equations by least squares as described earlier in the chapter. P and Q are both regressed on Z and Y. From the reduced form coefficients are derived the structural equation coefficients. For example b is found by dividing the reduced form coefficient

$$\frac{bf}{(b-e)} \text{ by } \frac{f}{(b-e)} \text{ thus: } b = \frac{\frac{bf}{(b-e)}}{\frac{f}{(b-e)}}$$

e is similarly found, i.e.

$$e = \frac{\dfrac{-ec}{(b-e)}}{\dfrac{-c}{(b-e)}}$$

The coefficients a and d similarly follow by transformation from the reduced form equation.

The method of indirect least squares is not appropriate for over-identified models, since we get several answers for the coefficients. Instead there are a number of other methods for reaching a solution. The main ones are

1. Full information, maximum likelihood
2. Limited information, maximum likelihood
3. Three stage least squares
4. Two stage least squares
5. Instrumental variables

These provide the coefficients for the structural equations: the over-identified model is in fact the most common. Computers enable the arithmetical calculations to be done in a matter of a few seconds. For a description of these methods see the Johnston reference at the end of the chapter.

In summary, simultaneous equation models have been found to be too complex and too costly for all but the largest firms and organizations. However, given the improved education of business managers, the growth in the number of personnel trained in statistics and the increased power of computers, econometric model building will likely become tenable for medium and large-size firms. At present most econometric work is carried out by government economists who, with the large resources at their disposal, have built very large models (involving many hundreds of equations) of the economy. This has allowed them to measure the impact of various economic policies that could be adopted on the economy as a whole. By incorporating the policies actually adopted into the model various economic forecasts are produced. These are usually publicly available and they can be incorporated into a firm's single equation regression model as an exogenously determined variable. In the Rainco example, for instance, the value of the personal disposable income variable would probably be taken from an official forecast produced by the government, which would be derived from their econometric model. Eventually, however, firms may find it economically valid to build their own sophisticated simultaneous equation models.

Curvilinear analysis

So far in this chapter we have only considered linear regression, that is data for which a linear relationship exists. However, some business variables may not have a linear form even when their logarithms or first differences are taken (these adjustments are described later). They instead may be represented by various forms of polynomial, such as those depicted by the curves in Figure 8.3. Having established what type of relationship exists

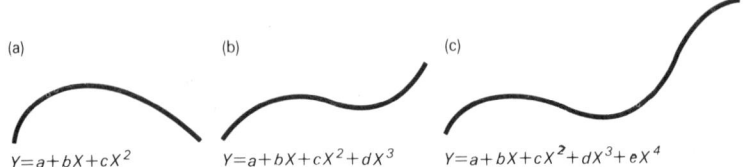

Figure 8.3

(i.e. 8.3 (a), 8.3 (b), 8.3 (c)), least squares regression can then be used to establish the coefficients. For example, the regression equation for Figure 8.3 (b) would be of the form

$$Y = a + bX + cX^2 + dX^3$$

where a, b, c and d are the coefficients found by least squares. If a linear relationship does not exist between the variables and if from both statistical and economic evidence it appears that a curvilinear relationship could exist, then this should be tested and used for forecasting purposes. In practice it is unlikely that many business variables will be curvilinear, hence the emphasis on there being economic as well as statistical grounds for believing that such a relationship exists.

Form of the variables

There may be many cases in which the independent variables do not have a linear relationship with the dependent variable. However, by transforming the data a linear relationship may be found to exist. The most common transformation is to convert the variables into their logarithmic form: many non-linear equations are found to be linear when logarithmic data is used. Model builders should therefore test log-linear relationships if the original data failed to find any linearity.

As will be seen in the next chapter, many variables are transformed into their logarithms purely for economic purposes. This is because in demand-supply relationships the regression coefficients of logarithmic data represent elasticities; if all the major explanatory factors are included as independent variables then the elasticity of individual factors can be assessed by holding the impact of the other factors constant.

Another transformation is to use the first differences of the data or the logarithms of the first differences. First differences are the difference between successive recordings of a variable. If a variable has the recordings 25, 18, 23 and 27 then the first differences are minus 7, plus 5 and plus 4. These are the data used in computing the regression coefficients. The use of first differences is often a method which is used to reduce or eliminate the undesirable properties of autocorrelation and multicollinearity. A common example of a trend model incorporating first differences of the independent variables is

$$V_t = V_{t-1} + A \Delta Z + b \Delta Y + c \Delta X$$

where V_t is the unit sales in period t
V_{t-1} is the unit sales in the immediately prior period
Z, Y and X are independent variables, e.g. temperature, rainfall and advertising expenditure
Δ = first difference
a, b, c are the regression coefficients

Additional techniques in regression

There are a multitude of techniques which can be used in regression analysis and simultaneous equation modelling in order to cope with specific problems. The major texts on statistics such as those referred to at the end of the chapter should be consulted for a description of these techniques. Since these are more specialized techniques, the manager using them will have to rely fairly heavily on the advice of a statistician. Two techniques which may be found helpful are the use of dummy variables and lagged models.

Dummy variables can be used to assess the impact of a qualitative factor or a major jump in an independent variable on the dependent variable. For example, if we want to know whether putting a dust jacket on a book increases sales we could do this by using a demand equation and a dummy variable. The equation might be

$$\text{book sales} = a + bZ + cY + dX + eDV$$

where DV represents the dummy variable. For books that use dust covers we could allocate the value 1 to the dummy variable and for books without dust covers we could allocate the value 0 to the dummy variable. In running the regression we will obtain a regression coefficient for the dummy variable and a t statistic. If the t statistic is significant we learn that the dust cover/no dust cover decision is important in creating sales. The use of dummy variables is fairly straightforward and allows the decision-maker to assess if a particular qualitative factor has any influence on the dependent variable.

Lagged models are formed when some of the variables in the equation are in a lagged relationship to the dependent variable. For example, in macroeconomic models the consumption function is specified as

$$C_t = a + bI_{t-1}$$

where consumption (C) in week t is a function of income (I) last week ($t-1$). Lagged models are of obvious use to the forecaster, since the value of the independent variable is known ahead of the dependent variable so a fairly accurate forecast can be made. An extension of a one period lag model is a distributed lag model, which is used if the adjustment of the dependent variable to the lagged variable takes beyond one time period.

Procedures in building regression models for forecasting

The organization of building regression models for forecasting can be broken down into the following steps:

1. Defining the problem to be solved and the forecast required. This is a general requirement of all forecasting. For example, we may require a forecast of our company's profits over the next five years, but we have to approach this by forecasting sales by regression modelling and then calculating the profits. Some thought must obviously be given to identifying ways of tackling the problem.

2. Building economically plausible causal models. This requires a detailed knowledge of the business and the markets or constraints within which it has to operate. This stage of the forecasting process is probably the most important and the one which requires the most skill and managerial judgement. The model building will probably require help from many executives within the firm. In considering the independent variables to be included in the model the following requirements should be kept in mind:

(a) That historical data on a variable is required so that its historical impact on the dependent variable can be quantified. Apart from the existence of data, there must also be some consideration as to its form. For example, if 20 annual recordings are available for a variable, this amount is generally sufficiently large to compute a satisfactory regression. However, the forecaster may feel that data more than five years old will be spurious for the relationships now existing, preferring to use quarterly data (i.e. 20 recordings in five years) or monthly data instead. The forecaster must look at the data availability in each case and use experience and judgment to decide its usefulness in the situation.

(b) For forecasting purposes we need to know the values of the independent variables ahead of the dependent variable. Thus the values of the independent variables need to be known in advance or need to be capable of being reliably forecast ahead of the dependent variable. The independent variables are likely to be those relating to the company's own operations and those relating to aggregate industrial and economic statistics. Those relating to variables under management's control (such as prices, advertising, marketing policies) may be interdependent with the variable being forecast and in these cases a simultaneous equation approach is theoretically required. As explained previously, however, single equation models usually suffice.

3. Quantifying the various causal models that have been postulated in step 2. The significance of the regression should then be assessed; this is automatically done in computer programs. The major significance tests are

(a) Examining the t values for the regression coefficients for significance; if any is not significant then ignore that variable and re-run the regression on the remaining significant variables.

(b) Examining the F value for the entire equation for significance; if the F value is not significant then we cannot use the equation as a causal or a predictive model. We determine the significance of both the t and F values by examining the t-statistic and F-statistic tables. If the computed values for t and F are above those appearing in the tables then the coefficients and the regression equation are significant at that level of confidence. The confidence level normally used is 95%, that is, we are certain that in 95 out of 100 cases the value of the true coefficient and the true value of R^2 is different from zero. Tables relating to t values and F values (and other statistics such as normal distributions, Durbin Watson and Von Neumann) are given in the standard statistical textbooks. The use of these tables is straightforward.

(c) Testing the requirements of ordinary least squares regression; if the requirements are not met then various adjustments to correct for this need to be undertaken. These were discussed on pages 119 to 122.

If none of the equations are statistically significant management should

(i) See if transformation of the variables into, say, logarithms or first differences provides a statistically significant equation. Regression programs normally have sub-routines which calculate logarithms or first differences of input data. Additionally various forms of curvilinear relationships can be tried if these seem plausible in economic terms. Again, regression programs have built-in sub-routines for handling standard types of curvilinear relationships.

(ii) See if there are any other independent variables that can reasonably be added to the model.

(iii) Completely reappraise the causal model building. This in fact is a feedback loop where the testing of causal model hypotheses are carried out at the regression stage and the results of these tests are used to reformulate models and hypotheses. If it is difficult to establish a significant model at all then the initial problem formulation should be reconsidered.

(iv) Collect more data, especially if the existing sample size is small. Sampling error is a major reason for equations and regression coefficients being non-significant and the collecting of additional data observations should greatly reduce the sampling error.

4. Selecting a model. The position is eventually reached where a number of statistically significant models have been developed and it is necessary to select the most useful for forecasting purposes. Although the equation with the highest R^2 gives the best explanatory model, this does not necessarily mean that it is the best one for forecasting. As has been explained previously, in order to forecast we need to know or be able to forecast accurately the values of the independent variables ahead of the dependent variable. It may well be that the independent variables of a model with a high R^2 are not capable of being accurately determined before the dependent variable becomes known itself. In such a case the forecasting ability of the model is worthless. Instead another model whose independent variables are known ahead of the dependent variable will have to be used, even though the R^2 statistic is lower. The appraising of the appropriate model can be done by testing the forecasting accuracy of the various models on prior data. The model giving the most accurate forecast for any particular time period should be chosen (it might be that one model is more accurate than another for some forecasting periods but not for others). The confidence limits for the chosen model should be calculated and probabilistic forecasts obtained. Because economic and business relationships change across time the model should be tested at regular intervals to see if it is still relevant. It can be expected that the coefficients of the variables will change somewhat over time and in some cases additional independent variables may become significant.

The above has given a summary outline of the steps to follow in using causal models in forecasting. The various stages should be used as feedback in carrying out the earlier steps, so that in building an adequate model the steps may well be repeated several times. While a trained statistician should normally take charge of stage 3 and possibly stage 4, the main skills for steps 1 and 2 are multi-disciplinary and numerous executives may contribute. The various statistics described in this chapter are all automatically produced in the various standard computer programs for regression, so the mathematics involved can be ignored by the business manager, although it is necessary to be able to understand the statistical results and know how to interpret them. The standard computer programs provided by both the computer manufactures and the computer bureaus have been highly developed and the forecaster and manager can run and test models in a matter of seconds.

Summary

This chapter has discussed methods of quantifying causal models so that they can be used for forecasting purposes. Although the theory behind the statistics is fairly complex, it is hoped that the chapter has shown that managers can understand and interpret the results. If they do not then the powerful techniques of regression may not be fully utilized in the processes leading to decision-making. The chapter has emphasized the importance of the initial model building and that regression is a purely mechanical method of quantifying the relationships. Techniques of model building are discussed in the next chapter, along with references to actual applications.

One of the major drawbacks in causal model building is that the output is perhaps difficult for managers to understand, although as stated above it is hoped that this chapter has at least ameliorated the position. Another drawback is the cost, mainly that of the initial development of the model, which includes the labour cost of deriving plausible relationships and collecting and analyzing data, and the computer time involved. Operating costs are relatively cheap and the re-evaluating of the model at periodic intervals is also usually inexpensive. Because of the expense involved with causal models, time series methods may be preferred in forecasting small value items over short periods of time. In the medium term however, and where management has control over various independent variables, regression models come into their own and the benefits normally exceed the costs.

Suggested reading

For a simple treatment of regression and correlation see the following texts:
1. Clark, C. T., and Schkade, L. L., *Statistical Methods in Business Decisions,* South West Publishing Co., 1969.
2. Croxton, F. E., Cowden, D. J., and Klein, S., *Applied General Statistics,* Pitman, 1968.

For more advanced texts on regression and econometrics see the following:
3. Ezekiel, M., and Fox, K., *Methods of Correlation and Regression Analysis,* Wiley, 1959.
4. Johnston, J., *Econometric Methods,* McGraw-Hill, 2nd edition, 1972.
5. Kane, E. J., *Economic Statistics and Econometrics,* Harper & Row, 1968.

6. Merrill, W. C., and Fox, K., *An Introduction to Economic Statistics*, Wiley, 1970.
7. Theil, H., *Applied Economic Forecasting*, North Holland Publishing Co., 1966.
8. Wonnacott, R. J., and Wonnacott, T. H., *Econometrics*, Wiley, 1970.

For a description of curvilinear trends see:

9. I.C.I., *Mathematical Trend Curves: an aid to forecasting*, I.C.I. Monograph No. 1, Oliver & Boyd, 1964, and the reference to Croxten, Cowden and Klein above.

9

The building of causal models

The most important aspect of causal model building is the actual model construction itself; this is the search for independent variables which explain the dependent variable. These descriptive models based on a detailed knowledge of the business represent hypotheses which are both quantified and tested by regression analysis. In the last two chapters we saw how regression analysis tackled this. Regression, however, is a mechanical process which ordinarily should not pose any problem to management (although it may do so for the firm's statistician or computer manager). The real skill in causal models comes in recognizing economic and business relationships and interpreting them into a model form.

This chapter sets out to show how model building can be tackled, although it must be emphasized from the outset that each problem is different and may require a different or modified approach. The forecasted variable used throughout the chapter is the demand for the company's products. This involves discussing major common determinants of sales and common problems that arise, and describing various applications of model building in practice. The reason for the emphasis on sales or demand models is that this is the single most useful parameter governing a company's growth—various types of costs and production levels are a function of the firm's sales. Thus forecasts of the amounts of costs, inventory levels, labour required and plant capacity would usually all be made after a forecast of sales has been made.

Macroeconomic forecasting

A firm operates within a national economy and this imposes certain constraints upon it: for example, a typical commercial company's volume sales are partially dependent upon the growth in real personal disposable income of the population. The government also imposes regulatory control over the economy, using measures such as taxes and public sector spending. Therefore in order to forecast a company's sales over the next few years we need to make some assumptions about or forecasts of the macroeconomic situation.

The forecasting of the growth in the national economy is a very specialized topic and interested readers should consult references 1, 8, 9, 13 and 14 at the end of the chapter. National economic forecasting involves a large amount of work to derive the model, since the economy is an interdependent system. However, a number of models exist, built by academic economists and economic institutes, and these provide forecasts of economic growth and various macrostatistics (e.g. productivity, capital expenditure). Among the major sources of macroeconomic forecasts are those produced by the Treasury, the OECD, National Institute of Economic and Social Research (these are published in the quarterly *Economic Review*) and the London Business School (published in the *Sunday Times*). These publish explicit forecasts for the immediate term, the medium term (say up to two years hence) and the longer term. Additionally the independent bodies usually suggest economic measures that the government should adopt in order to reach its goals.

While these forecasts are subject to a good deal of uncertainty they are still, on balance, useful to the firm in building models to predict its own sales growth (the use of the forecasts of personal disposable income for the forecasting of individual product demand is discussed later). The benefits of these forecasts for individual firms will vary: some will be very sensitive to changes in income (those with high elasticities of demand—this term is described later) while others will not.

In general it does not pay a company to develop its own macroeconomic forecasting model, since this is extremely expensive and the results are unlikely to be any better than those produced by the publicly available forecasts listed above. However, medium and large size firms may allocate one member of the planning department to look after economic forecasting. This role would involve monitoring the forecasts of the prior mentioned sources and estimating the impact on the firm. The role would also include the predicting of government measures in controlling the economy as these probably have an even greater effect on the firm.

Among the items that government uses to control the economy are
direct taxation
indirect taxation: value added tax (VAT) and customs and excise duty
interest rates
hire purchase and other credit controls
government spending on nationalized industries, education, defence, etc.
money supply
import-export duties and incentives
trade and economic pacts

Clearly the above have a significant impact on sales and corporate profitability. For example an increase in credit terms, an easing of interest rates and an increase in money supply will all lead to a growth in consumer demand and hopefully the company's sales. Other, non-economic government measures, such as the protection of the environment, may also have an impact on a company; for example, the gradual government pressure against smoking has caused cigarette firms to successively downgrade their estimates of future growth from this source. Thus the prediction of government legislation and the measuring of its likely impact on the firm is of great importance to many companies.

The forecasting of government action is often very difficult, but the following points may help the forecaster (see also references 1, 8, 9, 13, 14, 16, 17 and 18):

1. Government legislation is often leaked unofficially to the press.

2. Particular economic circumstances often call for standard type policies to be adopted (e.g. deflation, reflation). Press and media comment is often helpful in such cases.

3. Past history may indicate policies that the government may follow.

4. The political tone or mood of the government gives a broad hint of policies they may adopt.

Many of the regulatory controls exercised by the government are of a short-term duration (or at least the levels they adopt are short-term). Some, however, have longer-term ramifications; an example is the decision to join the European Economic Community.

Although macroeconomic forecasting is difficult, it should be incorporated in the process leading to the forecasting of the individual company's prospects. Movements in the economy under existing economic policies should be taken from publicly available forecasts. The prediction of government control measures is more subjective and the individual company must make its own forecasts of these and of the impact on the business. Apart from economic forecasts, it may also pay management to attempt some forecast of social and consumer taste changes. Clearly these are important in the longer term and accurate forecasting may lead the firm into new growth areas.

Forecasting of demand

The forecasts of the national economy and of government action form broad parameters within which the firm must operate. However, of more immediate importance is the demand for the type of products it makes, or could make, and its share of this market. This section of the chapter relates to the former: that is the forecasting of market demand for a product.

The basic simple model of demand for an existing product can be expressed as

quantity demand $= f(P, I)$ 9.1

where $P =$ the price of the product and
$I =$ income of consumers

If the price of a product falls we expect the quantity demanded to rise as customers switch their buying from substitute products, which are now more expensive in a relative sense. Consumers will also have relatively more to spend given that the price has dropped. Conversely, if the price of a product rises we would expect the demand to fall as customers switch to competing goods which become relatively cheaper. Occasionally this relationship may be found to be spurious: for example, an increase in price may increase demand because (a) consumers associate the increased price with increased quality or increased status and (b) consumers, on seeing a price rise, may predict from this that prices will rise even further and so they buy now. These cases are likely to be rare, however, and exist for only short periods of time.

In order to quantify the relationship, we compute what is known as the price elasticity of demand; this is the percentage change in demand for a one per cent change in price. In virtually all cases firms are interested in the elasticity of relative prices, thus the percentage change in demand is measured for a one per cent change in relative prices. The reasoning here is that many products have some substitute that consumers will turn to if there is a price advantage. This means of course that a product can become more or less expensive purely as a result of price changes in substitute products. The forecaster needs to define a 'product' and 'competing or substitute products' carefully. In many cases a 'product' may be defined as a group of very similar items (e.g. brands of motor car). Thus a single 'product' for forecasting purposes may be made up of slightly differing items (this type of classification often occurs in consumer durables and luxuries; it should be contrasted with basic commodities such as petrol and many foodstuffs where the products are identical). Similarly, the definition of competing products which can be substituted for the product can vary. In the case of electricity for heating purposes the competing products are likely to include gas, coal and solid fuel. A good guide to identifying competing goods is to examine the markets the product serves. The forecaster needs to exercise a fair amount of judgment in deriving appropriate relatives. The relative of the product to competing products is also used for other independent variables such as advertising and quality; these are discussed later. For existing products, where there are adequate statistics stretching back over some time, the elasticities are derived by regression analysis, as discussed in the previous chapters. Specifically we regress the logarithm of the quantity demand on the logarithms of relative prices, as follows:

$$D = f\left(\frac{Pi}{Ps}, V\right) \quad \quad 9.2$$

where Pi = price of the product
Ps = price of substitute products
V = any other variable in the model

By using logarithms we obtain the coefficients in proportionate form and thus the regression coefficients represent the price elasticity of the product. The elasticity of a product will vary depending upon where it is situated on a demand curve. Where there is a significant change in price the regression equation should be re-run to evaluate the new elasticities. Also elasticities may change over time, so again the regression should be re-run to obtain up-to-date measurements. The various tests of significance for regression should also be run. In practice we may well find difficulty in isolating a relative price, for while the price of the product is known, there is a multitude of possible substitutes which could be used in the denominator of equation 9.2. This especially applies when there are a number of competing products whose prices change independently of each other. For example, an index of the costs of gas, coal and solid fuels would be needed or else a separate relative for each could be computed. There are however price elasticity functions for various broad based products available in official statistics (prepared by civil service economists, academic economists and trade associations) and these greatly ease the work of the forecaster if they are appropriate to the situation. If they are not appropriate then the forecaster will have to use judgement based on knowledge of the business in order to formulate relative price statistics. The regression analysis will help determine whether the hypotheses put forward are reasonable. If the elasticities are very small, i.e. the quantity demanded varies very little for wide changes in relative prices, this implies that the relative price variable is virtually useless in the causal model and will not aid the forecasting process.

The income variable in equation 9.1 is the other major common factor in demand analysis. In general the higher consumers' incomes are, the greater will be the demand for a product. This assumption is less marked than the relative price factor, since the marginal increase in incomes may be spent on new classes of products such as luxuries. However, there is always likely to be at least some increase in demand for a product if consumers' incomes rise. One of the major statistics used for income is personal disposable income (income less tax and national insurance), adjusted to real terms (i.e. with allowances made for inflation). Personal disposable income statistics are produced by the Central Statistical Office and so are readily available to the forecaster. Often the statistic is computed per head of the population: I, the total personal disposable income, is divided by N, the population. Again we compute the elasticity of demand, that is the percentage increase in demand for a 1% increase in the income variable.

The model is now in the form

$$\frac{D}{N} = a + b\left(\frac{Pi}{Ps}\right) + c\left(\frac{I}{N}\right) \qquad 9.3$$

where a, b and c are derived from multiple regression analysis and b and c represent elasticities. The forecaster now wishes to use this basic model for forecasting. As described in the prior chapters, the independent variables need to be known or forecast ahead of demand. The company will know of the likely prices of the product but difficulty may be found in predicting the prices of competing goods. If the competing goods are those which are normally priced in advance, then sales catalogues may be useful in estimating relative prices. In the absence of any advance pricing it will be difficult to estimate relative prices. The personal disposable income variable can be obtained from official forecasts, although these forecasts are subject to error, a factor which should be borne in mind when examining the results.

Other factors

Up to now we have only discussed a simple model of demand although this contained the two most influential and common factors. Other independent variables should be added when they make a significant impact on the causal model and on forecasting accuracy: significance is measured by the regression tests. The identification of these other factors depends upon the forecaster's and management's skill and judgment: we examine some of them below.

Complementary goods
If a product is complementary to another, then the inclusion of the other as an independent variable should make the causal model better and could improve the forecast. For example, the demand for electricity is partly associated with the number of electrical household appliances sold, so we can include a price variable Pe/Pf which gives the relative price of electrical appliances to other types of appliance. The lower the relative price of electrical goods the more they will sell and the higher will be the demand for

electricity. The model is now in the form

$$\frac{D}{N} = f\left(\frac{Pi}{Ps}, \frac{I}{N}, \frac{Pe}{Pf}\right) \qquad 9.4$$

The elasticity is again derived from the regression coefficient of the data in logarithmic form.

Management must use its skill and judgement in identifying significant complementary goods. The rewards from this effort can be very high, especially if the complementary good is in a lag relation, since this aids accurate forecasting: for example, the sale of electrical appliances will lead to an increase in the consumption of electricity for a number of years hence.

Population
For many products the total number of the population may be one determinant of demand. In such cases the population needs to be entered as an independent variable, as follows:

$$D = f\left(\frac{Pi}{Ps}, I, \frac{Pe}{Pf}, N\right) \qquad 9.5$$

where N is the population.

Instead of total population, other statistics may be incorporated, such as the number of households; the average size of a household; the 'retired' population; the population in full-time education; the teenager population. These segments are useful for determining the markets for particular products, such as the pop record market for teenagers or the textbook market for full-time students.

Income distribution and social structure
It is useful to segment the population into spending habits, since this greatly aids the model building relating to products other than those considered as necessities. Thus the demand for consumer durables and luxuries is partly a function of the number of people in the income bracket who can afford these products and the social class who desire them. Among the methods of incorporating the above are

1. The threshold idea. Once a person or a household earns above a certain figure, it becomes a potential customer for a specific product.

2. Discretionary income. This relates to that which is left after buying the necessary goods of life, i.e. the amount available for buying consumer durables and luxuries.

The forecaster must now try to estimate these thresholds or levels of discretionary income, possibly through using consumer surveys, i.e. asking individuals what their buying habits are and recording these against their income level or social class (various measures of social class have been derived and official statistics are available on them). The analysis is generally very difficult but a simple segmentation into income and social groups may sometimes give a good forecasting device.

Advertising

Advertising a product can have an impact on the demand which diverts sales away from competing goods. The advertising may improve the quality of the product as perceived by consumers, as well as creating product awareness if the product has not been around for many years. Thus another variable which can be included in the model is relative advertising, that is, the total advertising expenditure on a product as a percentage of the total advertising expenditure on competing goods. Again, difficulty will probably be found in obtaining statistics to quantify this variable and thus to measure the advertising elasticity of demand. The model incorporating advertising is now of the form

$$\frac{D}{N} = f\left(\frac{Pi}{Ps}, \frac{I}{N}, \frac{Pe}{Pf}, \frac{Ai}{As}\right) \qquad 9.6$$

where Ai = advertising expenditure on the product
As = advertising expenditure on competing goods

Advertising is also an important variable in deciding market share; this is dealt with later on page 156, along with descriptions of other methods of measuring the impact of advertising.

Changes in consumer tastes

This is a very difficult item to measure and quantify, nevertheless it represents a real influence on market demand. One method of quantifying it is to use consumer surveys in which consumers are asked to express preferences and their reasons. In general, however, changes in taste can only be handled qualitatively by the forecaster, who uses them to modify the quantitative forecast produced by the model.

Consumer durables, goods sold to other firms and new products

We have now considered a number of the variables which are commonly found to influence the demand for a product. However, management and the forecaster will have to use their skill and judgment in thinking of other factors which may help in explaining and forecasting demand. Some will be particular to the specific product while others may be common to standard situations. Among these standard situations are the demand for consumer durables, goods sold to other firms (i.e. not sold direct to the final con-

Consumer durables demand

These items are purchased to give satisfaction over some period of time after which they are replaced. Thus demand in any period is a function of the replacement of durables plus the demand for new durables. One method of computing this is to determine the demand for a durable (Dd) and then to forecast how much of this demand has been met by existing stocks (Ds). The difference reflects demand for additional goods (Q) as follows:

$$Q = (Dd - Ds) \qquad 9.7$$

The existing stock variable is equal to the stock at the beginning of a period less depreciation (scrapping) of this stock during the period. The depreciation figure is usually found either from statistical sources or from consumer surveys. For example, the forecast stock demand for television sets at the end of the forthcoming year is 13 million, which may represent 90% of the total households in the country. At the beginning of the period there is an existing stock of 12 million sets, the figures being derived from official statistics. From past statistics it may be calculated that televisions are scrapped in the fourth year. Again from official statistics it might be shown that the number of four year old televisions is $2\frac{1}{2}$ million. The demand for new televisions therefore becomes

$$Q = (13 \cdot 0 - (12 - 2 \cdot 5)) \text{ million}$$
$$= 3 \cdot 5 \text{ million}$$

Thus there is a replacement demand of 2·5 million sets and a demand by new users of 1 million. For applications of the forecasting of consumer durables using stock level variables, see the work by Chow on automobiles and Burstein on refrigerators (both these studies reported in Harberger (6 (a), (b)).

In addition to the presence of existing stocks of a product, there are a number of other factors which have an influence on consumer durable sales, including the following:

1. Changes in the quality of a product need to be recognized. This should be done as objectively as possible, but in the end it may come down to a purely subjective judgement.

2. Credit terms granted have an important impact on demand. Thus the forecaster needs to assess credit terms given for a product and for competing products. The main constraints on the granting of credit are likely to be credit controls imposed by the government, such as over down payments and repayment terms. The sensitivity of demand to changes in credit terms

can be estimated from prior experience using regression analysis. The likelihood of there being changes in credit terms is largely a macroeconomic matter, thus the methodologies mentioned at the beginning of the chapter should be followed.

3. The threshold or discretionary level of income factor discussed previously is often an important indicator of consumer durables demand, these products having the air of being semi- or full luxuries. Additionally, an analysis of the social classification of consumers may help indicate demand for various types of consumer durable.

In forecasting demand for consumer durables it will often be found that consumer surveys provide very good indicators of short-term demand. Well structured market research surveys should therefore be utilized in demand analysis: the use of this technique is covered in Chapter 13.

Goods not sold direct to the public

So far we have discussed demand analysis where the product is sold to the final consumer. The majority of firms, however, sell their output to other companies, either for further processing or some final input (e.g. plant and machinery). In forecasting this type of demand we will in fact have to make a forecast of our customers' sales as well: if industry A supplies products to industry B which converts the products into finished goods sold to the public, then we need to forecast the demand for industry B's output. Even if industry A is only selling goods to industry B as a final product (e.g. fuel or capital equipment) the level of these sales will still be a function of the demand for industry B's products. Thus the demand for industry B's products will be a major variable in predicting the demand for industry A's products. A number of other variables also need to be incorporated into the model, especially if industry B has a choice between the products of industry A and other industries' products, as inputs. Among the variables to be considered are technical advertising, credit terms, technical back-up services and quality.

The analysis becomes more complex when industry A makes a number of products which are sold to a number of other industries, some of which are final consumers and some of which are intermediaries (i.e. firms which add value to a product and then sell it to a customer). In such a case a model for each type of product should be derived, although data problems and the costs involved become considerable. The model may be in the form

$$\frac{D}{I} = f\left(\left[\frac{PBi}{PBs}, \frac{ABi}{ABs}, \frac{VBi}{VBs}\right], \frac{Pi}{Ps}, \frac{I}{N}, \frac{Ai}{As}\right) \qquad 9.8$$

where PBi = price of finished product

PBs = price of goods which are competing with product B

ABi = advertising on finished product
ABs = advertising on goods which are competing with product B
$\dfrac{VBi}{VBs}$ = index of other variables influencing the demand for the finished product
$\dfrac{Pi}{Ps}, \dfrac{I}{N}, \dfrac{Ai}{As}$ = factors relating to the demand of products produced by industry A, by industry B

The term in the squared brackets represents the demand function of industry B, while the other factors represent factors which influence B's purchasing decisions. The forecasting is now becoming more complex in the amount of detail it has to consider, although the input-output analysis techniques discussed in Chapter 10 may help to analyze some of the detail. For an example of the use of a simple input-output analysis in forecasting the demand for steel, see an article by Miles and Hailey (10).

New products

In analyzing the demand for new products the forecaster is faced with the major problem of having no numerical data with which to quantify relationships. In these cases the forecaster may adopt the following forms of analysis:

1. New products are often only modifications to existing products, hence market demand can still be estimated.
2. Even if a product is revolutionarily new, it may still only serve an existing market; for example hovercrafts, although technologically unique, only serve an existing transportation market and it is doubtful whether they induced substantial new demand themselves.
3. Comparisons with overseas experience may help. For example the USA has in recent years led the world in adopting various types of consumer durables and luxuries. By examining the progress of new products in America forecasters can obtain some idea of the level and rate of adoption in their own country.

As described in the first two points, the potential market for a new product is often known and the problem is to predict what share of this market will be taken by the new product and over what length of time. To do this requires considerable marketing knowledge and judgement as to the learning and acceptance processes of customers. Although there have been a number of theoretical studies into these, the practical application of learning and acceptance processes has been left largely to subjective appraisal and experience. If a firm is continually bringing out new products (e.g. types of motor cars or consumer durables) then it will have some experience of the level of consumer awareness and consumer acceptance of new products. It is this type of analysis which is likely to be the most useful until a lot more research has been conducted into consumer behaviour. Sometimes it is possible for a new product acceptance curve to be fitted to the data. The major type of curve used in this analysis is the S-shaped curve (see reference 2 for an example of the use of growth curves in forecasting new products). These techniques only provide a very approximate forecast and are only of use in the case of new products which have no existing market and where there are no similar competing products. Chapter 12 covers the particular growth curves in more detail and gives examples of their application. Although the forecasting of new products involves additional problems the factors mentioned above should help the forecaster in this work. If the product is completely new or if the firm is introducing its first new product for many years then the forecasting will be very difficult. In such cases management may adopt a defensive strategy (such as undertaking a pilot scheme) or engage in a lot of market research and consumer surveys.

The assessment of market share

Having established the demand for a product, management will now want to assess how much of this demand will accrue to their firm. The suggested methodology is the same as that used in forecasting product demand, namely the building of a causal model which in this case explains the market share obtained by a firm. As will be seen, many of the variables in the market share model are those that appeared in the market demand equation, i.e.

$$MS_F = f\left(\frac{PF}{Pi}, \frac{AF}{Ai}\right) \qquad 9.9$$

where F stands for the individual firms and MS stands for market share. In the market share model, however, the relative expenditures on advertising, etc. will be

$$\frac{\text{expenditure by firm } (AF)}{\text{expenditure by all firms making the product } (Ai)}$$

as opposed to

$$\frac{\text{expenditure on product } (Ai)}{\text{expenditure on competing products } (As)}$$

The demarcation between when a product is in a homogenous group and when it is a competing product is one of degree. Demand for a product is likely to be made up of several slightly differing products (i.e. many firms will have brand differences, such as motor cars, household furniture). The demarcation of products is a subjective matter to be handled by the forecaster and the management; no insuperable problems should arise. It is possible that the market demand and market share models be combined into one, thus for the relative price variable we may have the price charged by the firm divided by an index of the prices of similar products charged by competing firms and prices of different but competing goods charged by other firms. For example, the price of Company A's electric heater may be expressed as a relative of a composite index made up of the prices of electrical heaters produced by firms B, C, and D and the prices of gas heaters and smokeless fuel heaters made by firms E, F, G, H. In practice, however, this type of relative is likely to be unwieldy and give a poor causal explanation and a poor forecasting model. Thus except in very simple situations, the forecaster should forecast market demand and then forecast market share.

The elasticities of each variable need to be computed, i.e. the percentage change in market share expected from a one per cent movement in the price relative. Given adequate historical data these elasticities are given by regression coefficients. A major advantage of using regression analysis is that the other known influencing variables on market share are held constant, so the elasticity of the individual factor can be identified. If the past data is insufficient, because the variables have varied very little or because the product is new, then other methods will have to be used to compute elasticities. One method is to experiment with the variable and another is to use a consumer survey. These two methods are reviewed in the next section on the relative price variable.

Relative price

The next few subsections discuss some of the major variables in determining market share. Many have been met before in the section on market demand, so this discussion will be confined to the specific applications in market share models.

The price charged by the firm relative to the prices charged for identical or similar products by competing firms is an obviously important variable. Consumers almost certainly buy the product which is cheapest. However, there is a major difficulty in assessing the impact of relative prices in many cases, because competing firms charge exactly the same amount for their brands (e.g. petrol, basic foodstuffs). In such cases it is difficult to assess elasticities since the past data is inadequate. However, for forecasting purposes it does not matter greatly, since we know that all the firms react to

154 *Forecasting methods in business and management*

any price cutting almost instantaneously and by the same amount.

If differentiation does exist in pricing then there is likely to be some quality or styling difference to account for this. However, this may allow elasticities to be computed, since the differentiation in prices may vary over time (the regression analysis holding constant the impact of quality).

For identical goods, prices are likely to be the same. However some price competition may arise though the granting of discounts and credit terms. By a careful analysis of the data it may be possible to measure a variable incorporating discounts, trade-in values of old products and credit terms and thus the elasticity could be computed on market share. The section on market demand for consumer durables discussed a variable of credit terms and the impact of this has now to be assessed at the individual firm level.

If there are no differences in the pricing policies of the various firms then regression analysis is fairly useless in deriving elasticities. The forecaster may, however, be able to get an estimate of the elasticities by the following means:

1. Experimenting with prices, i.e. increasing or decreasing prices by varying amounts and measuring the impact on quantity sold. This experiment will probably have to be conducted in a fairly narrow geographical area as otherwise competing firms will almost certainly alter their prices as well. Additionally the experiment will have to last some time so that customers become aware of the revised prices; the longer the period, however, the more likely competitors will alter their prices.

2. A market survey could be undertaken whereby consumers are asked how they would react to changes in relative prices. If the survey is well constructed (see Chapter 13) then it could give fairly good estimates of elasticities.

It must be remembered, however, that in the case of identical products and in duopolies and oligopolies price differentiation may be impossible. (The fewer the number of firms competing in a market, the easier it is to keep a check on the prices each is charging.)

Product quality

As previously mentioned, there are often quality and styling differentiations within product groupings and any changes in these can have a significant impact on market share. This especially applies in the market for more expensive goods such as consumer durables. Thus in the motor car industry there are numerous brands of cars with different 'quality' characteristics. What the forecaster has to do is to forecast changes in qualities of competing manufacturers' cars and assess the public's demand for these qualities. This is a very difficult task and one which is often handled subjectively by management.

In some cases it may be possible, with a lot of research, to construct a quality index. This would involve quantifying the quality characteristics of the firm's product and measuring this against the composite quality characteristic of all makes of the product. (For example, Brems (5) used horsepower as a measure of quality in his study of the US car market. This is a very simplified variable and one which is unlikely to be very satisfactory today.) By incorporating this variable in a regression model, the impact of movements in the quality index can be measured after holding other factors (such as price) constant. This gives the quality elasticity of demand and by forecasting future movements in the quality index the impact on market share can be established.

An added difficulty in this analysis is that consumers' tastes change over time and so the elasticity of the quality variable will also change. Unless it is possible to construct a consumer taste variable, then the elasticity of quality needs to be checked at fairly close intervals. The construction of a quality index is likely to be extremely difficult and it is perhaps unlikely that many firms will attempt to do so. Some trade associations have derived elasticity figures for quality variables and these can be used by the individual firms, although for forecasting purposes they will still have the difficult problem of predicting changes in the quality index.

Distribution policies and after-sales services

Apart from the price and quality of the company's product, market share is also determined by the number and type of distribution outlets and the after-sales service facilities. The distribution outlets can be measured as some function of the number of outlets, the square footage of the outlets and the location of the outlets. This is then measured against the statistics for all the firms selling the product. The construction of an index for numbers and square footage of outlets should be feasible, although the location factor will involve qualitative judgement.

After-sales service can be a very important factor in purchasing decisions and its influence should be assessed if possible. Among the items making up after-sales services are

1. Repair services
2. Replacement services
3. Training in the use of technical products
4. The planning and installation of a product
5. The replacing of machines with newer, improved versions

Again this variable is difficult to quantify, but if it is feasible it can lead to a significant improvement in the causal model and the forecasting.

Advertising

Advertising is an obviously important determinant of market demand and market share, although the measurement of its impact is difficult. Various studies have been made into advertising effectiveness and the major ones are briefly discussed below; these studies are also relevant for advertising a product which is competing with substitutes (page 148).

One method of measuring the impact of advertising is to compute the expenditure of a firm for a particular period as a percentage of the total advertising expenditure by all firms making the product. This period is usually one year, since statistics relating to total advertising are normally only availabe on an annual basis (possibly calendar year): for an example of this form of approach see reference 15. Various modifications can be made to the approach, such as disaggregating the advertising expenditures into various component parts. For example, market share might be expressed as

$$MS_F = f\left(\frac{AP_F}{APi}, \frac{AT_F}{ATi}, \frac{AO_F}{AOi}, \frac{AG_F}{AGi}\right) \quad 9.10$$

where $\frac{AP_F}{APi}$ = press advertising relative

$\frac{AT_F}{ATi}$ = television advertising relative

$\frac{AO_F}{AOi}$ = other type advertising relative

$\frac{AG_F}{AGi}$ = free gift or other promotional relative

In addition, the model could be restricted to one type of product sold by the firm (i.e. a causal model for each product produced) and could include the advertising relatives of prior periods. Obtaining the data to quantify the above detailed model will be very time-consuming and may involve using some estimates. Having constructed it, however, the forecaster will get an estimate of the advertising elasticity. By incorporating future values or estimates of the variables into the model, the impact of various possible advertising campaigns can be assessed. As with the other explanatory variables, however, it will not be easy to form estimates of the future values of the advertising variables. In the above model, for example, various estimates of total advertising are required; this will involve estimating what their competitors' advertising budgets are. It is also possible to use a consumer survey approach, i.e. asking consumers how they react to advertising, however this should only be used as a general guide.

One independent variable discussed above was the advertising in prior periods. This is an important factor, since continuous advertising of a product builds up a quality image and customer loyalty: it is similar to the demand model for consumer durables (see page 149). The model can be specified as

$$\text{sales}\,(S_t) = A_t + ZA_{t-1} + YA_{t-2} \ldots \qquad 9.11$$

$Z, Y \ldots$ are weights attached to advertising expenditures in prior periods

or

$$\text{sales}\,(S_t) = bA_t - \lambda S_{t-1}$$

where λ is a series of exponential weights (i.e. exponential smoothing as described in Chapter 3). The coefficients can be calculated by regression analysis: see Palda's use of this form of model in reference 12. Thus sales (or market share) during the current period is determined partly by the level of advertising in the current period and partly by the level of advertising in prior periods.

An alternative method of allowing for the cumulative impact of advertising is to formally estimate the stock level of advertising goodwill. This stock depreciates over time but is replenished by current advertising expenditures (A_t). The model is described notationally as

$$AS_t = A_t + (1 - \lambda)\,AS_{t-1} \qquad 9.12$$

where λ is a depreciation factor and AS is the advertising stock in a particular period. Various values of λ are tried until the regression gives the best statistical fit. For examples of this approach see Nerlove and Arrow (11) and Ball and Agarwala (3).

Other models have also been used in attempting to measure the impact of advertising. Among the variations are the use of simultaneous equation models and the use of the threshold idea on advertising effectiveness. Simultaneous equation models have been suggested because many firms base their advertising expenditure on the level of sales, so the cause and effect relationship is unclear. For an example of this approach see an article by Bass and Parsons (4). The threshold model is based on the premise that below a certain level of expenditure advertising has no impact, and that it also has no impact above a certain level, since a saturation level is reached. Attempts have therefore been made to estimate what these levels are, so as to optimize the advertising effort. An example of this methodology can be found in a paper by Emshoff and Mercer (7).

Market share estimated by salesmen

If it is found that the quantitative methods discussed above are too uncertain for predicting market share, it may be advisable to use market surveys. This topic is discussed briefly in Chapter 13 and references are made there to additional readings. Basically the firm's salesmen are asked to give their opinions on what they think sales will be or what the market share will be over various future periods. These forecasts need to be handled with care, however, as the salesmen's opinions are likely to be biased to some degree. Care must also be exercised in stating clearly what forecasts the salesmen have to make.

Summary

This chapter has attempted to identify the major variables that influence demand and give readers an insight into model building in general. Clearly the forecaster needs to assess each individual situation and look for additional factors that help determine market demand and market share. Model building for forecasting other variables follows much the same principles.

In making use of models we need to be able to quantify the relationships and this involves the regression techniques discussed in the two prior chapters. Specifically

1. We need past data on the variables.

2. We need to be able to make reliable forecasts or know the values of the independent variables ahead of the dependent variable. This is aided when the independent variables are in a lagged relationship with the dependent variable. For example, quantity demanded may be a function of the prices charged in a prior period (i.e. customers basing purchasing decisions on the relative cheapness of a product in the immediately prior period). Many of the variables discussed in the chapter may have a lagged relationship and the forecaster should experiment to examine for this.

3. The elasticities of various factors may change over time or over large movements in the value of the factor. The elasticities therefore need to be reappraised at regular intervals or after certain events.

Given that we can quantify relationships, causal model building represents the most sophisticated and usually the most accurate forecasting device. It is also the most complex and expensive method, so the discussions in Chapter 14 on selecting appropriate techniques need to be kept in mind.

References

1. Ash, J. C. K., and Smyth, D. J., *Forecasting the United Kingdom Economy*, Saxon House, 1973.
2. Bain, A. D., *The Growth of Television Ownership in Britain*, Cambridge University Press, 1964.
3. Ball, R. J., and Agarwala, R., 'An econometric analysis of the effects of generic advertising on demand for tea in the UK', *British Journal of Marketing*, Winter, 1969.
4. Bass, F. M., and Parsons, L. J., 'Simultaneous equation regression analysis of sales and advertising', *Applied Economics*, May, 1969.
5. Brems, H., *Product Equilibrium under Monopolistic Competition*, Harvard University Press, 1951.
6.(a) Burstein, M. L., 'The Demand for Household Refrigeration in the United States' and
   (b) Chow, G. C. 'Statistical Demand Functions for Automobiles and Their Use for Forecasting' both in Harberger, A. C., *The Demand for Durable Goods*, University of Chicago Press, 1960.
7. Emshoff, J. R., and Mercer, A., 'Aggregate Models of Purchases', *Journal of the Royal Statistical Society*, Series A, 133, Part I, 1970.
8. Hilton, K., and Heathfield, D. F., (eds.), *The Econometric Study of the U.K.*, Macmillan, 1970.
9. McMahon, C., *The Techniques of Economic Forecasting*, OECD (*HMSO*).
10. Miles, T. P., and Hailey, M. J., 'Demand Forecasting in the Short Term', *British Steel*, November, 1969.
11. Nerlove, M., and Arrow, K. J., 'Optimal Advertising Policy Under Dynamic Conditions', *Economica*, 1962.
12. Palda, K. S., *The Measurement of Cumulative Advertising Effects*, Prentice Hall, 1964.
13. Renton, G. A., (ed.), *Modelling the Economy*, Heinemann, 1975.
14. Surrey, M. J. C., *The Analysis and Forecasting of the British Economy*, Cambridge University Press, 1971.
15. Weinberg, R. S., 'Multiple factor breakeven analysis', *Operations Research*, April, 1956.
16. Ball, R. J., and Burns, T. 'An economic approach to short-run analysis of the UK economy 1955–1966', *Operational Research Quarterly*, September, 1968.
17. Bratt, E. C., *Business Forecasting*, McGraw-Hill, 1968.
18. Lewis, J. P., and Turner, R. C., *Business Conditions Analysis*, 2nd edition, McGraw-Hill, 1967.

10

Other techniques: input-output analysis, leading indicators

Forecasting with input-output tables

Input-output analysis consists of tables which show the transactions between component forms of a system: for example, the transactions between various industries within a national or regional economy can be shown in an input-output table form. This shows the extent to which one industry is dependent upon another for the purchases of its inputs and the sales of its products. Inputs into a firm can also be classified by categories such as imports, commodities and labour, while outputs of a firm can be classified by exports, investment and consumption. It is essentially an accounting exercise where the original sources of all the inputs into an industry and all the outlets for the industry's output are shown.

The main use of input-output analysis is in the planning process and it has achieved a high rate of adoption at the national economy and regional economy level, thus we find that many countries which make heavy use of centralized planning are deeply involved with input-output analysis. At the micro level few firms have found it worthwhile to compute their own input-output tables as the expenses are very high and the benefits not so great. Firms can, however, make use of existing input-output tables and a brief discussion of this is presented later. Before describing the ways of forecasting from input-output tables, a brief simplified example on the make-up of a table is given.

A simplified example of input-output tables

Table 10.1 shows the profit and loss accounts of industries X, Y and Z which constitute the sole activities of a simple economy. The left-hand side of the accounts represent the various expenses incurred by the firms and the profits made. The right-hand side of the accounts represent the sales

Table 10.1

Industry X

	£		£
Purchases from industry Y	100	Sales to individuals	400
Purchases from industry Z	200	Sales to industry Z	100
Wages	100		
Profits	100		
	500		500

Industry Y

	£		£
Purchases from industry Z	200	Sales to industry X	100
Wages	400	Sales to individuals	900
Profits	400		
	1000		1000

Industry Z

	£		£
Purchases from industry X	100	Sales to industry X	200
Wages	400	Sales to industry Y	200
Profits	300	Sales to individuals	400
	800		800

made by each. From these accounts an input-output table for the economy is constructed and this is shown in Table 10.2. The inputs into each industry are shown in the columns: industry X receives £100 of input from industry Y, £200 from industry Z and £100 of labour. The outputs are shown in the rows; for example, £100 worth of sales are made to industry Z, and £400 worth of sales to private individuals. The example is of course

Table 10.2 Input-output table

	Inputs £				
Outputs £	Industry X	Industry Y	Industry Z	Individuals	Total
Industry X			100	400	500
Industry Y	100			900	1000
Industry Z	200	200		400	800
Wages	100	400	400		900 ⎫ 1700
Profits	100	400	300		800 ⎭
Total	500	1000	800	1700	

extremely simplified, but it does represent the basic idea of input-output analysis. The table shows the various interactions between the component forms of the economy. In order to facilitate tight planning control the industry groupings should be narrowly specified, thus giving a lot of industry types.

From the initial table a number of other tables can be computed. Firstly there is an output distribution table which shows the output in percentage terms: Table 10.3 shows an example relating to the data in Table 10.2.

Table 10.3 Output distribution table

	Industry X	Industry Y	Industry Z	Individuals	Total
Industry X	·00	·00	·20	·80	1·00
Industry Y	·10	·00	·00	·90	1·00
Industry Z	·25	·25	·00	·50	1·00

Similarly, a percentage input table, known as a direct requirements table, can be computed: this is shown in Table 10.4. Here the columnar figures appearing in Table 10.2 are divided by their total, e.g. Y's £200 purchase from industry Z is 20% (·2) of Y's total inputs. Thus in order to produce £100 more output from industry Y we must incur the following expenses: £20 worth of industry Z's products and £40 of labour. There should be an increase of £40 in profits resulting from the transaction.

Table 10.4 Direct requirements table

	Industry X	Industry Y	Industry Z
Industry X	·000	·000	·125
Industry Y	·200	·000	·000
Industry Z	·400	·200	·000
Wages	·200	·400	·500
Profits	·200	·400	·375
Total	1·000	1·000	1·000

When planning in the national context the decision maker will want to know the impact on all the factors of production for any increase in an output. If industry Y's production rises by 10% then the total impact on the economy is different from that specified in Table 10.4, because Y needs the products from Z (an increase of £20 worth) and Z has to incur inputs to meet this demand. Specifically Z would have to increase production by 2·5% (that is 20/800). This involves costs of purchases from X

(102·5/100·0 × £100 = £102·5) and labour (102·5/100·0 × 400 = £410·0), which in turn increases the costs of X in order to meet the demand. X incurs purchases from both Y and Z and so these in turn have to increase their production. The calculations are continued (in practice, using matrix algebra and a computer) and a total requirements table can eventually be constructed. This table shows the indirect as well as the direct input requirements of each industry for a given increase in sales to

Table 10.5 Total requirements table

	Industry X	Industry Y	Industry Z
Industry X	1·058	0·026	0·132
Industry Y	0·212	1·005	0·026
Industry Z	0·466	0·212	1·058

final consumers. The total requirements table is shown in Table 10.5. The figures within the table are known as the input-output coefficients.

Assumptions involved with forecasting from input-output tables

In using the input-output tables the forecaster must be aware of the assumptions involved. The major assumptions are

1. That the cost relationships are the same for all levels of production. Thus no matter how much the final sales (to outside customers) of industry Y are increased, the cost of input goods supplied from industry X will always be 0·026 × the increase (from Table 10.5). In practice, however, this is unlikely to be strictly so because of economies of scale and fixed and variable expenses differentiation: for example, annual fixed costs for an industry are only likely to change when production reaches particular levels and are unlikely to rise in exact proportion to production for all levels of production.

2. That the relationships hold true over time. Thus the tables are constructed on historical data and these are assumed to hold for the current and future periods. In these days of rapidly changing technology the above assumption for longer-term forecasts is likely to be spurious.

In addition to these assumptions the forecaster has to recognize the industry grouping used and examine how appropriate this is for the forecast required. This is usually a major problem for individual firms, since the input from industry X to their particular industry, say industry Y, may not be applicable to themselves. For very large firms within an industry grouping the problem is perhaps not so severe, since they are usually much more representative of the overall industry. A further consideration of using published input-output tables is the measurement used in the tables, i.e. whether the figures are inflation-adjusted or not.

Forecasting with existing input-output tables

As described previously, very few companies find it feasible to construct their own input-output tables, so recourse is made to those published by government, trade and academic sources.

At the macro-level the impact of forecasted or assumed growth rates of a number of industries can be measured on the remaining industries and also the impact of various economic measures on various sectors of the economy can be established. The tables enable the planner to evaluate the impact of any policy or decision on individual industries. This analysis can be extended to regional investigations and employment forecasts, such as forecasting the demand for labour by geographical area.

At the micro-level the forecaster can be helped in a number of ways:

1. If there are any official forecasts made for an industry or a sector, then by using the tables the impact of this forecast for the industry under scrutiny can be established. The tables are especially helpful where one industry indirectly supplies another. For example, a steel manufacturer sells its products to an engineering company which supplies the motor industry with engine components, thus the steel industry is both a direct supplier to motor manufacturers (sheet steel for car bodies) and an indirect supplier (via the engineering company). The input-output table gives the total requirements (inputs), both direct and indirect, for each industry or sector. This helps a firm to forecast its sales (e.g. by estimating the total sales of other industries and knowing their input requirements of steel a forecast of sales of steel can be made.) The forecaster must of course be aware of the caveats expressed earlier.

2. The forecaster may use the tables to help the forecasting, and hence the planning, of inputs into the industry (and firm). If, for example, the firm forecasts that its sales are to double in the next year, then the inputs (indirect as well as direct) can be approximated from the input-output table (assuming the firm can be allocated to a single industry or other classification in the table). This may, in the case of a very large firm, suggest possible bottlenecks and constraints on sales, so appropriate action can be taken in plenty of time.

Input-output tables for 1971

Tables 10.6 and 10.7 are extracted from official input-output tables appearing in *Economic Trends*, No. 258, April 1975, and relate to the year

1971, the latest tables available. The figures are partially based on an extrapolation of the 1968 input-output tables which used original data taken from the census of production. Table 10.6 shows the industry categorized inputs into each purchasing industry (equivalent to Table 10.2). The food industry (column 5) bought £1126·4 million output of the agricultural industry, £90·1 million output of the chemical industry (such as colouring and preservatives), £167·4 million output of the paper and printing industry (for packaging purposes) and so on. Row 36 shows the imports into each industry and, as expected, food has a very high import content at £914·1 million. Row 38 gives the total purchases of goods and services from other industries: the other expenses that an industry has to incur are shown in rows 39 and 40, these being taxes and wages paid respectively. Row 41 shows gross profits. The total expenses (including the profit element) of the food industry in 1971 comes to £4859·7 million.

The sales made by various industries are shown along the rows; for example, the sales of the food industry classified by the type of consumer are shown in row 5. The agricultural industry took £531·2 million of the food industry's output (such as food for animals), the drink and tobacco industry took £21·5 million, and so on. The total sales of the food industry to other industries was £693·0 million in 1971. Column 37 shows that direct sales of the food industry to the public was £3775·1 million, not surprisingly the largest customer. Column 38 shows the purchases by public authorities, while column 39 relates to gross domestic capital formation (fixed assets).

The food industry sells little to this source, while the construction industry (row 27) is a major supplier. Column 40 relates to the addition (plus sign) to or the depletion (minus sign) of stocks during the year. Column 41 shows that exports of food amounted to £310·0 million and column 43 shows the total output of the food industry. Note that the total inputs into the food industry shown in column 5 (£4859·7 million) equal the total outputs by the food industry shown in row 5 (£4859·7 million). The total transactions between British industry including imports in 1971 comes to £35 839·5 million (row 38, column 36).

Table 10.7 shows the total requirements table by industry grouping for 1971; this is an actual example of Table 10.5 in use. It shows the direct and indirect inputs into each industry per £1000 of output to the final consumer (these are shown in the columns below the industry classification). The food industry, for example, requires £245·4 of direct and indirect input from the agricultural industry to obtain a final food output to consumers of £1000. The diagonal line represents the output of an industry X to achieve £1000 sales to the final consumer from industry X. Thus in order for the food industry to increase its output to the final consumer by £1000 it must

166 Forecasting methods in business and management

Table 10.6 Reproduced by permission of the Controller of Her Majesty's Stationery Office

Summary industry x industry flow matrix 1971

£ million

Sales by \ Purchases by	Agriculture	Forestry and fishing	Coal mining	Other mining and quarrying	Food	Drink and tobacco	Mineral oil refining	Coke ovens	Chemicals, etc.	Iron and steel	Non-ferrous metals	Mechanical engineering	Instrument engineering	Electrical engineering	Shipbuilding, etc.	Motor vehicles, etc.	Aerospace equipment	Other vehicles	Other metal goods	Textiles
	1	2	3	4	5	6	7	8	9	10	11	12	13	14	15	16	17	18	19	20
1 Agriculture	—	—	—	—	1,126.4	37.6	0.1	—	4.1	—	—	—	—	—	—	—	—	—	—	4.2
2 Forestry and fishing	—	—	—	—	21.7	—	—	—	2.4	—	—	—	—	—	—	—	—	—	—	—
3 Coal mining	0.5	—	—	0.9	6.4	2.4	—	78.8	20.3	46.3	0.9	2.4	0.2	1.8	0.2	1.6	0.8	0.6	1.1	8.8
4 Other mining and quarrying	6.9	—	—	—	0.8	—	1.3	—	13.8	28.0	1.7	1.2	—	—	—	—	—	0.5	—	—
5 Food	531.2	0.8	—	0.2	—	21.5	1.2	0.1	71.7	0.5	0.1	0.3	—	2.7	—	0.2	—	—	0.2	4.5
6 Drink and tobacco	0.2	—	—	—	5.4	—	—	—	2.5	—	—	—	—	—	—	—	—	—	—	0.1
7 Mineral oil refining	39.9	6.6	2.8	16.6	35.1	8.7	—	1.2	125.0	51.3	9.9	22.1	2.3	13.1	2.5	19.1	6.3	1.5	14.2	23.2
8 Coke ovens	0.3	—	0.1	0.1	0.6	0.1	0.1	—	11.5	58.9	0.9	2.2	—	0.4	0.2	0.4	0.1	0.1	0.9	0.6
9 Chemicals, etc.	190.8	0.2	3.6	24.3	90.1	6.6	34.6	1.2	—	33.4	9.1	42.8	4.7	55.0	3.9	34.0	1.8	2.5	35.6	135.6
10 Iron and steel	0.1	—	36.9	8.8	11.1	0.2	—	0.3	9.5	—	4.7	467.6	10.4	103.5	34.5	317.2	16.1	21.6	402.3	0.7
11 Non-ferrous metals	1.0	—	0.1	0.3	25.3	7.1	0.2	—	32.4	38.7	—	133.8	14.5	173.1	8.6	76.6	18.1	4.9	166.5	0.9
12 Mechanical engineering	20.5	0.4	22.7	18.4	34.5	14.1	10.1	1.7	50.0	66.4	14.4	—	7.1	138.1	41.5	75.3	13.7	28.0	49.9	29.5
13 Instrument engineering	0.1	—	0.3	0.1	0.2	0.1	1.1	—	0.5	2.2	0.4	28.9	—	18.4	3.3	8.1	5.4	0.5	1.1	0.5
14 Electrical engineering	0.6	0.1	9.2	0.9	2.9	0.9	2.9	—	3.5	6.0	25.7	109.4	89.0	—	18.5	105.6	69.3	13.4	15.3	0.4
15 Shipbuilding, etc.	—	9.7	—	2.0	—	—	—	—	2.1	2.5	0.1	—	—	0.1	—	0.4	—	—	—	—
16 Motor vehicles, etc.	11.2	0.3	0.9	2.5	6.4	1.8	0.4	—	3.0	13.7	4.3	28.0	0.6	5.9	3.1	—	1.8	0.9	4.8	1.7
17 Aerospace equipment	—	—	—	—	—	—	—	—	0.4	1.0	—	—	—	—	—	—	—	—	—	—
18 Other vehicles	—	—	—	—	0.1	—	—	—	0.1	2.7	0.9	1.0	—	4.6	0.1	4.1	—	—	0.2	0.3
19 Other metal goods	7.4	0.7	15.1	17.3	99.2	23.6	7.1	0.4	74.0	84.8	31.8	334.8	13.8	234.8	9.8	231.8	10.1	11.0	—	9.2
20 Textiles	6.0	7.4	0.1	0.3	3.1	0.2	—	—	13.8	0.2	0.1	8.0	3.7	6.5	2.4	27.3	1.5	0.6	7.9	—
21 Leather, etc.	—	—	—	—	—	—	—	—	0.8	—	—	—	0.5	—	—	2.4	—	0.2	0.8	5.8
22 Clothing and footwear	0.6	—	3.4	0.1	1.5	0.4	—	—	3.8	—	0.3	—	—	0.4	—	0.5	—	—	0.1	11.4
23 Bricks, etc.	32.0	—	2.2	2.3	41.8	19.7	0.3	0.3	27.0	45.4	0.7	30.3	5.5	62.2	2.1	30.2	1.2	0.8	102	1.2
24 Timber and furniture	21.6	0.2	8.5	1.1	7.2	15.6	0.1	—	8.4	2.6	2.4	17.9	0.6	31.1	7.2	18.1	1.2	2.7	10.5	3.2
25 Paper and printing	9.2	0.1	1.1	4.7	167.4	71.8	0.8	0.1	100.6	7.3	5.9	42.0	9.4	45.1	1.7	16.7	3.6	1.5	22.5	32.5
26 Other manufacturing	10.6	—	—	3.8	2.3	38.5	10.2	0.8	0.2	64.4	16.1	4.4	42.5	10.2	70.2	2.0	171.8	8.0	3.9	32.3	23.8
27 Construction	50.6	2.6	48.1	11.8	8.9	12.5	0.3	—	9.3	4.2	1.2	112.7	1.2	7.5	3.0	6.5	2.9	0.5	4.9	6.6
28 Gas	0.5	—	0.1	0.1	6.1	0.3	—	5.7	4.9	70.2	6.1	10.8	1.1	5.5	1.2	6.8	1.3	1.2	13.3	1.8
29 Electricity	21.4	0.6	32.8	7.9	29.9	5.9	3.9	1.7	71.8	58.4	17.9	35.4	4.4	24.5	6.2	28.0	8.3	2.8	28.1	35.7
30 Water	8.0	0.2	0.2	0.2	4.8	1.8	0.9	0.3	15.1	2.8	0.7	3.7	2.2	2.8	—	1.4	0.5	—	1.7	3.9
31 Transport	73.3	9.4	16.7	8.2	196.3	33.3	219.8	20.0	138.7	107.2	35.1	55.5	5.2	27.7	3.4	31.0	3.6	2.3	46.4	53.3
32 Communication	8.5	0.6	1.0	1.9	11.3	4.1	0.5	—	13.7	3.9	2.1	30.2	5.3	17.4	1.4	8.2	3.3	0.5	12.5	9.4
33 Distributive trades	39.3	0.6	3.1	7.6	330.8	18.2	1.7	—	44.8	100.6	75.4	139.7	8.0	70.8	8.4	68.6	5.1	5.7	94.5	80.1
34 Miscellaneous services	91.2	15.2	1.0	4.6.7	384.0	281.1	27.6	2.5	384.0	96.2	27.5	348.4	37.9	186.8	24.1	109.2	20.8	1.0	147.0	178.9
35 Public administration, etc.[1]	—	—	—	—	—	—	—	—	—	—	—	—	—	—	—	—	—	—	—	—
36 Imports of goods and services	130.3	1.6	12.1	14.2	914.1	144.9	802.1	2.5	466.3	240.6	361.8	250.1	55.6	298.8	37.3	185.6	57.1	14.8	190.3	341.0
37 Sales by final buyers	1.5	—	2.8	0.8	13.6	3.4	3.3	0.7	10.1	100.3	95.3	12.1	1.5	8.9	1.8	9.0	19.6	0.1	9.8	8.4
38 Total goods and services (1 to 37)	1,315.5	57.3	228.7	202.8	3,625.4	748.2	1,121.2	118.0	1,801.9	1,291.5	745.2	2,313.6	294.9	1,617.7	228.3	1,596.6	281.5	124.1	1,335.0	1,017.2
39 Taxes on expenditure less subsidies	−226.8	−4.7	1.5	62.1	88.0	26.8	19.4	3.3	74.4	39.4	12.1	54.8	11.1	41.7	−3.5	48.5	10.0	2.3	35.3	44.3
40 Income from employment	394.0	58.0	484.0	86.0	865.0	253.0	61.7	22.3	746.0	683.6	208.4	1617.0	249.0	1,095.0	303.0	898.1	374.6	96.3	753.0	737.0
41 Gross profit and other trading income	871.0	54.0	97.0	58.0	281.3	366.8	61.4	4.2	449.7	63.5	66.0	444.2	50.6	287.7	26.4	60.2	14.7	3.0	210.8	205.7
42 Total input (38 to 41)	2,353.7	164.6	811.2	408.9	4,859.7	1,394.8	1,263.7	147.8	3,072.0	2,078.0	1,031.7	4,429.6	605.6	3,042.1	554.2	2,602.8	680.8	225.7	2,334.1	2,004.2

[1] Public administration, domestic services, ownership of dwellings.

Other techniques: input-output analysis, leading indicators 167

	Leather, etc.	Clothing and footwear	Bricks, etc.	Timber and furniture	Paper and printing	Other manufacturing	Construction	Gas	Electricity	Water	Transport	Communication	Distributive trades	Miscellaneous services	Public administration, etc.[1]	Total intermediate output	Consumers	Public authorities	Fixed	Stocks	Exports	Total final output	Total output
																	\multicolumn{5}{c}{Final demand}		
																	\multicolumn{2}{c}{Current expenditure}	\multicolumn{2}{c}{Gross domestic capital formation}			
21	22	23	24	25	26	27	28	29	30	31	32	33	34	35	(1-35) 36	37	38	39	40	41	(37-41) 42	(36+42) 43
19.9	—	0.7	0.1	—	0.7	—	—	—	—	6.5	—	—	11.6	—	1,211.9	977.5	19.9	27.0	21.7	95.7	1,141.8	2,353.7
—	—	—	11.6	4.4	—	—	—	1.7	—	0.8	—	—	—	—	42.5	65.5	2.6	—	43.7	10.3	122.1	164.6
0.5	0.5	22.8	0.5	10.2	3.3	1.0	11.2	348.4	0.7	0.5	—	—	0.5	—	574.1	147.9	30.7	11.3	34.1	13.1	237.1	811.2
—	—	58.3	—	3.9	0.8	149.0	79.6	—	—	0.9	—	—	—	—	346.6	3.6	12.2	2.8	2.4	41.3	62.3	408.9
—	—	1.3	—	7.4	3.1	2.4	—	—	—	12.2	—	7.0	24.0	—	693.0	3,775.1	90.8	1.0	-10.3	310.0	4,166.7	4,859.7
—	—	—	—	—	0.1	—	—	—	—	3.3	—	74.8	—	—	86.8	1,019.4	0.7	1.0	3.1	283.8	1,208.0	1,394.8
1.6	2.9	46.8	6.7	22.7	10.2	37.8	25.2	97.7	0.5	78.7	1.8	27.1	34.8	—	795.9	139.9	38.6	—	44.8	244.4	467.8	1,263.7
0.1	0.1	3.1	0.2	0.4	0.3	0.5	3.4	0.3	0.1	—	—	0.5	0.9	—	87.4	37.6	13.5	—	3.4	5.9	60.4	147.8
9.2	8.2	39.1	23.0	96.9	201.4	72.9	2.8	9.0	2.7	17.3	—	41.4	116.9	—	1,350.6	445.1	223.4	42.5	12.8	997.6	1,721.4	3,072.0
0.3	1.7	9.2	7.4	2.2	5.5	168.4	17.5	1.4	9.3	9.2	2.2	0.5	0.9	—	1,681.4	25.1	12.4	11.5	-39.3	386.9	396.6	2,078.0
0.2	0.4	3.9	3.9	12.1	7.2	36.4	1.6	0.7	1.3	0.1	—	0.4	0.9	—	770.9	3.7	4.4	0.7	22.6	229.4	260.8	1,031.7
1.3	5.9	24.1	7.4	29.5	17.1	447.6	5.0	11.9	6.0	10.5	2.3	20.1	24.6	—	1,249.6	27.0	168.6	1,522.5	-7.0	1,468.9	3,180.0	4,429.6
—	0.3	0.2	0.2	0.3	2.6	1.2	1.1	0.1	0.8	1.4	1.2	8.8	—	89.8	27.8	101.0	163.6	2.5	221.0	515.8	605.6
—	0.8	3.7	2.6	1.2	3.2	86.6	0.7	78.6	0.3	43.2	86.8	71.6	111.3	—	964.4	271.8	291.6	813.8	-2.3	702.8	2,077.7	3,042.1
—	—	—	—	—	—	1.5	—	—	—	44.0	—	—	1.9	—	64.4	0.1	193.9	154.0	21.6	120.2	469.8	554.2
0.2	0.3	2.8	1.5	1.3	1.6	15.3	0.7	0.7	0.5	35.4	1.4	7.0	66.8	—	226.9	409.5	67.3	764.1	-32.8	1,167.8	2,375.9	2,602.8
—	—	—	—	—	—	—	—	—	—	24.8	—	—	—	—	26.2	0.1	392.4	32.5	-18.6	248.2	654.6	680.8
—	—	—	—	—	—	—	—	—	—	103.9	—	0.1	2.5	—	121.4	17.1	4.3	17.0	4.8	61.0	104.3	225.7
4.6	21.4	46.0	38.5	15.2	62.6	109.3	12.8	6.1	1.3	11.3	23.4	36.5	52.5	—	1,658.3	228.1	15.9	81.4	0.3	350.8	675.8	2,334.1
1.8	276.9	3.9	32.6	19.3	48.5	4.1	—	0.9	0.8	2.3	—	91.2	69.4	—	641.0	738.5	23.9	0.1	-14.9	615.5	1,363.2	2,004.2
—	54.0	—	0.4	1.1	1.0	—	—	—	—	—	—	—	6.9	—	73.8	51.8	0.1	—	3.7	78.4	134.1	207.9
0.3	—	0.4	—	0.2	0.3	—	0.6	—	0.4	10.2	3.5	28.4	16.3	—	83.1	851.1	36.4	0.1	8.5	206.2	1,102.2	1,185.3
—	0.1	—	15.9	0.7	6.7	689.9	1.0	6.1	5.3	9.5	2.3	—	24.5	—	1,077.4	91.7	29.7	3.7	4.6	163.4	293.0	1,370.4
0.5	2.9	8.1	—	7.6	8.7	371.3	0.2	0.2	—	2.5	0.8	23.6	56.5	—	642.8	351.8	37.3	90.4	-5.3	37.3	511.5	1,154.3
2.3	19.0	34.1	13.1	—	47.1	28.1	2.8	7.1	0.9	18.3	13.6	277.2	663.9	—	1,681.7	452.3	142.0	—	-7.3	246.4	833.4	2,515.1
3.2	27.5	11.0	24.3	12.6	—	64.0	0.6	1.0	3.2	53.8	1.5	51.2	96.0	—	866.1	285.8	39.2	-0.1	12.9	282.8	620.7	1,486.8
0.3	2.3	3.9	2.5	6.6	2.7	—	94.2	3.4	4.4	4.5	6.2	39.8	38.2	—	504.1	834.8	305.7	4,506.8	12.7	58.1	5,718.2	6,222.3
0.1	1.2	10.2	0.6	2.4	2.0	3.3	—	4.7	0.1	0.4	0.7	25.4	43.1	—	231.0	441.4	20.2	45.5	—	3.4	510.6	741.6
1.6	5.7	41.9	9.0	24.5	21.4	17.6	5.5	—	10.8	41.3	8.7	185.4	86.2	—	888.1	786.1	114.4	128.0	-0.2	—	1,028.2	1,913.3
0.2	0.3	0.8	0.1	1.9	1.7	—	0.2	1.0	—	2.3	0.4	19.7	12.5	—	92.2	95.6	13.1	43.5	—	0.5	152.8	245.0
4.8	12.4	169.9	37.6	88.0	43.9	105.1	8.5	48.3	0.3	—	73.7	671.1	81.8	—	2,431.7	902.4	81.7	59.0	-0.9	1,863.8	2,506.0	5,337.7
0.8	6.2	5.4	6.0	29.3	9.0	23.1	4.3	7.5	1.4	21.2	—	152.6	437.0	—	839.7	398.0	96.8	230.7	—	50.3	775.8	1,615.5
17.6	27.9	15.1	35.3	108.8	25.6	58.8	7.0	8.7	1.4	23.7	63.6	—	271.6	—	1,796.3	5,289.6	149.9	69.2	0.1	474.4	6,003.3	7,459.6
8.9	61.5	111.7	91.1	222.5	122.2	232.3	89.1	97.3	3.4	121.8	26.6	271.6	—	—	3,871.6	4,114.9	1,489.5	596.2	0.2	1,362.4	7,543.2	11,434.8
—	—	—	—	—	—	—	—	—	—	—	—	—	—	—	—	3,434.0	6,072.0	—	—	—	9,506.0	9,506.0
54.2	122.0	75.3	281.5	386.7	169.4	142.9	14.7	47.1	1.1	1,488.6	52.2	35.1	560.3	—	7,952.2	2,579.6	331.0	1,013.3	-10.1	—	3,911.8	11,864.0
0.7	3.6	3.7	3.2	7.9	3.7	20.3	2.0	5.6	0.5	14.2	23.1	19.9	16.1	—	427.5	664.3	-755.3	-515.1	—	178.6	-427.5	—
135.1	665.9	757.5	657.1	1,127.8	831.8	2,892.3	392.2	796.5	56.8	2,218.0	396.5	2,105.7	2,742.3	—	35,839.5	29,585.7	9,911.9	9,936.0	111.0	12,580.7	62,525.3	98,364.8
4.5	26.3	42.4	35.3	47.5	27.8	285.0	10.1	66.4	16.9	129.7	30.0	502.9	664.5	—	2,229.3	4,895.3	441.1	243.0	—	64.3	5,643.7	7,873.0
55.0	427.0	442.0	365.0	959.0	466.0	1,983.0	208.0	400.0	77.0	2,204.0	819.0	3,197.0	5,085.0	6,812.0	33,484.0	—	—	—	—	—	—	33,484.0
13.3	66.1	128.5	96.9	380.8	161.2	1,062.0	131.3	650.4	94.3	786.0	370.0	1,694.0	2,943.0	2,694.0	14,947.0	—	—	—	—	—	—	14,948.0
207.9	1,185.3	1,370.4	1,154.3	2,515.1	1,486.8	6,222.3	741.6	1,913.3	245.0	5,337.7	1,615.5	7,499.6	11,434.8	9,506.0	86,500.8	34,881.0	10,353.0	10,179.0	111.0	12,645.0	68,169.0	154,669.8

168 *Forecasting methods in business and management*

Table 10.7 *Reproduced by permission of the Controller of Her Majesty's Stationery Office*

Total requirements per £1,000 of final industrial output in terms of gross output 1971[1]

	Agriculture	Forestry and fishing	Coal mining	Other mining and quarrying	Food	Drink and tobacco	Mineral oil refining	Coke ovens	Chemicals, etc.	Iron and steel	Non-ferrous metals	Mechanical engineering	Instrument engineering	Electrical engineering
	1	2	3	4	5	6	7	8	9	10	11	12	13	14
1 Agriculture	1,056.3	1.8	0.3	1.1	245.4	33.0	0.9	0.8	7.8	0.6	0.4	0.6	0.6	0.8
2 Forestry and fishing	1.4	1,000.1	0.2	0.2	4.9	0.4	0.1	0.2	1.1	0.1	0.1	0.2	0.1	0.2
3 Coal mining	5.9	2.4	1,011.1	10.2	6.1	5.0	1.8	542.9	15.5	46.7	6.7	10.0	5.2	7.3
4 Other mining and quarrying	5.5	0.9	3.2	1,002.7	2.6	1.7	1.5	6.5	6.0	19.4	3.1	4.5	1.9	3.0
5 Food	241.3	6.1	0.6	3.1	1,057.3	24.2	2.4	2.1	26.2	1.6	0.9	1.3	1.2	2.3
6 Drink and tobacco	1.1	0.8	0.2	1.1	2.1	1,001.5	0.4	0.4	1.9	0.6	0.4	0.8	0.6	0.7
7 Mineral oil refining	28.3	44.4	10.2	49.4	16.8	11.9	1,004.9	19.1	47.2	34.5	14.4	14.0	9.7	12.3
8 Coke ovens	0.9	0.4	1.9	1.9	0.8	0.5	0.3	1,001.5	4.3	29.3	1.5	4.4	1.2	2.2
9 Chemicals, etc.	97.8	9.7	10.8	69.4	48.4	17.5	30.1	17.2	1,012.7	26.2	14.5	21.3	19.6	30.4
10 Iron and steel	8.9	8.6	58.3	40.8	11.6	8.1	4.3	38.5	13.9	1,020.1	16.4	127.4	34.1	58.5
11 Non-ferrous metals	5.8	3.1	6.3	9.2	10.0	8.9	2.2	5.2	15.2	25.8	1,006.0	42.5	37.8	67.8
12 Mechanical engineering	18.1	11.7	37.8	54.8	15.5	15.7	10.7	35.0	22.5	41.4	19.5	1,013.3	24.0	54.4
13 Instrument engineering	0.4	0.7	0.9	1.1	0.4	0.5	1.1	0.8	0.6	1.7	0.9	7.2	1,001.3	6.8
14 Electrical engineering	5.5	6.2	16.9	9.9	6.3	6.2	5.6	12.6	7.4	10.9	29.7	32.7	152.5	1,008.6
15 Shipbuilding, etc.	0.7	59.6	0.4	5.4	1.0	0.4	1.5	1.4	0.7	1.9	2.9	0.6	0.4	0.6
16 Motor vehicles, etc.	6.9	3.8	2.5	8.3	4.4	3.5	1.9	3.0	3.0	8.7	5.4	8.9	2.8	4.2
17 Aerospace equipment	0.3	0.3	0.2	0.2	0.3	0.2	0.8	0.8	0.3	0.6	1.3	0.2	0.2	0.2
18 Other vehicles	1.3	1.5	0.8	1.1	1.5	0.9	3.5	3.3	1.5	3.0	2.0	1.3	0.9	2.4
19 Other metal goods	17.6	10.2	29.3	55.6	30.1	24.6	9.4	23.1	33.0	53.7	38.6	91.1	43.0	92.1
20 Textiles	5.9	46.4	2.6	3.9	5.1	3.8	0.9	2.2	3.0	2.9	2.4	4.9	8.9	5.7
21 Leather, etc.	0.2	0.3	0.3	0.2	0.2	0.3	0.1	0.2	0.5	0.1	0.1	0.2	0.9	0.2
22 Clothing and footwear	1.0	0.7	4.4	0.9	1.2	0.9	0.5	2.8	1.9	0.8	0.8	0.6	0.5	0.7
23 Bricks, etc.	21.6	3.4	12.4	12.6	15.4	17.9	1.6	10.4	11.8	25.8	3.1	15.1	14.7	24.6
24 Timber and furniture	13.2	4.2	15.2	6.8	6.3	14.3	0.8	9.1	5.1	4.3	4.0	8.1	4.4	12.8
25 Paper and printing	24.9	10.1	6.3	26.9	51.5	69.2	5.2	7.9	46.8	15.1	14.0	22.9	27.8	27.8
26 Other manufacturing	12.6	4.0	8.7	12.5	14.8	12.5	4.2	8.8	25.8	13.6	8.4	16.7	24.1	29.2
27 Construction	25.7	17.7	62.0	32.8	10.1	12.2	1.3	39.5	0.7	12.4	4.1	29.3	5.0	6.6
28 Gas	2.0	1.2	2.9	3.3	3.2	2.0	0.5	40.9	3.6	37.1	7.5	8.7	4.5	5.8
29 Electricity	18.5	8.3	45.6	27.8	16.5	10.6	6.4	39.2	30.2	38.1	23.0	18.8	14.8	17.6
30 Water	4.7	1.6	0.7	1.3	2.7	2.0	1.0	2.8	5.5	2.1	1.2	1.6	4.3	1.7
31 Transport	64.1	72.0	34.2	45.8	72.3	40.9	178.7	159.9	67.8	80.1	49.8	37.9	25.5	32.3
32 Communication	10.5	9.3	4.0	13.1	11.5	14.0	3.0	5.0	12.7	8.3	6.7	14.3	15.3	12.5
33 Distributive trades	41.4	10.3	12.7	30.2	84.3	23.3	4.8	10.5	25.3	59.2	79.5	49.7	27.5	41.2
34 Miscellaneous services	89.6	110.0	22.5	147.0	119.9	225.2	34.4	44.5	150.3	79.1	45.7	110.0	92.8	94.7

[1] The entry in row i (a typical row) and column j (a typical column) represents the value of gross output of industry i, required to produce £1,000 of final output by industry j.

Other techniques: input-output analysis, leading indicators 169

	15	16	17	18	19	20	21	22	23	24	25	26	27	28	29	30	31	32	33	34	
	Shipbuilding, etc.	Motor vehicles, etc.	Aerospace equipment	Other vehicles	Other metal goods	Textiles	Leather, etc.	Clothing and footwear	Bricks, etc.	Timber and furniture	Paper and printing	Other manufacturing	Construction	Gas	Electricity	Water	Transport	Communication	Distributive trades	Miscellaneous services	
	0.4	0.8	0.3	0.6	0.6	4.0	102.0	5.9	1.6	0.8	1.5	2.6	0.7	0.6	0.4	0.3	2.0	0.2	0.7	2.1	1
	0.2	0.2	0.1	0.2	0.2	0.2	0.3	0.2	0.3	10.2	1.9	0.3	0.7	0.2	1.0	0.1	0.2	0.1	0.2	0.2	2
	7.6	12.1	6.6	13.2	13.1	10.2	6.7	5.2	26.8	4.6	7.7	9.2	7.2	23.1	185.3	14.4	2.6	2.2	5.9	2.8	3
	2.5	4.4	1.6	6.0	4.9	1.0	1.3	0.9	44.6	1.5	2.3	2.4	30.3	112.4	1.4	2.7	0.7	0.6	0.9	1.0	4
	0.9	1.8	0.8	1.3	1.5	5.5	25.2	3.2	3.1	1.6	4.8	6.8	1.8	1.4	0.8	0.8	3.1	0.5	1.9	3.4	5
	0.5	0.6	0.4	0.4	0.7	0.9	0.6	0.7	0.9	0.7	0.8	1.0	0.6	1.1	0.5	0.3	0.8	0.2	0.4	6.7	6
	10.9	18.6	14.2	16.4	17.0	18.3	15.6	9.9	44.6	11.7	14.0	18.0	17.1	44.9	55.3	8.7	16.9	3.9	8.6	6.2	7
	2.9	4.8	1.4	4.4	5.9	0.8	0.9	0.6	3.2	0.8	0.6	1.3	1.9	5.9	0.8	1.9	0.3	0.3	0.3	0.3	8
	15.4	34.2	11.3	24.7	27.2	75.1	61.1	33.7	40.5	30.2	44.1	145.6	26.0	19.9	11.4	17.7	7.6	4.1	11.9	16.5	9
	81.0	150.1	37.7	129.9	182.5	6.4	9.6	8.7	21.9	16.7	6.1	17.2	46.5	40.8	16.3	46.3	8.0	8.6	4.6	4.5	10
	25.2	45.5	37.3	38.6	78.8	3.5	5.0	4.0	9.0	8.1	7.3	12.0	14.4	8.1	5.4	9.1	2.7	5.4	2.5	2.7	11
	83.3	43.8	29.8	137.3	33.2	19.4	11.9	12.6	26.7	11.5	15.4	19.4	81.7	27.1	30.6	7.4	6.3	6.7	5.8		12
	7.0	4.1	8.9	3.8	1.2	0.6	0.5	0.6	0.7	0.5	0.4	0.7	1.3	2.3	1.2	0.8	0.5	1.4	0.4	1.0	13
	40.7	48.7	107.7	68.9	14.6	5.1	4.7	4.7	10.0	6.6	5.1	7.8	20.5	8.8	6.6	12.0	56.4	14.3	13.7		14
	1,000.4	0.8	0.3	0.6	0.9	0.4	0.4	0.3	1.5	1.1	0.6	0.5	0.9	1.0	0.5	0.3	8.3	0.5	0.8	0.3	15
	7.7	1,002.9	4.2	7.0	5.0	2.3	2.5	1.7	4.7	2.8	1.9	2.9	4.9	3.8	1.8	3.0	7.2	1.8	2.2	6.4	16
	0.2	0.3	1,000.1	0.2	0.3	0.2	0.2	0.1	0.7	0.2	0.2	0.3	0.2	0.2	0.2	0.1	4.7	0.3	0.5	0.1	17
	0.8	2.8	0.7	1,001.1	1.4	1.1	1.0	0.7	3.0	1.1	1.0	1.2	1.2	0.9	1.0	0.4	19.7	1.2	2.0	0.6	18
	35.1	111.2	31.2	76.0	1,018.5	11.9	29.5	26.0	44.7	40.1	11.8	52.2	38.2	33.4	14.9	14.3	7.4	21.5	9.8	9.9	19
	6.6	15.6	4.2	6.2	6.4	1,004.2	12.3	237.2	5.7	31.4	10.0	36.1	4.9	2.8	2.0	5.3	2.0	1.9	14.6	8.0	20
	0.1	1.2	0.1	1.2	0.5	3.3	1,000.2	46.4	0.2	0.5	0.6	1.0	0.1	0.2	0.1	0.2	0.2	0.2	0.3	0.8	21
	0.4	0.9	0.3	0.5	0.7	6.3	2.2	1,001.9	1.1	0.7	0.7	1.1	0.5	1.4	1.1	2.0	2.1	2.5	4.3	1.7	22
	9.1	18.9	6.6	11.1	10.9	3.2	6.0	2.3	1,003.8	16.0	2.3	8.2	115.5	19.3	7.3	25.9	3.0	3.8	2.1	3.9	23
	15.5	10.5	4.4	15.3	7.0	3.5	5.1	4.6	8.4	1,001.8	4.6	8.2	62.4	10.4	4.1	2.3	1.6	2.0	4.5	6.1	24
	12.5	21.8	13.5	18.2	26.3	29.0	24.1	30.7	37.2	22.8	1,011.1	47.8	17.8	18.8	10.6	9.1	7.3	13.9	42.7	62.0	25
	9.4	74.0	17.3	25.6	19.9	16.6	20.8	30.1	14.2	25.3	8.8	1,007.5	17.4	7.5	4.9	16.0	12.4	4.3	10.1	11.0	26
	9.8	7.6	7.0	9.4	7.3	6.2	4.9	8.9	4.4	5.0	5.2	1,005.4	133.9	14.4	20.6	1.9	5.0	7.2	5.0		27
	6.1	9.9	4.4	11.5	13.6	2.2	2.1	2.5	9.5	2.3	2.1	3.4	4.2	1,003.0	3.7	2.9	0.9	1.4	4.1	4.4	28
	18.6	24.1	18.0	23.8	24.6	24.1	15.7	14.3	39.0	14.0	15.0	23.8	13.6	16.8	1,011.0	49.2	10.1	8.9	28.4	10.5	29
	0.6	1.6	1.2	0.9	1.6	2.7	2.1	1.3	0.7	1.4	2.4	0.7	0.9	0.9	1,000.4	0.6	0.6	2.9	1.4		30
	23.5	42.9	19.3	36.5	49.4	43.4	46.8	30.9	145.7	48.6	48.9	51.8	48.4	37.4	45.4	15.3	1,007.5	54.2	98.2	16.8	31
	7.9	10.6	9.2	8.0	12.3	11.4	10.4	12.3	11.2	11.4	17.7	13.8	9.9	14.7	8.0	8.4	6.0	1,003.1	24.0	40.4	32
	28.7	49.4	19.2	47.2	61.3	46.6	94.5	43.0	21.5	38.7	48.7	29.8	23.9	21.0	10.7	13.2	8.2	44.2	1,006.4	7.5	33
	71.0	87.2	53.9	48.5	96.0	113.1	72.5	93.3	114.1	101.7	105.8	122.4	79.1	157.3	66.0	32.7	31.5	29.4	52.6	1,017.2	34

in fact produce more than this amount (£57·3 more). This is because in order to produce more it requires more inputs, and some of these inputs require purchases from the food industry; for example, the food industry will sell such items as animal feedstuffs to the agricultural industry in order that the agricultural industry can supply it with increased quantities of meat, etc. The figures in Table 10.7 are known as input-output coefficients.

Various other tables are produced by the Central Statistical Office and the latest cover industry and commodity balances, industrial output in terms of primary input, industrial composition of final expenditure in terms of net output, the proportion of net output exported and final output in terms of primary input, in addition to the two described above.

The major table for forecasting purposes is the total requirements table (Table 10.7 above) although the others do give useful additional information.

The firm can now use the tables for forecasting purposes along the lines discussed. They can form a broad parameter for forecasting or can be used as a check on forecasts produced by other methods. In the latter case the input-output analysis may indicate that a forecast produced by some other forecasting technique is clearly unattainable; this could arise because the original forecast did not realize the dependence of the firm on some industry (possibly supplying indirect inputs) which has some sort of problem attached to it.

Problems in utilizing input-output tables in forecasting

Utilizing input-output tables at the micro-level may be difficult, especially for smaller firms. Among the practical problems are the following:

1. The assumptions involved in using the relationships expressed in input-output tables are not strictly tenable, especially in the longer term.

2. Input-output tables are published infrequently, so the forecasts must be based on old relationships. The latest input-output tables for the UK relate to 1971 and even these use estimates extrapolated on the 1968 tables. Although the coefficients have remained very broadly the same over the various published tables (at different dates), this may not be really precise enough for accurate forecasting.

3. The industry groupings are very wide and so it is the large firms, who are widely spread across an industry, that are able to make the best use of input-output tables. Smaller firms may feel the tables are virtually useless for their needs. (The wide industry groupings are one reason why the coefficients have been reasonably stable over time. If the groupings were disaggregated the coefficients would probably become much more volatile.)

Some firms or trade associations may undertake to construct input-output tables themselves with the aim of making them more appropriate to their own forecasting and planning situations. This may take the form of a large firm with just a few large customers computing tables. Using forecasts of the large customers the firm can, from the tables, estimate the likely demand requirements on itself. Input-output tables can also be used for large, vertically integrated firms where subsidiaries supply fellow subsidiaries with certain inputs. By constructing tables the impact of any forecast for subsidiary X can be measured on the other subsidiaries very quickly. These developments in input-output analysis are likely to continue, although only within large firms.

Summary of forecasting using input-output analysis

Up to the present not much use has been made of input-output tables in forecasting at the individual firm level. A good part of this is due to the lack of really suitable tables, i.e. those that are disaggregated into many small groups and are produced annually (with a small time lag before publication). If improvements can be made here then the use of input-output tables for micro-forecasting will develop quickly. At the moment input-output analyses are mostly used by economists in forecasting broad economic and industrial factors, although these of course are often eventually utilized in forecasts by individual firms. For a detailed description of input-output analysis see the reference to Leontieff (2).

Leading indicators

Leading indicators relate to industrial and economic statistics from which we can obtain an indication of the value or direction of another variable (a variable of interest to the firm). For example, we may find that the statistics relating to money supply indicate the future level of consumer durable sales, so by monitoring the statistics relating to money supply we can gain rough first approximates of the value of consumer durable sales and their turning points (such as where sales start to turn up or turn down). Figure 10.1 shows a very simplified example in graphical form. Here the leading indicator appears to peak and bottom around about nine months ahead of the variable being forecast. Thus when we see that the indicator starts to decline (month 27), we predict that the variable will peak and start to decline in about nine months time (month 36). Similarly, the leading indicator bottoms out at about month 46 and from this we predict the variable will bottom out at about month 55. In addition, the magnitude of the peaks and troughs appear to be associated, indicating that regression methods might well be useful. (Regression should always be used if possible (i.e. where it gives a statistically satisfactory model) since it gives better quantitative forecasts. Leading indicators are used when the relationship is not good enough to make regression methods suitable.)

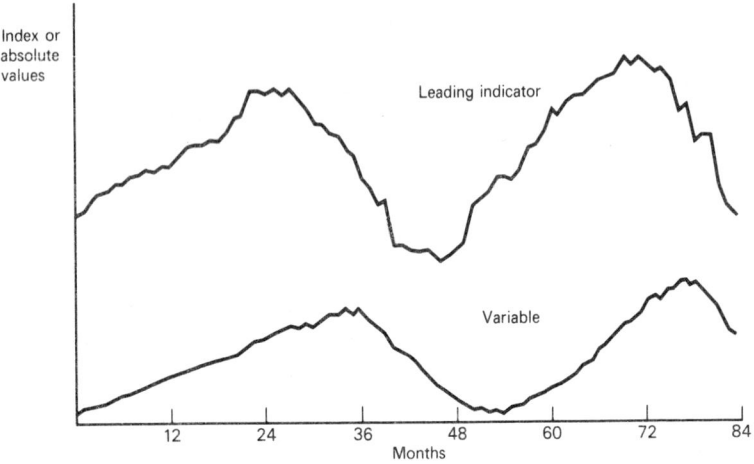

Figure 10.1

In practice lead-lag analysis is more difficult to apply than shown in Figure 10.1. Specifically

1. The lead-lag relationship is more volatile, i.e. it varies.
2. The turning point in the leading indicator may be more difficult to identify quickly; for example, it is difficult to know if a decrease in the leading indicator represents a turning point or just a temporary fall. Any error here can be very expensive, therefore considerable experience and judgement on the part of the forecaster is required. If the lead-lag relationship is fairly precise then regression methods should be used.

The forecaster must use common sense in searching out likely leading indicators; the possibilities should be fairly obvious. It is also necessary to experiment in finding the degree of lead-lag in the indicator-variable relationship. In doing this it will probably pay to run a correlation and regression analysis on the indicator and the variable in order to quantify the relationship, as opposed to using solely visual means (correlation and regression were introduced in Chapter 7). The major sources of economic and industrial statistics are described in Chapter 13.

In practice it has been found that leading indicators (sometimes the technique is referred to as lead-lag analysis) are most useful as pointers to the turning points in a variable. Because of this the method has gained its greatest relative importance in measuring the cyclical aspect of business variables (the time series being deseasonalized as described in Chapter 4). The reliability that can be placed upon lead-lag analysis should be assessed by the forecaster, by using historical data. Some firms have found that leading indicators are quite useful, while in others they have been of little help; it is therefore necessary for individual firms to assess the relevance of the method to their own circumstances.

In many situations the forecaster may find a number of indicators which have some association with the variable to be forecast. These can be used collectively either in multiple regression models (discussed in Chapter 8) or as a barometer (hence the term barometric forecasting). In barometric forecasting the various indicators are given either equal or individual weightings and then a consensus of them is used in forecasting the variable under consideration. If a barometer consists of, say, seven indices, then when four of them indicate that sales will start turning down in three to four months time, this will become the forecast. (One technique for reaching a 'consensus' is known as a diffusion index.) The forecaster must experiment with various weightings and measures for the diffusion index.

The leading indicator technique has been found useful by a number of forecasters, so the technique should be pursued for relevance in new situations. In many cases the indicators will be fairly weak and the forecaster will have to also use other methods and/or judgement in conjunction with lead-lag analysis. For a further discussion of this topic see references 3 and 4.

References

1. 'Summary input-output tables for 1971', *Economic Trends,* No 258, HMSO, April 1975.
2. Leontieff, W., *Input-Output Economics,* Oxford University Press, 1966.
3. Moore, G. H., ed., *Business Cycle Indications*, Princeton University Press, 1961.
4. Moore, G. H., and Shiskin, J., *Indicators of Business Expansions and Contractions,* National Bureau of Economic Research, 1967.

11

Subjective probabilistic forecasting and decision analysis techniques

The future is uncertain and future values of sales, costs and profits can cover a fairly wide range of quite feasible outcomes. This range of outcomes is uncertain because of the unknown market conditions, technological developments and regulatory policies that may be adopted in the form of governmental legislation. For some forecasts the future is more uncertain than for others, such as long-range forecasts, technological predictions and forecasts of consumer acceptance of a new product. In such cases management is greatly aided by some indication of the likely range of outcomes and their probabilities of occurrence. For example, the forecast of a new household domestic product might be stated as

Probability	Outcome £000	
	Sales	Profits
·05	1	−2
·10	10	+1
·50	25	+6
·20	35	+8
·15	40	+10

There is a five per cent chance of sales being only £1000 and the final column shows that such an outcome would result in a trading loss of £2000 (the profits-losses can be calculated for any given level of sales); there is a ten per cent chance of sales being £10 000 in which case a profit of £1000 would ensue, and so on. The reader should recognize the approximations in the forecast, i.e. there will be an enormous number of sales outcomes between say £1000 and £40 000, each with some probability of occurrence. Thus the true distribution of future outcomes is likely to be a curve of the form of Figure 11.1, from which the probability of any given level of sales can be determined. Clearly the information given above is of far more value to management than is a single point estimate, which in this case is likely to

Subjective probabilistic forecasting and decision analysis techniques

have been £25 000 sales and £6000 profit (the outcome which is more likely than any other). Single point forecasts give the decision maker no information whatsoever about the possible outcomes apart from the single point forecast. Thus in the example the manager would not have realized there was the chance of losing £2000, even though there is only a five per cent

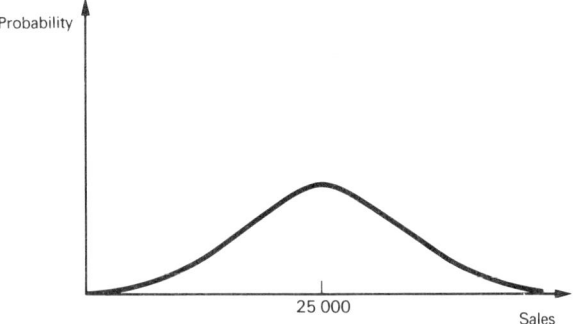

Figure 11.1

probability this would happen. Had this been known the manager might have decided to abandon the promotion of the new household product.

Probabilistic forecasts and other forecasting techniques

All the major types of forecasting techniques discussed in this book can either output probabilistic results as part of their normal mechanical process or incorporate probabilistic data in their answers. Regression models, for instance, are usually programmed automatically to compute confidence limits for the dependent variable, i.e. we can be 95% certain that a variable will fall within ± 1.96 standard deviations of the mean value (the single point estimate given by the model). Additionally regression models can be re-run to test the sensitivity of the results to the changing values of independent variables (such as changes in government investment plans, foreign currency realignments, etc.).

Qualitative forecasts rely on the human judgement of experts in the specific field. It is very easy to get the experts to give a range of outcomes, indeed many experts may only be prepared to make forecasts in the form of probabilities. Thus in forecasting the demand for, say, housing in the year 2000 the forecaster would probably produce a range of possible outcomes and specify probabilities for these. Qualitative forecasts can also easily incorporate subjective sensitivity testing.

176 *Forecasting methods in business and management*

Time series methods give single point estimates for variables, however the forecaster can apply a range of outcomes to the single point estimate. For example the sales of a particular food product may be forecast by time series methods at £10 million in one year's time, around which the forecaster can apply a range of £9·75 to £10·25 million. This range may be based on the past errors of the technique, possibly using the error measurements discussed in Chapter 2.

Objective and subjective probabilities

The probabilistic forecasts used in the above techniques fall into two distinct types. Firstly, there are objective probabilities derived from past data, such as standard deviations and confidence limits. These are highly applicable to causal models and have been referred to in previous chapters. Secondly, there are subjective probabilities; these correspond to qualitative forecasts using human judgement and skill. Subjective probabilities are used when objective probabilities are unavailable; additionally, subjective adjustments can be made to existing but rather indefinite objective data.

Subjective probabilistic forecasting can be dealt with in an implicit manner; for example, the manager arriving at a forecast can appraise the various possible outcomes mentally and produce a 'most likely' result or a particular decision. While this is a very crude method, it does represent a very common analysis carried out by many managers. Subjective probabilistic forecasting can also be carried out at an explicit level and it is with these methods that the current chapter will involve itself. The methods described later have already been adopted by many large and medium-sized companies, especially for use in qualitative forecasting. Subjective forecasts can be used by management as input knowledge when making a decision or alternatively can be incorporated in a formal model which produces the course of action that is to be adopted. In the former the manager can decide to disregard the probabilistic forecasts; in the latter, however, the probabilistic forecasts are automatically incorporated into the decision-making process. The latter is known as decision analysis or decision theory and subject to the accuracy of the input data (forecasts and probabilities) it gives the optimum decision. The elements of decision analysis are given later.

The basic interpretation of probabilistic forecasts

We will begin with a simple example to explain the process. Alpha Ltd. is contemplating launching a completely new product for which there is no competition. As there is no historical data, management uses qualitative estimates of the likely sales over the first five year period, in the form of possible outcomes. These consist of a low estimate (if the product is a complete failure), a mean value (the expected sales given by the consumer surveys) and a high value (which might arise if a lot of the major retail stores stock the product). From these figures the accountant works out the associated profits after all fixed expenses. The forecasts are

Sales	Profits
£10 000	−£80 000
£200 000	+£40 000
£500 000	+£200 000

Management's subjective probabilities of these outcomes are ·1, ·6, ·3, i.e. there is one chance in ten of sales of £10 000 occurring, and so on. It should be noted that the total of the probabilities must equal 1·00 and that the

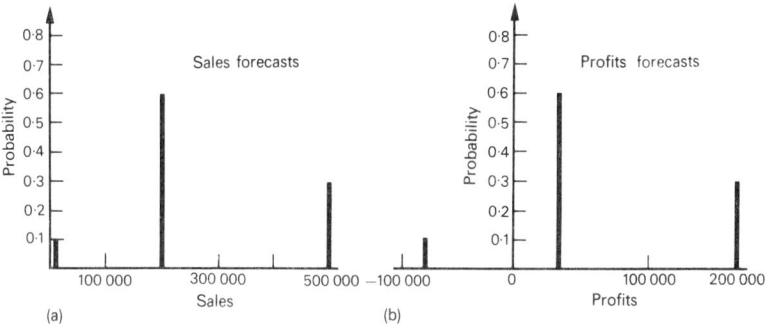

Figure 11.2

probability of any individual outcome must be greater than 0 (otherwise it does not count at all) and less than 1·00 (otherwise it is the only outcome). If the probabilities do not add up to 1 then the analysis is incomplete and the objective models met later will not be valid. The possible sales outcomes and the associated profits are shown in Figure 11.2. These forecasts are extremely simplified: in practice sales and profits can take any value within certain ranges. In Alpha's case the sales may range from £10 000 to £600 000 with a distribution as in Figure 11.3 (a). Profits likewise may take the value of −£90 000 to +£230 000 and a typical distribution may look like Figure 11.3 (b). The simplified case of Alpha Ltd., however, makes the description of the techniques less complex and so we have assumed that only three outcomes can possibly occur.

178 *Forecasting methods in business and management*

Probabilities represent the frequency with which a particular variable will arise. Most people are familiar with the use of probability in tossing a coin or rolling dice. For example, in tossing a coin it is equally likely that a tail or a head will appear; that is, the probability of a head is ·5 and that of a tail is ·5. Although there is a chance of obtaining a sequence of, say, four consecutive heads, in the long run the probability is that there will be an equal number of heads and tails. With dice there is a one-sixth chance that the figure 3 will turn up; that is, in a long number of dice rolls (say 1000), 3

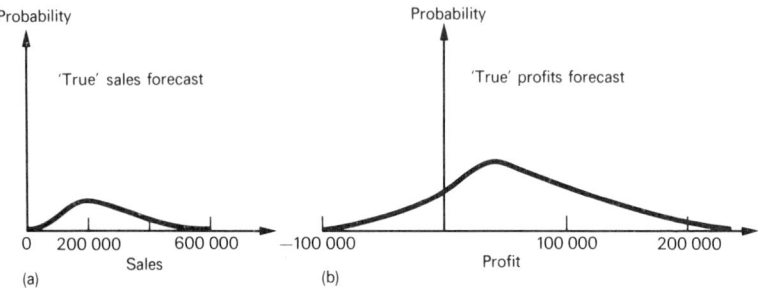

Figure 11.3

will appear in one-sixth ($16\frac{2}{3}\%$) of cases. Thus probability represents the long-run frequency pattern of a variable.

In business situations, however, the use of probabilities is more complex. Firstly, there is the problem that probabilities are subjective and cannot be tested. In the example, Alpha's management has assessed the probability of sales of £200 000 as ·6, but there is no way of checking this. If sales did materialize at £200 000 this does not mean that the probability of ·6 was correct, or that the probability should have been 1·0. Without being able to repeat the event it is not possible to say whether the probability was correct or not. In tossing a coin we can obtain the probability of ·5 for heads by mathematical means or by repeating the experiment; if we only tossed the coin once we would have inadequate information on the probability of occurrence (apart from the mathematical means), indeed our best estimate might be that if a head turned up then a head will always occur. In many business situations there is no mathematical means of determining probabilities and there is no chance of repeating the event in exactly the same circumstances. As regards Alpha Ltd., there is no similar product and so there is no historical data on which to base probabilities. Although Alpha may have data on other product promotions, these products were so far different and related to, say, a period at least a year prior, that this gives no information on which to base objective probabilities. Sometimes data

Subjective probabilistic forecasting and decision analysis techniques

does exist which is objective or which at least greatly aids the subjective forecast; examples are dealt with later.

The second problem in business situations is that large sums of money may be involved and the event cannot be repeated in order to recoup any losses (which is possible if the probabilities were correct; probabilities represent the long-term frequencies). In gambling on the toss of a coin individuals can adopt a strategy whereby it is impossible to lose (i.e. doubling the stakes to recover losses). This is not so in most business situations, since it is not possible to re-run the event; other product launches will be different and do not therefore represent a repetition of the event. Thus in using probabilities management must not only appraise the expected value, but must also measure the impact of the various possible outcomes on the business and specify the firm's risk-bearing attitude.

Expected values

Returning to the example of Alpha Ltd., management is faced with three possible outcomes and it has now to use these forecasts in reaching a decision on whether to go ahead with the product launch. One way of handling the information is to compute the expected value. This statistic represents the average return that would occur in a long-run repetition of the event. The expected value is computed by multiplying the outcomes by the probability of occurrence. For Alpha Ltd. the expected value (or mean expected value) of profits is calculated as follows:

Profits £	Probability	Profits × probability
−80,000	·1	−8,000
+40,000	·6	+24,000
+200,000	·3	+60,000
	Expected value	£76,000

The expected value of the profits from the new product launch over the next five year period is £76 000. There are two specific points that must be borne in mind in using this result:

1. The expected value may not correspond to any possible outcome, i.e. in rolling a die the expected value is $3\frac{1}{2}$, calculated as

$$(1 \times 1/6) + (2 \times 1/6) + (3 \times 1/6) + (4 \times 1/6) + (5 \times 1/6) + (6 \times 1/6) = 3\frac{1}{2}$$

although there is no face on a die which has the value $3\frac{1}{2}$. If the variable under consideration can only take certain discrete values then the expected value remains a statistical average which will never be achievable in a single event. If the variable can take any value within a certain range (i.e. sales are expected to be anywhere in the range £10 000 to £600 000) then the expected value will actually be achievable.

2. The major characteristic of the expected value is that it is a long-run average, i.e. if an event is repeated many, many times the results will average towards the expected value. In the case of Alpha Ltd., if the probabilities and outcomes were accurate and if the product launch could be repeated many times, then the expected profits would average out at £76 000. As described previously, however, most business decisions cannot be repeated and so, unlike gambling on dice or cards, the expected value criterion cannot be relied upon solely. The expected value gives a guide to management's decision making, but it is necessary to look at all the possible outcomes and marry these to their risk bearing attitudes in the light of the company's circumstances and objectives.

In the example, Alpha's management would have to look at a number of factors apart from the expected value:

1. The range of dispersion of the results (− £80 000 to + £200 000 profits).
2. The high and low forcasts (+ £200 000 to − £80 000) and their probabilities.
3. Other possible outcomes, especially those which represent losses, and their probabilities. (The forecasts for Alpha are extremely simplified. In practice the possible outcomes would take any value in a certain range; for example, profits could be −£90 000 to +£230 000.)
4. The size of the profits/losses and the resources involved, in the context of the company's other activities and assets.

Perhaps the major item in these factors is the extent of possible losses and their probabilities of occurrence. Although a project may have a high expected value, there may be a one in ten chance that a large loss would arise which might force the company into bankruptcy. In such a situation management would have to measure the returns and the risks involved against the company's or organization's objectives. Figure 11.4 shows three projects which all have the same expected value and on this criterion alone they are all equally desirable. However, the range of possible outcomes is different for each of the various projects; project A, for example, has no probability of making a loss although its maximum possible profits are lower than for the other two projects. In deciding between the projects, which are equally desirable on the grounds of expected values (and assuming only one can be undertaken), management must view the possible losses in the context of their impact on the company, i.e. using the systems

Subjective probabilistic forecasting and decision analysis techniques 181

approach of Chapter 1. If the worst outcome arises (i.e. the figures £10 000, −£30 000 and −£40 000 in projects A, B and C), but this only represents a

	Project A			Project B	
Profits	Probability		Profits	Probability	
£			£		
10 000	·1	1 000	−30 000	·1	−3 000
20 000	·3	6 000	30 000	·4	12 000
60 000	·5	30 000	65 000	·4	26 000
90 000	·1	9 000	110 000	·1	11 000
Expected value of profits		£46 000	Expected value of profits		£46 000

	Project C	
Profits	Probability	
£		
−40 000	·1	−4 000
−10 000	·2	−2 000
40 000	·5	20 000
160 000	·2	32 000
Expected value of profits		£46 000

Figure 11.4

very small fraction of the company's resources, then management may not be exceptionally worried about which project it accepts. In Figure 11.5 for example the company would probably accept project F, which has the highest expected value; although this project has a chance of showing a loss, it only represents a small fraction of the company's resources (£50 000 out of capital employed of £100 million), so the expected value criterion can be expected to be a major determinant in the decision analysis.

Having viewed the impact of possible losses on the business, management must now decide whether to go ahead with the launch. This will depend upon the mangement's attitudes to risk. If the worst outcome would wipe out the company, then management may ignore the project altogether. Alternatively, it may be decided that the possibility of earning exceptionally high returns is worth pursuing, even though there is also the possibility of making a loss which will bankrupt the company. Thus management makes subjective judgements based on the probabilistic forecasts; decisions made on this basis are likely to be far better than those using single point forecasts alone.

	Project D			Project E	
Profits	Probability		Profits	Probability	
£			£		
50 000	·2	10 000	5 000	·1	500
100 000	·4	40 000	100 000	·2	20 000
120 000	·3	36 000	200 000	·5	100 000
200 000	·1	20 000	250 000	·2	50 000
Expected value of profits		£106 000	Expected value of profits		£170 500
Capital invested in project		£50 000	Capital invested in project		£50 000
Capital employed		£100 million	Capital employed		£100 million

Project F

Profits	Probability	
£		
−50 000	·2	−10 000
100 000	·1	10 000
200 000	·3	60 000
300 000	·4	120 000
Expected value of profits		£180 000
Capital invested in project		£50 000
Capital employed		£100 million

Capital employed in this case represents the total assets minus the liabilities. It therefore represents the value of the business to shareholders. It should be noted that there are a number of other definitions of capital employed.

Figure 11.5

The use of utility or preference theory in probabilistic forecasting

In addition to the subjective evaluation of probabilistic forecasts, there are a number of quantitative methods which, given the accuracy of the inputs, give 'objective' decisions; that is, decisions are made automatically. One major method is the use of utilities; this is fairly complex in nature and so only a simple introductory analysis is given here.

Utility or preference theory (the terms are interchangeable in this chapter) acknowledges that the marginal utility or the change in satisfaction for a unit increase in money income differs at different levels of in-

Subjective probabilistic forecasting and decision analysis techniques

come. In general shareholders and management are held to be risk averse; that is, as money income (profits) grows, the rate of increase (generally referred to as the marginal increase) in satisfaction starts to decline. Figure 11.6 gives a utility curve, with income or wealth shown on the horizontal axis and the utility, expressed in terms of utiles, shown on the vertical axis. The risk-averse investor has a declining marginal utility of money and this is shown by the concave curve A. As can be seen, a loss of £1000 gives a utile reading of −2 while a profit of £1000 gives a recording of +1·4. Thus

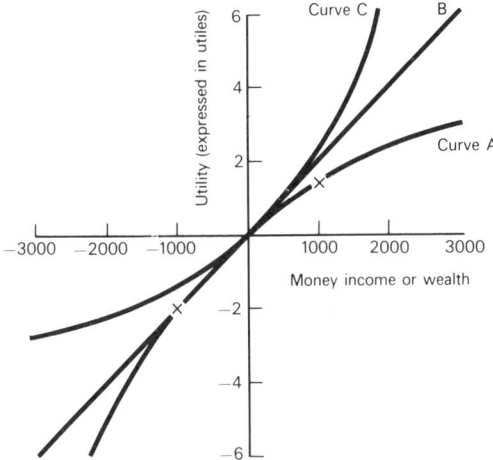

Figure 11.6

the investor gets more 'pain' from £1 lost than he does 'pleasure' from £1 gained. Clearly in this case investors place substantial weight on losses.

However, an investor need not be risk averse (although experience shows this to be the general case); the alternatives are a constant utility (shown as the straight line B) where the utility rises linearly with income, and an increasing utility for money (shown as the convex curve C) which is indicative of a gambler.

A preference or utility curve gives a complete summary of a decision maker's attitude toward risk over a particular range. Each shareholder and manager is likely to have a different preference curve. However if the firm's objectives are fairly explicit, then some consensus will prevail (if not, then the decision maker's preference curve will be used). For the purposes of the rest of the chapter the description 'decision maker's preference' will be used; it should be understood that this represents the risk preference of the business as represented by the various interested parties.

The preference curve, once specified, can be used to determine objectively the decision relating to probabilistic information. This is done by substituting the utilities for the money outcomes (i.e. for the profits figures of −£80 000, £40 000 and £200 000 for Alpha) and multiplying by the respective probabilities to obtain the expected value of the utility.

A preference curve can be built up by establishing the decision maker's preference between a certain sum and uncertain sums of money. For example, two incomes may be selected, say −£100 000 and +£900 000, and assigned arbitrary utilities, say 0 utiles and 1 utile respectively. Next, an intermediate income may be selected, say, +£200 000 and then the decision maker is offered the choice between (1) a α chance of −£100 000 and a (1−α) chance of +£900 000, or (2) a certain sum of £200 000. The value of α

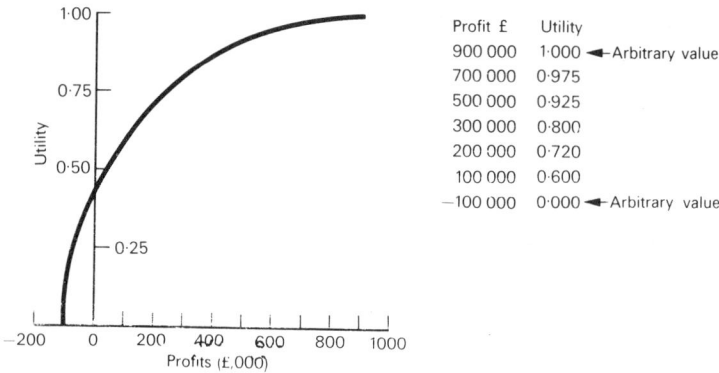

Figure 11.7

is varied until the decision maker is indifferent between the two. If the indifference value of α is ·280 then it follows from the hypothesis that

utility (u) of +£200 000 = $\alpha\, u\,(-£100\,000) + (1-\alpha)\, u\,(+£900\,000)$
$u\,(+£200\,000) = ·28\, u\,(-£100\,000) + ·72\, u\,(+£900\,000)$
$= ·28 \times 0 + ·72 \times 1$
$= ·72$

In this way a utility can be attached to every income between −£100 000 and +£900 000. Figure 11.7 gives a hypothetical utility (or indifference) curve for a decision maker. It is possible to derive other preference curves, for example a minus utility term could be attached to losses as in Figure 11.6. The utility to each level of income is then used in the expected value decision-making process: an example is shown in Figure 11.8. Although the analysis still uses subjective preferences, it does force the decision

Subjective probabilistic forecasting and decision analysis techniques 185

maker to express explicitly a risk preference at each level of uncertain income.

Profits forecast	Utility	Probability	Utility × probability
£			
900 000	1·000	·1	0·1000
700 000	·975	·1	0·0975
500 000	·925	·2	0·1850
300 000	·800	·3	0·2400
100 000	·600	·2	0·1200
−100 000	·000	·1	0·0000
		Expected value of utility	0·7425

The utility for any other probabilistic forecast can be ascertained from the graph in Figure 11.7 (i.e. a profit of £400 000 would have a utility of ·875 approx).

Note: the money value equivalent to the expected value utility is obtained from Figure 11.7. In this case the utility of ·74 gives a profits figure of £225 000.

Figure 11.8

Probability trees

In real life situations the number of variables that make major contributions towards the profit and loss figure is very large. Figure 11.9 shows an example of the various components of costs and each requires a

Sales			10 000	
Less:	Operating costs		3000	
	Administrative costs		1000	
	Financial charges		1000	
	Depreciation		1000	
	Taxes		2000	8000
	After tax profits		2000	
	Operating costs:		Raw materials	
			Bought-in components	
			Wages	
			Sub contracting	
			Heat, light and power for factory	
	Administrative:		Salaries	
			Rent, rates	
			Printing, postage, stationery	
			Office running expenses	
	Financial:		Interest charges	
	Depreciation:		Plant and machinery	
			Buildings	
			Office equipment	

Figure 11.9

forecast. These forecasts are often made in probabilistic terms themselves and Figure 11.10 gives a typical example of the factors that may influence wages and salaries. Clearly the profits figure has many 'quite possible' different outcomes (theoretically, the number is infinite). Management, however, cannot possibly hope to ascertain and predict all the possible outcomes, so a simplified model has to be built. Guidelines in the derivation of

---

Included in the operating costs and the administration costs, there will probably be a charge for wages and salaries. Future wage and salaries bills will be determined by a number of factors. Amongst the foremost of these will be the following:

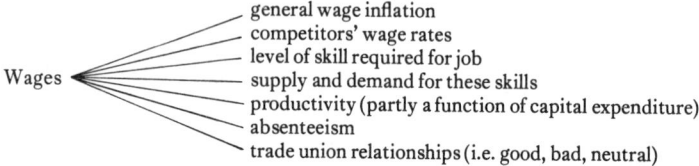

In forecasting future wage expenses the forecaster should appraise the above factors if possible.

Figure 11.10

---

probabilistic information are given later. The probabilistic data relating to Alpha was an example of a very simplified model: here just three outcomes of sales were expected and profits were dependent solely on sales (i.e. it assumed the costs for any given level of sales were known with complete certainty). In practice, most forecasting departments are able to build more sophisticated forecasting models than the Alpha example and of course this should mean much better data for decision making.

In considering more components of profits and more possible outcomes, the handling of the input data becomes quite complex and the relationships are often difficult to assimilate. In order to clarify the situation, the forecaster can draw up a probability tree. This gives a pictorial network of all the possible outcomes that are to be incorporated in the model, their probabilities of occurrence and the relationships of the variables. Figure 11.11 gives an example of a probability tree. Here the relationship of the variables is shown by the terms sales and costs which, when matched, give the profits. Each sales and costs combination gives a profit outcome and is represented by a separate branch on the tree. The forecasts of the possible outcomes are shown for each factor along with the probabilities. Thus in Figure 11.11 there are three possible outcomes of cost which the management feels able to identify, i.e. £80 000, £85 000 and £90 000. These possibly relate to low, middle and high estimates. Management also specifies subjective probabilities for these cost outcomes and they are ·3, ·4, and ·3 (note these add up to 1·00, i.e. these are the only three outcomes).

Subjective probabilistic forecasting and decision analysis techniques 187

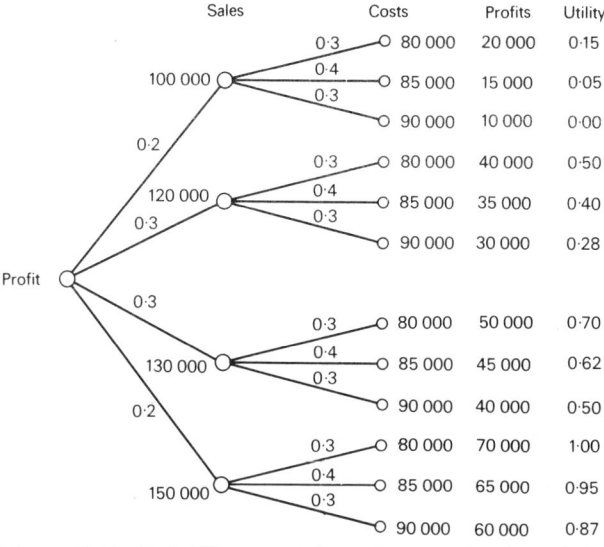

Figure 11.11 Probability tree relating to forecast sales of an existing product

It also feels confident enough to forecast four likely outcomes of sales (£100 000, £120 000, £130 000 and £150 000) and their probabilities (·2, ·3, ·3, ·2 respectively).

The decision tree draws up a logical sequence of events and thus costs are matched against revenues in computing profits. In the example the probabilities of the cost outcomes remain the same no matter what the level of sales (i.e. there are the same three probable costs for each level of sales). In practice, however, it may be that the probability of high costs increases if the sales are high. This can be logically supported if there is a high level of general inflation pushing up sales values and cost expenses. If management feels there is some degree of correlation between sales value and costs then the probabilities should reflect this (i.e. the probabilities of the cost outcomes when sales are at a level of £150 000 could be say ·2 (80 000), ·4 (85 000) and ·4 (90 000)).

The figures at the right-hand side of the tree represent the possible profit outcomes, i.e. sales price minus cost (e.g. £100 000–£80 000 = £20 000 for the top branch). This shows management the range of outcomes and the best and worst figures can be ascertained. Various averages can be computed from the tree. The major average used is the mean or expected value and in this case it turns out to be £40 000: it is computed by multiplying the various outcomes by their probabilities of occurrence, as shown in Table 11.1. The probabilities of the possible profits is obtained by multiplying the various probabilities along a branch together; for example, the probability

188 *Forecasting methods in business and management*

of obtaining a profit of £20 000, (i.e. the top route) is ·3 (the probability of costs of £80 000) times ·2 (the probability of a sales figure of

Table 11.1

Profit	Probability of profit	Profit × probability
£		
20 000	·06	1200
15 000	·08	1200
10 000	·06	600
40 000	·09	3600
35 000	·12	4200
30 000	·09	2700
50 000	·09	4500
45 000	·12	5400
40 000	·09	3600
70 000	·06	4200
65 000	·08	5200
60 000	·06	3600
	1·00	
	Expected (mean) value of profits	£40 000

£100 000) = ·06. If management has determined any preference or utility functions, these can be incorporated in the place of the profits outcomes. Figure 11.11 shows an example of possible utilities for the various profit figures and Table 11.2 shows the expected value of utility.

Table 11.2

Utility	Probability	Utility × probability
·15	·06	·0090
·05	·08	·0040
·00	·06	·0000
·50	·09	·0450
·40	·12	·0480
·28	·09	·0252
·70	·09	·0630
·62	·12	·0744
·50	·09	·0450
1·00	·06	·0600
·95	·08	·0760
·87	·06	·0522
	Expected value of utility	·5018

A utility of ·5018 gives a monetary value of very slightly over £40 000. In this example the expected utility is very near to the expected monetary value of profits.

Subjective probabilistic forecasting and decision analysis techniques 189

The advantages of probability trees are

1. They provide a logical network of the factors involved, enable the forecaster to carry out more easily the analyses and help prevent overlooking various input data.

2. Because of their pictorial and logical framework, they facilitate the comprehension of functional and general management. It was emphasized in Chapter 1 that the output forecast needs to be comprehensible and credible for management if it is to be at all useful.

More sophisticated probabilistic forecasting exists in the form of risk analysis, sensitivity testing and simulation. Each of these techniques requires considerable input data and the use of a computer to handle the calculations. They are thus fairly expensive and management has to weigh up the additional benefits received against the costs. Brief explanations of these techniques are given later.

Decision trees

Probability trees have been defined as a pictorial representation of probabilistic forecasts. Once in possession of the results (the various outcomes and the expected value) the management then has to make a decision, such as whether to launch a new product or whether to continue the manufacture of an established product. In the example in Figure 11.11 management must decide whether to continue production of the product or whether to abandon it. In many cases, however, decisions are not that simple and many alternatives may be open to management: examples might include (1) At what price should we bid for a contract? (2) What size of plant should we build? As regards the bidding for a contract, the company will usually secure the job only if its bid is the lowest, but in order to maximize its profits it needs to pitch its bid only just below the next lowest bid. There exist many prices at which a company can make its bid (the lower the bid the greater chance of winning the contract) and each has an associated profit (the lower the bid, the lower the profits). In building a plant, management must decide upon its size, which is based largely upon the forecast sales. The optimum plant to construct is that which produces just enough goods to cover demand, minimizing the cost of the plant and yet incurring no opportunity loss of missed sales (due to insufficient production).

In order to help forecasters and managers evaluate the various alternatives (i.e. bid prices or plant sizes) a decision tree can be constructed. An example of a decision tree for a bidding contract is shown in Figure 11.12. It is similar to the probability tree in appearance, but there is one major

190 Forecasting methods in business and management

difference: the decision tree has decision forks which represent events where management has to make a decision (i.e. the bid value, the size of plant to construct). In the example, decision forks are shown by a square. In the probability tree shown in Figure 11.11 all the outcomes of sales and costs were due to chance, these being variables over which the management had no real control, such as inflation. In the decision tree of Figure 11.12, however, the mangement does have control of the value of the bid it makes.

The example in Figure 11.12 represents a situation where a clothing manufacturer is tendering for a contract to supply uniforms for the Army.

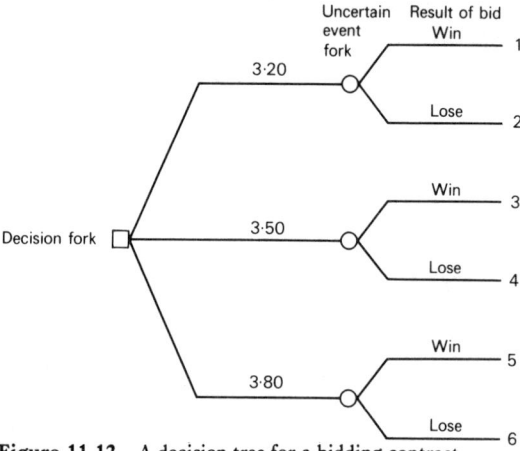

Figure 11.12 A decision tree for a bidding contract

The tender calls for the supply of 100 000 uniforms and the lowest bid gets the contract. The cost price per uniform is £3. Management now has to decide at what level to price its bid and three bid values are thought feasible. The three values are £3.20, £3.50 and £3.80 and these are shown as branches at the decision fork (represented by a square). However, there is a chance that the bid will fail, since a competitor may offer a lower price. So for each decision route there is chance event of the bid failing and the bid succeeding; these are drawn in as branches of the uncertain event fork (sometimes known as the chance event fork). Figure 11.12 therefore shows the possible alternatives open to the company (the decision events) and the possible outcomes of these decisions.

The next step that management must take is to assign probabilities to the chance events. These are subjective estimates based on experience and possibly on knowledge gained from prior tenders. The probability of winning the tender is obviously higher for the lowest bid, £3.20. The decision

Subjective probabilistic forecasting and decision analysis techniques

tree incorporating the assigned probabilities is shown in Figure 11.13. From this an expected value can be computed for each uncertain event fork, in the same way as for the probability tree discussed previously, i.e. if the bid is made at £3.80 the expected value of profits is £16 000. The

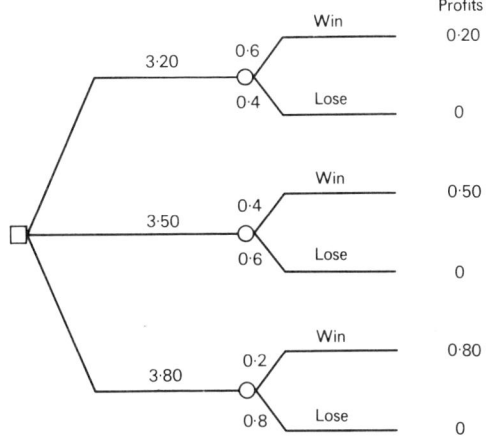

Figure 11.13

calculations for the various decisions are shown in Table 11.3. As can be seen from this table, the bid at £3.50 gives the highest expected value profits.

As will be recognized, the expected value of a decision is the result of a probabilistic forecast, i.e. the probability tree described earlier is part of a

Table 11.3

		Profits on 100 000 uniforms £	Probability	Profits × probability £
Decision: bid at £3.20	Win	20 000	·6	12 000
	Lose	—	·4	—
		Expected value of profits		12 000
Decision: bid at £3.50	Win	50 000	·4	20 000
	Lose	—	·6	—
		Expected value of profits		20 000
Decision: bid at £3.80	Win	80 000	·2	16 000
	Lose	—	·8	—
		Expected value of profits		16 000

decision tree. The decision which has the highest expected value gives the optimum bid value; that is optimum in the sense of statistical probability theory (as explained earlier other considerations are likely to come into play such as the risk aversion profile of management). Again management

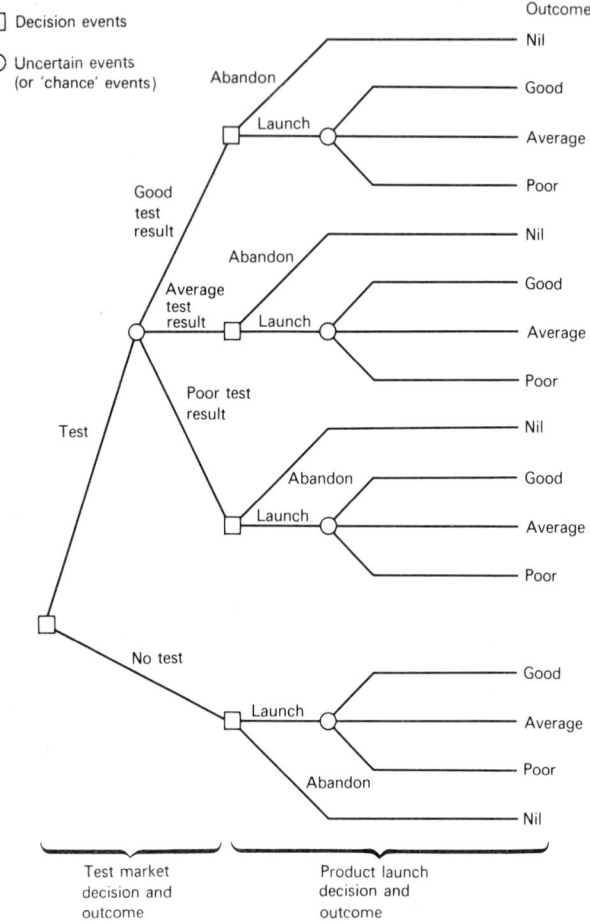

Figure 11.14

can assign utilities to the various possible profit outcomes and the decision showing the highest expected utility value represents the optimum bid price.

In practice, business situations are far more complex than the one in our example; while this likewise makes decision trees more complex, it also highlights their usefulness as an aid in decision analysis. An example is shown in Figure 11.14, in which a pharmaceutical firm is contemplating a

Subjective probabilistic forecasting and decision analysis techniques 193

product launch. The first decision faced is whether to test market the product or not. If a test market is done then the result (an uncertain event) could be good, average or poor. For each of these chance events the company has to decide whether still to go ahead with the launch (since they may not place substantial reliance on the test run) and so another decision has to be taken. From here there is the uncertain event of the future returns: in Figure 11.14 they are termed good, average or poor. If the company does not undertake a test market then it still has to decide between launching or abandoning the project.

Steps in building decision and probability trees

1. Construct a tree showing all the relevant decisions and all the possible uncertain events, putting them in their proper sequence. (As explained earlier, there are often any number of decisions that can be taken (e.g. bids at any price) and any number of uncertain events that can occur. However, management cannot consider all these in a decision tree and so only a few outcomes are chosen. A description of how a forecaster chooses these figures is given later.)

2. The value of each route must be determined and is expressed in the terms that the management require, e.g. money profits, quantity sales, utilities.

3. Probabilities are assigned to uncertain events (chance events). These will generally be subjective probabilities based on past experience and human judgement.

4. Calculate the expected value (in money, utility or other measurement terms) of each uncertain event point, working from the right-hand end of the tree backwards (towards the left-hand end).

5. At a decision point, choose the decision with the highest expected value. Repeat the processes of uncertain events and decision events back along the tree.

6. The optimum decision at the decision fork at the left-hand side of the tree is the one with the highest expected value or utility. Although a tree can become very complex, these rules, if applied consistently and correctly, will enable the optimum decision to be reached. The reader should recognize the assumptions involved in interpreting probabilistic information, which were discussed earlier in the chapter. When the data inputs become very heavy a computer can be used and this can output the answer in the form of a graphical decision tree.

194 *Forecasting methods in business and management*

Risk analysis

The probabilistic forecasts described in Figures 11.13 and 11.14 were fairly simple and could be handled by manual calculations. In reality however many forecasting departments determine a far larger number of possible outcomes for a variety of factors influencing profits. The calculations in these cases become enormous and risk analysis programs have been designed to handle them. The various factors and their relationships (e.g. sales minus costs equals profit) are put into the program. The forecaster then has to specify the range of values these factors can take. This can be in the form of

1. High, median and low values or quartile values.
2. Probabilistic forecasts of any kind. The probabilities have to be specified.
3. Mean values and standard deviations. If the variable is assumed to have a normal distribution then all of its possible outcomes can be ascertained and utilized in the model.
4. Other statistical distributions.

The risk analysis program then appraises all the possible combinations and computes a distribution of outcomes such as in Figures 11.15 and

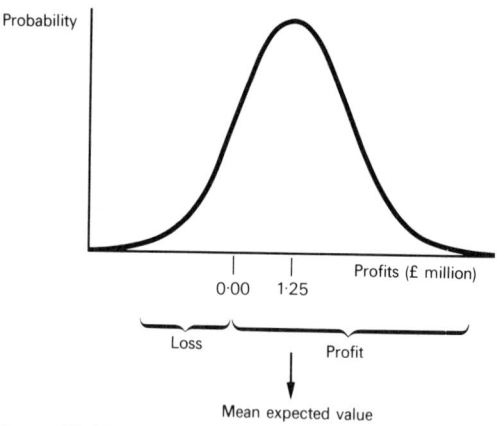

Figure 11.15

11.16. Figure 11.15 shows the results in the form of a probability distribution and Figure 11.16 shows the results in the form of a cumulative probability distribution. This represents all the possible outcomes given the data input into the model (the various factors, their range of outcomes, their probabilities and their inter-relationships). From Figure 11.16 we find that the expected value of profits is £1·25 million and that there is a 26% chance of a loss occurring.

The most sophisticated manner of dealing with risk analysis is Monte Carlo simulation which involves using random numbers to generate possible probabilities. Using a computer the model is run several thousand times after which a probabilistic distribution of outcomes can be drawn out, as in Figures 11.15 and 11.16. The method allows the assignment of values that

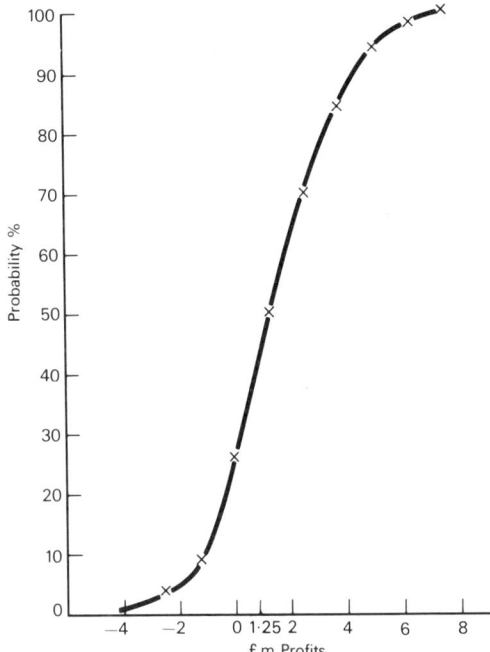

Figure 11.16 Cumulative probability distribution of profits

reflect differing degrees of dependence between events and other subsequent events; for example, it allows the forecaster to specify correlation between say sales quantity and sales prices, or to specify serial correlation (e.g. if sales are high in one year then sales in the following year will also be high). Although such mobility in the technique adds to the quality of the output, it requires considerable effort in deriving the data input.

The risk analysis and simulation approaches facilitate the use of sensitivity analysis and this is yet another sophisticated tool in aiding management decision making. Sensitivity testing tells us what the impact is on an output forecast (i.e. profits) for a change in the value of an input variable. If

196 *Forecasting methods in business and management*

the impact is minimal for a major change in an input variable then that input variable probably requires little analysis or control. On the other hand, if a small change in an input variable causes a dramatic change in the forecast output then this variable will have to be closely controlled. Sensitivity analysis is especially appropriate when the input data consists of expected values, since the impact of the various individual possible outcomes can be measured. A computer can speedily and easily compute the sensitivity to changes in input data.

Decision analysis

Apart from decision trees there are a number of other techniques for determining decision situations, some being used in conjunction with decision trees. The following paragraphs will briefly explain these.

Firstly, there is a criterion known as *maximin* which sets out to minimize losses. For a company faced with a decision tree as shown in Figure 11.17 there are nine outcomes (three uncertain outcomes relating to each of three possible decisions). The negative outcomes relate to fixed costs; these are incurred even if a company makes no sales and thus losses occur. The various outcomes can be shown in matrix form as follows:

Decision pay-off matrix

	S1	S2	S3
O1	0	−3	−3
O2	0	5	15
O3	0	5	−10

S = strategy which is decided upon (Note: strategy 1 is do nothing)
O = outcome—an uncertain or chance event

The maximin strategy says that the decision event to follow is the one that shows the highest minimum return. In this case it is S1, do nothing. According to this criterion the company will not undertake any of the projects.

This strategy is very conservative and is rarely applicable to progressive companies. The strategy can give ridiculous answers to some sets of data. Using the maximin strategy the company would choose S1 in the following decision pay-off matrix, but most people would choose S2, since this gives a high probability of obtaining large profits.

Subjective probabilistic forecasting and decision analysis techniques

	S1	S2	Probability of occurrence
O1	−5	−10	·1
O2	20	150	·9
Expected value	17·5	134	

The expected value criterion plainly prefers strategy 2

$((·1 \times -10) + (·9 \times 150) = 134; S1 = (·1 \times -5) + (·9 \times 20) = 17·5)$

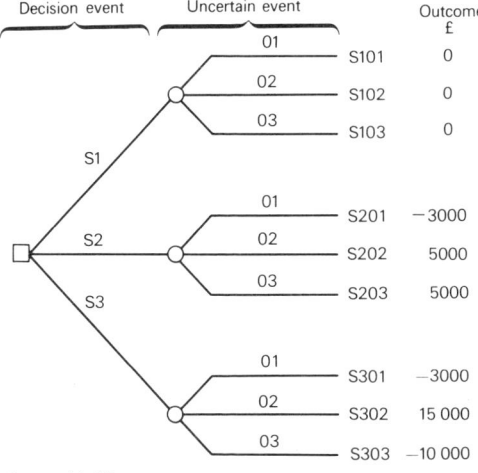

Figure 11.17

Another criterion based on similar lines is the *minimax regret strategy* or, as it is sometimes known, opportunity loss appraisal. A matrix is formed which shows the opportunity loss of having adopted a decision (i.e. how much you regret having adopted the strategy). The matrix below shows the opportunity losses by having adopted the different strategies for each chance event (using the data from the prior decision pay-off matrix).

	S1	S2	S3
O1	0	3	3
O2	15	10	0
O3	5	0	15

Thus if the uncertain event O1 occurs, then strategy 1 will have been best and so there is no opportunity loss. Strategy 2 and 3, however, have both suffered opportunity losses (i.e. they should have adopted strategy 1 if the uncertain event proves to be O1). For each strategy the maximum regret (opportunity loss) is calculated. The strategy which shows the minimum maximum regret is the one to follow; the maximum regret for each strategy is

	S1	S2	S3
Maximum regret	15	10	15

Thus strategy 2 is adopted as this has the minimum maximum regret.

This method can lead to rash decisions if there is a small chance of a very high return for a particular strategy. If the pay off table looks like this

	S1	S2	Probability of occurrence
O1	200	10	·01
O2	−40	20	·99

then the regret matrix will be

	S1	S2
O1	0	190
O2	60	0
Expected value	−37·6	19·8

The criterion would select strategy 1, since this has the minimum regret (60 as opposed to 190). However, after considering the probabilities most decision takers would prefer S2.

Clearly both the maximim and the minimax strategies can lead to absurd results if very high or very low returns are associated with just one of the strategies and if the probabilities are very high or very low. However, both strategies do provide some guideline in decision taking and in the absence of more sophisticated methods they deserve to be used. They are objective methods and are therefore not subject to the personal bias which can be in evidence in, say, utility or preference measures.

Another method which can be used to determine decisions is to construct a *risk return analysis* for each decision alternative. The expected return for each alternative is calculated; this is the expected value which has been described previously. However, the risk of a decision alternative is more complex. Amongst the measures that are generally taken are the standard deviation, the variance and the semi-standard deviation or the semi-variance of the forecasts. The use of the semi-standard deviation or the semi-variance is advocated on the grounds that it is only the deviation below the expected value that represents undesirable risk. The risk and the expected return of rival projects (alternatives) are then plotted on a graph as in Figure 11.18 (numbered 1 to 8). The company's risk preference

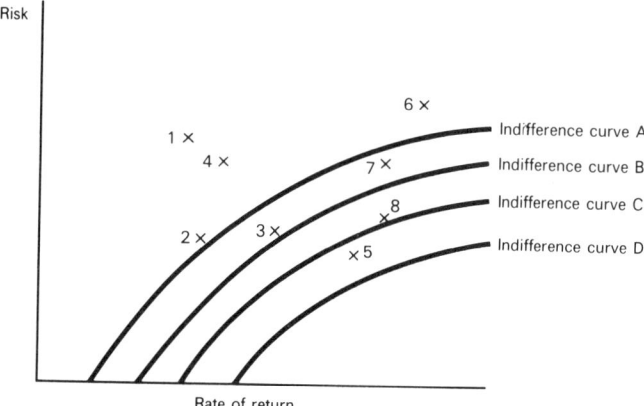

Figure 11.18

curves are then drawn in (curves A, B, C, D). Each curve represents risk return combinations to which the company is indifferent. (These are determined subjectively according to the organization's risk bearing attitude. The approach is similar to that of utilities described earlier in the chapter.) Thus if two projects lie on curve B the company will be indifferent between them. Clearly curve D is preferable to the others, since there is less risk for a given expected return. The decision which lies at a tangent to the curve nearest to the bottom right hand corner of Figure 11.18 is the optimum strategy, i.e. strategy 5 (assuming only one project is capable of being undertaken and this meets the minimum risk-return requirements).

Deriving subjective probabilistic information

Having discussed the nature and analysis of subjective probabilistic forecasting, we are now left with the obtaining of the input data. While the methods described above can be regarded as objective in some sense, the assessment of probabilistic forecasts is very subjective. The forecaster is reliant on the various functional managers and the experts in a specific area to make the forecasts and their associated probabilities. This contrasts with time series methods and, to a lesser extent, causal models, where the forecasts can be derived purely from historical data without any recourse to the subjective judgement of functional managers.

In some situations subjective forecasting is very difficult and only broad predictions will be possible. These situations include those described in Chapter 12 on qualitative forecasting, i.e. technological forecasting and long-range forecasting. In other situations there are various guidelines which can help the manager in making the forecast and aid the co-ordinating forecaster to assist in the forecasting process. The main guidelines are as follows:

1. Sometimes there is past data which can give some indication of the future. For example, the forecasting of a product launch of a new soap powder may use, with some degree of validity, past information of other soap powder introductions. It will be found that for many subjective forecasting situations there exists historical data which can be used as one input into the probabilistic forecast assessment. The value of this past data will vary in quality but should give some guide in deriving subjective estimates. The past data will give guidelines to both possible outcomes and their probabilities.

2. Although there may be a vast number of outcomes the forecasts can be cut down in a number of ways. Amongst the most common are

(a) A mean forecast, a high forecast and a low forecast. The high and low forecasts could represent either the very best and very worst expected outcomes or the upper and lower quartile figures. Both of the prior statistics could be given, making it a five point forecast. This type of data gives valuable information to management, i.e. the best, worst and expected values and their impact on the business as a whole. Any intermediate item can be subjectively extrapolated. The probabilities attached to these outcomes will have to be appraised subjectively: if the high and low estimates are the very extreme outcomes then small nominal probabilities will probably suffice (e.g. 5% chance of occurrence).

(b) The manager could specify a number of outcomes to which the forecaster may be able to attach a known statistical distribution such as the normal. In any event the standard deviation and the variance can be computed from the manager's forecasts. If a normal distribution can be validly applied to the data this will be extremely valuable as the probability of every possible outcome can be specified. (If the distribution is normal then all the forecaster needs to know is its mean and standard deviation. From

Subjective probabilistic forecasting and decision analysis techniques 201

these every possible outcome can be computed along with its probability.)

It is impossible for the manager and forecaster to explicitly specify all the outcomes that are possible, however, the above methods provide a broad guide to the range of outcomes and can be incorporated in the computer modelling approaches; this especially applies when a normal distribution can be attached to the probabilistic forecasts.

3. The co-ordinating forecaster should liase with the manager making the probabilistic forecast so as to obtain consistent data and knowledge of how the forecasts were made. In making forecasts of the business as a whole it may be that the forecaster requires certain types of forecast (such as high, mean and low estimates) and this must be communicated to the specific managers making the component forecasts.

In many cases the manager may have little or no idea of statistics, probabilities and forecasting techniques. It is therefore important that the forecaster works with the managers if they are unsure about preparing forecasts. This will ensure more valid results (in case the managers misunderstand, say, probabilities), enable the forecaster to have the forecasts prepared in the manner desired and help educate the managers for future forecasting.

4. Some measure of the managers' and the forecasters' predictive accuracy should be made. Measures of forecasting accuracy are discussed in Chapter 2 and these should be applied to the forecasts made. These particular techniques only give reliable results if there is a fair amount of data (such as historical forecasts) on which the measurement can be made. Thus if a manager only makes the occasional forecast, no reliable estimate can be made of forecasting ability. Additionally, if the type of forecast being asked for differs substantially from the other type of forecasts previously made, then historical forecasting accuracy measurements may be irrelevant.

The co-ordinating forecaster now has to incorporate any 'accuracy' measure into the current forecast. This can be done at a subjective level (e.g. 'the manager is always too optimistic'), in which case the forecast is scaled down by some amount, or at a more objective level. If the sales manager makes forecasts of the sales of a non-seasonal food product each month then their predictive accuracy can be measured, as shown in Figure 11.19. The standard deviation is computed as 5·64. If the forecast for January 1972 is 120 then we know that in 99·7% of cases the actual value will be within the range 103·08 and 136·92. (From statistical distribution theory we know that 99·7% of cases will occur within $\pm$ 3 standard deviations of the mean in a normal distribution).

These error measurements are based on the expected value information given by the forecasters. (There is no way in which probabilistic forecasts

Month 1971	Forecast	Actual	Error	Error²
January	110	115	5	25
February	120	115	−5	25
March	130	120	−10	100
April	110	120	10	100
May	120	125	5	25
June	120	120	0	
July	130	130	0	
August	130	125	−5	25
September	120	125	5	25
October	140	135	−5	25
November	120	120	0	
December	110	110	0	
			0	350

$$\text{Standard deviation} = \sqrt{\frac{\Sigma(x-\bar{x})^2}{N-1}}$$

$$= \sqrt{\frac{(350-0)}{(12-1)}}$$

$$= \sqrt{\frac{350}{11}}$$

$$= \sqrt{31 \cdot 8}$$

$$= 5 \cdot 64$$

Figure 11.19

can be quantitatively appraised.) Any valid figure obtained on forecasting ability can give valuable corrective data in deriving a final forecast.

Apart from deriving subjective probabilistic forecasts the forecaster will want to ensure that the users of the information can comprehend it. This can be a significant problem, since probabilistic forecasting usually involves a lot of output; decision makers may be faced with ten outcomes for a specific event, each with a probability of occurrence, or they may be faced with a statistical distribution of outcomes. The forecaster must therefore be prepared to explain the forecast and its basis of derivation to the decision maker and to the people who implement decisions. This will involve presenting the forecast in a comprehensible way.

The above guidelines will give some help to managers and forecasters in preparing subjective probabilistic forecasts. The involvement of the coordinating forecaster with the manager making the specific forecast needs to be emphasized: this should enable the forecasting ability of the manager to be realized to its full potential.

As described earlier in the chapter, subjective forecasting can be applied to the results obtained from other methods of forecasting. Time series methods often give quite accurate forecasts of the near future but they become less reliable for longer-term periods. In this case the time series result can be used and a subjectively based modification can be made for the longer time period. This also applies to causal models although these can themselves produce ranges of outcomes. In addition, the independent variables in regression models are often forecast by subjective or qualitative means.

Summary

This chapter has outlined the making, and the interpretation, of subjective probabilistic forecasts. The references at the end of the chapter provide more specialized readings on the topics discussed. Although the basic forecasting requires a lot of human judgement, the ensuing probabilistic forecasts and decision analysis is fairly formalized and objective. The role of subjective forecasting in an organization therefore needs to be treated analytically and systematically; the results from such an approach make subjective probabilistic forecasting a powerful and substantial aid in decision making.

References

1. Coyle, G., *Decision Analysis*, Nelson, 1972.
2. Hertz, D. B., 'Risk Analysis in Capital Investment', *Harvard Business Review*, XLII, January–February, 1964.
3. Hillier, P. S. and Lieberman, G. J., *Introduction to Operations Research*, Holden–Day, 1967.
4. Magee, J. F., 'How to use Decision Trees in Capital Investment', *Harvard Business Review*, XLL, September–October, 1964.
5. Raiffa, H., *Decision Analysis: Introductory lectures on choices under uncertainty*, Addison–Wesley, 1968.
6. Schlaifer, R. O., *Analysis of Decisions under Uncertainty*, McGraw-Hill, 1967.

12

Qualitative methods of forecasting

Qualitative approaches to forecasting consist of techniques which do not depend upon numerical historical data. They are applicable in circumstances where numerical data does not exist (i.e. where quantitative methods are not usable) or for very long-term forecasts (where the historical data cannot be extrapolated sufficiently far into the future with any certainty, i.e. where the underlying relationships of a time series are likely to change substantially over the longer period). Examples of typical forecasts which would require qualitative techniques include technological forecasting, corporate planning, consumer tastes, fashion changes and changes in longer-term social attitudes. Many of the examples relate in fact to technological change and to social change where consumers develop or change their tastes; these longer-term factors are rarely forecastable by quantitative means alone.

Whereas quantitative forecasts rely upon establishing patterns or relationships in historical time series, qualitative forecasting relies largely on human judgement. This human judgement, which is common to all qualitative forecasting, is generally brought to bear by obtaining the views and opinions of many experts, both inside and outside the organization. In some forecasting situations, especially those involving long-term predictions of existing items, the qualitative forecasts can be made on the back of quantitative forecasts; for example, the demand for electricity to the year 2000 could be based on time series or regression analysis and then qualitative factors could be attached. These factors might include human judgement as to possible competition from other energy sources, opinions as to consumer taste and judgements of what technical developments are likely in industry and in what form their energy sources will be needed. In other situations, however, there is no historical data on to which qualitative judgement can be superimposed.

Explorative and normative models

Qualitative forecasting is usually divided into two distinct subgroups, explorative and normative, and there are a number of techniques within each classification (some straddle both the exploratory and the normative descriptions). Explorative methods start with the current state of affairs and knowledge, and attempt to predict what will happen in the future and at what particular time. This is done by projecting and developing the present state of technology or another variable into the future. Normative methods, however, start by determining a desired scenario at some future period and then working back to the present to consider the various alternative ways by which the goal (given in the scenario) can be achieved. This highlights possible constraints and problems to the successful achievement of the future goal, as well as often suggesting various subgoals or developments on the way to the future scenario. These subgoals can then be examined to see if they are feasible; if not then the future desired objective must be reappraised (the reappraisal should only take place if the subgoals are clearly unrealistic). In very general terms explorative methods often tend to concentrate on technological change (in practice they usually concentrate more on examining technological barriers to progress), whereas normative methods tend to concentrate on social change. Examples of the more popular techniques within these two classifications will be described later.

For any longer-term forecasts some assumption or forecast of the socio-economic future has to be incorporated in a technological prediction, i.e. although a technical breakthrough is foreseeable, it may be negated by both economic and social requirements (these can change substantially over a long period). Examples might include technological products costing far too much for the mass consumer or products causing pollution above the level tolerated by society.

The types of results given by qualitative forecasting

Because of the lack of historical data or because of the very long-term nature of the forecast, qualitative methods give results which are very broad estimates or guidelines of possible occurrences. The reader should recognize that the error term is far larger in these situations and so the potential rewards from any long-term decision taking should allow a premium for the increased uncertainty. Examples of such broad guideline forecasts include the following:

1. An estimate of the date when a current invention or new product will be accepted by the consumer. This allows the company to plan its stockholding policies, build after-sales service facilities and prepare an advertising promotion campaign at the appropriate time.

2. An estimate of what new technological changes are expected and when. Chemical and engineering companies will be interested in forecasts

of likely changes in processes and technologies within the next 10 to 20 years. This will help them plan their research and development programmes, current capital expenditure projects (i.e. if a new process technology is expected to breakthrough in say five years time, then major expenditure on an existing type process may not be thought worthwhile) and help them appraise what type of developments their competitors are likely to come up with. In all of these cases it will also be useful to have some idea of when the development breakthrough is likely to occur.

3. An idea of the amounts involved. For example, long-term sales demand is necessary when considering major capital expenditure projects or when contemplating changing or adding to the company's sphere of activities. Although such estimates are likely to incur large errors they will almost certainly be better than doing no forecasting at all.

The above types of forecasts will often be given as a range of outcomes: for example, 'commercial use of space travel expected in the years 2000 to 2015'; 'sales in the year 2000 will probably be in the range £20m to £40m'. These are very broad estimates but they do indicate areas of likelihood with which management can work. In the making of these qualitative forecasts some economic, social or technological assumptions may have been made; in these cases the assumptions should be stated and the sensitivity of the forecast to different assumptions noted. For example, estimates of sales of electricity in the year 2000 in the UK may be based partly upon some quantitative forecast of the population; the changes in the consumption of electricity for changes in the level of the population should therefore be estimated. In some cases qualitative forecasting is done within pre-set quantitative predictions: for example, some planning departments may think they can predict with some accuracy the growth in personal disposable income over the period to 1990. They can then use this as a parameter to their qualitative forecasting of sales of, say, sports leisure equipment.

The normal ultimate desired objective of a forecast is to optimize profit or efficiency (if a non-profit making organization, or if constrained in profit maximization by some governmental, social or legal factors). In reaching this objective certain variables (such as sales) are forecast into the future. As with quantitative forecasting methods, however, care has to be exercised in choosing a variable to forecast. A well referenced example of the choice of the wrong forecasting variable is that of the aircraft piston manufacturer who rejected the developing technology of the turbo-jet because on a fuel-engine efficiency comparison it was inferior to existing engines. As was shown in due course, the determining feature proved to be the cost per ton-seat mile and here the advantage lay sharply with the turbo-jet (see reference 17).

The adoption of qualitative forecasting methods

The formal use of qualitative techniques has grown rapidly alongside quantitative methods throughout the past two decades. Research by Jantsch (1967), Gerstenfeld and Blumberg (1968) and Cetron (1969) has shown the level of adoption of the techniques to have covered more than half of the medium and large corporations in the United States. Jantsch has credited this increase to the fact that the rate of technological change has been increasing rapidly, consequently the life of many projects is now substantially shorter than in previous years. This along with the increased costs involved in capital projects has emphasized the rewards of formal forecasting procedures.

Apart from formal qualitative forecasting, management has long been making rudimentary qualitative estimates of the future. These may have involved little more than a few hour's thought but they do represent, in a very simplified way, qualitative forecasting.

Perhaps the major applications of qualitative forecasting are in the areas of corporate planning and technological forecasting. Corporate planning involves decision taking which has a long-term impact and thus requires predictions of the long term. Typical decisions were described in Figure 1.4 and clearly technological change has an impact on the corporate plans.

Technology can be broadly defined as the application and exploitation of science, and technological forecasting attempts to measure and predict the rate of its commercial development. There are a number of reasons for the

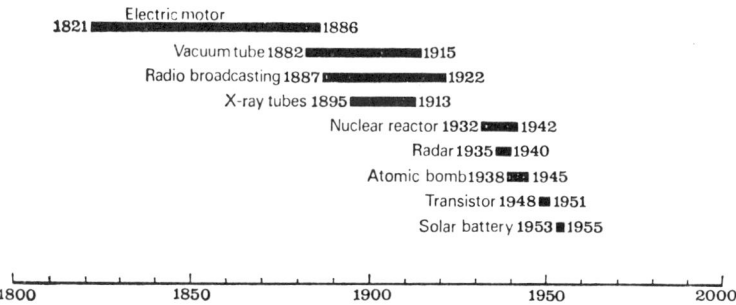

Figure 12.1
Source: *The Role of Forecasting in Corporate Planning* by Ashton and Simister, Crosby Lockwood Staples, 1970.

importance of technological forecasting. Firstly there has been a narrowing of the interval between discovery and invention and commercial application; Figure 12.1 shows an example for the physical sciences. This narrowing of the interval between discovery (invention) and commercial application, added to the high rate of discoveries (and inventions)*, has meant that various technologies become obsolete far more quickly. Thus there is a substantial risk of a project not earning a proper return over its life. Secondly, the development of scientific discoveries into commercial products costs an ever increasing amount of money. Even more expensive, though, is the building of processes and plants to produce the products in the desired quantities. The rate of expenditure on successful research to the expenditure on development and the expenditure on the commercialization of the product has been put at 1:10:100 in the chemical industry (reference 5). Other industries may have lower ratios than this but as they become more science-based their ratios will rise. The ratio is also expected to increase over time as development and commercialization grow ever more proportionately expensive. Any serious discrepancies in the forecasting of the success of the research and development, the cost of the capital plant and the eventual consumer product acceptance can and do bankrupt many firms.

Extrapolation of trends

The quantitative forecasting methods discussed previously in the book have relied upon establishing a pattern in a time series. In many cases, however, there are too few historical data points with which to operate the technique, so the alternative is often used of extrapolating the data in a freehand, subjective manner. Figure 12.2 gives an example of an extrapolation curve forecasting the efficiency of man-made light (Cetron 1969). Here there are only seven data points available, a number which is clearly inadequate for any quantitative forecasting method. However, the various technological advances did lie somewhere near a straight line when plotted on a logarithmic scale, therefore an extrapolation of this line offers one prediction of the future, to be used by management as an approximate yardstick of potential development. Human judgement on technological and sociological matters should be exercised in conjunction with the forecasts especially if the trend is weak anyway. As regards the development of man-made illumination, there is in fact a theoretical limit to the lumens per watt achievable and the forecaster has to incorporate this on the mechanical projection.

---

* Technological Forecasting and Research and Development planning are highly interwoven. At any one time there are many more basic scientific discoveries awaiting commercial application than there is room to develop. This leads management to select between numerous scientific advances the one to develop. This of course requires very accurate forecasts in order to accept the most profitable projects.

The projection of the trend in Figure 12.2 tells the manager what the capability of the product (in this case, lighting) must be in any particular period, if it is to remain competitive; it does not tell the manager how this capability (lumens per watt) is to be achieved. However, some guidance can be given by forecasting the development of each of the technological advances. As will be described later, many technologies' development approximately follows an S-curve pattern (or some other pattern) and this

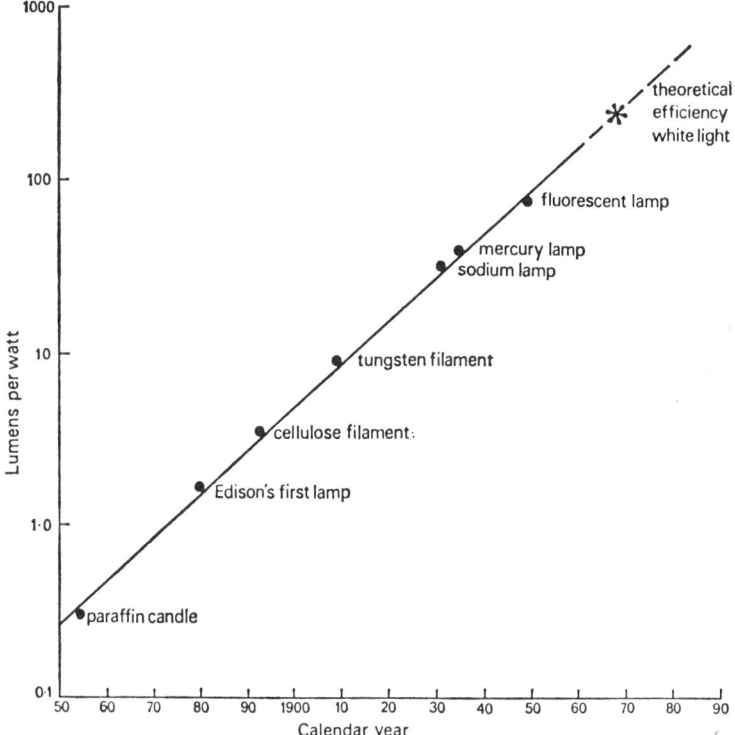

Figure 12.2 Developments in the efficiency of man-made white light
Source: *Technological Forecasting* by M. J. Cetron, Gordon and Breach, 1969.

can be used to forecast its particular growth. Figure 12.3 shows a technical capability trend for incandescent lamps and mercury vapour fluorescent lamps. From this it appears unlikely that the fluorescent lamp will achieve the theoretical limit to illumination capability, so management deduces that some other technology will be needed. Thus from the two forecasts management can establish a future scenario for 1980 of a lighting technology in terms of lumens per watt and also that this technology will

210 *Forecasting methods in business and management*

not be any development of the fluorescent lamp. This at least reduces to some degree the uncertainty of the future.

Extrapolative forecasting involves determining a curve or trend that is appropriate to the item being forecast and then projecting the future from this. The forecaster, however, interacts with the mechanical extrapolation to incorporate his own technical judgement; for example, in Figure 12.2 the extrapolation of white light illumination will be curtailed at the known theoretical efficiency of white light and some other, possibly horizontal, trend formed.

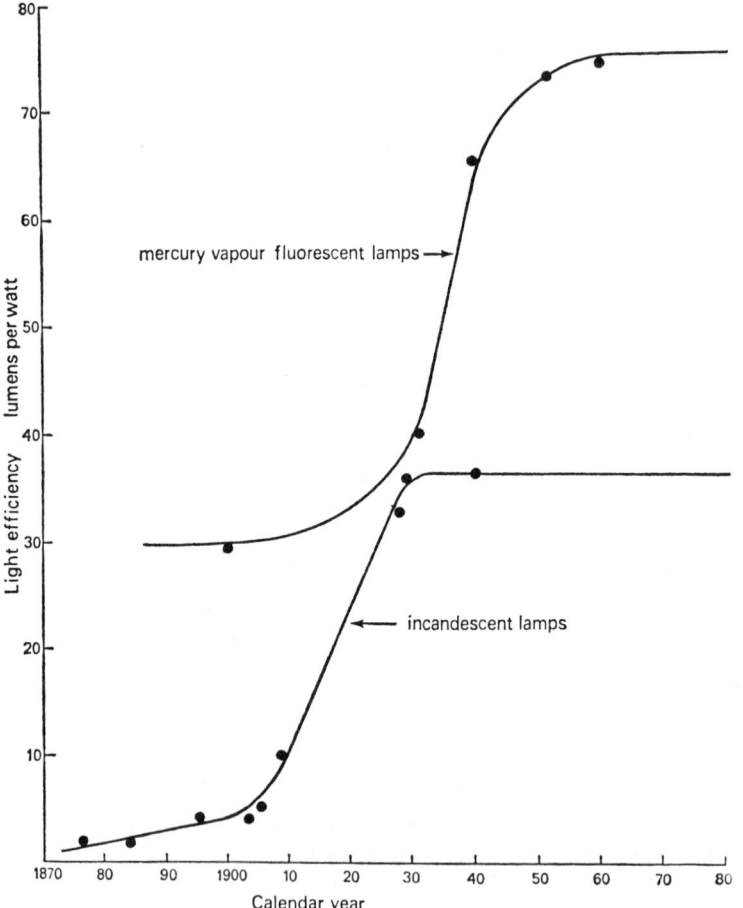

Figure 12.3 Technical capability trend for incandescent and mercury vapour fluorescent lamps.
Source: *Technological Forecasting* by M. J. Cetron, Gordon and Breach, 1969

Qualitative methods of forecasting 211

The determining of an appropriate curve is usually done on a subjective basis, since there is often insufficient data from which to establish a trend. For some occurrences, 'typical' curves have been found to exist and these are used in the forecasting process. For example, many technologies and many products' life cycles are said to follow an S-shaped curve. This is intrinsically explained by five process stages; research and development, product introduction, market growth, market maturity and sales decline. This produces a graph with a slow take off (customer awareness), a rapid middle stage (growth) and then a stable stage where the adoption of the

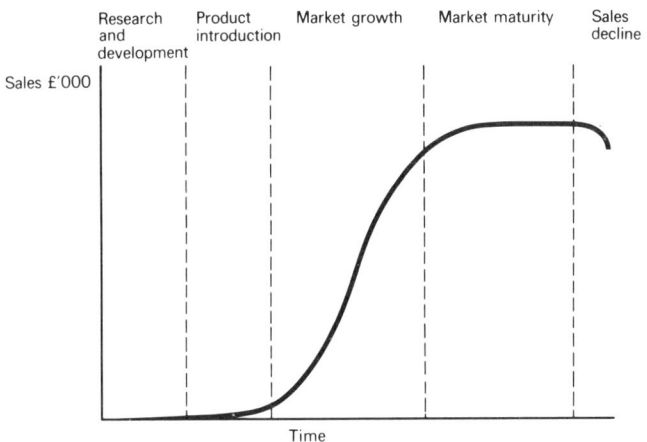

Figure 12.4 A typical life cycle (S-curve) of a product

technology or the sales of the product becomes saturated. Many products and technologies have been found to follow such a curve (see Ayres, reference 2, and Jantsch, reference 12). An example of an S-curve is shown in Figure 12.4. One adaption of the S-shaped curve is known as an envelope S-curve, which is formed from a number of individual S-shaped curves representing, say, different technological advances in a particular field. The envelope S-curve is formed by connecting the tangents of the individual S-curves. An example is shown in Figure 12.5, which shows a forecast of the maximum speed of transport (see Ayres 1960 and 1969). Other patterns are often applied in qualitative forecasting and among the most common are exponential and logarithmic curves.

Extrapolative curve fitting is a very difficult task, which requires considerable human judgement. Among the problems that the forecaster must tackle are decisions over what is the appropriate curve for the data, which stage of the curve the variable is in at the moment, what the constraints or limits to the curve are, what the length of the curve is and which dates it covers. With there being so few data points, no obvious trend will be dis-

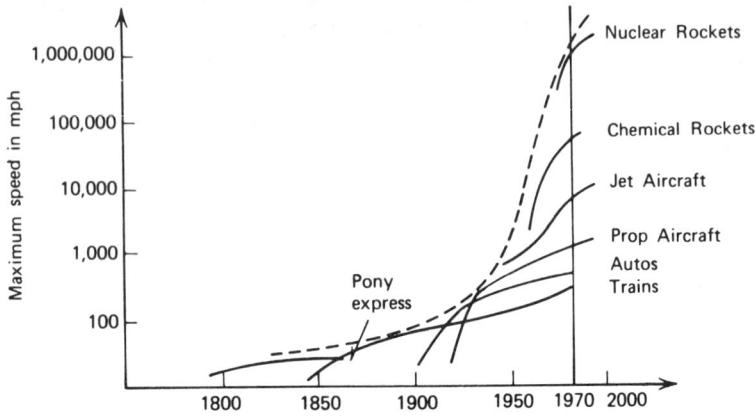

Figure 12.5 Envelope S-curve fitted to the maximum speed of transport
Source: *Technological Forecasting and Long-Range Planning* by R. U. Ayres, 1969. Used with permission of McGraw-Hill Book Company.

cernible, indeed if one exists at all in such long-term data. As an example, Figure 12.6 shows a set of six data points which could as easily be extrapolated into a curve of the form of Figure 12.7 as that of Figure 12.8 or even a straight line. Clearly these curves will lead to very different conclusions, so considerable skill or judgement is required. This problem is frequently met with in practice and Ayres (1969) refers to a case of two

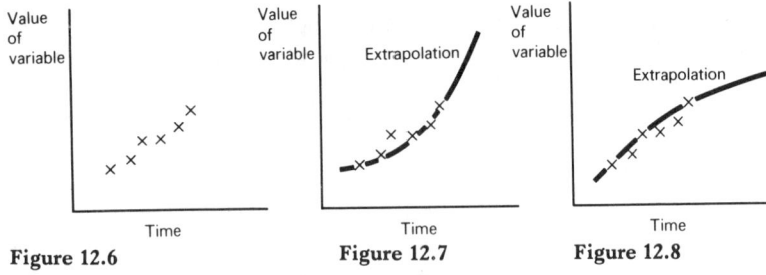

Figure 12.6 **Figure 12.7** **Figure 12.8**

different forecasters who, by using different scales, produced very different extrapolation trends. In practice management frequently use standard patterns to extrapolate over the long term, but even these standard patterns require individual judgement. For example, an S-curve could be very short or very elongated (see Figures 12.9 and 12.10) and the different forecasts would be very wide apart. The length of the curve also affects the dates when, say, particular capabilities are forecast to be reached (e.g. £20 000 sales in Figures 12.9 and 12.10 are reached in February 1975 and December 1973 respectively). The envelope S-curve demands some opinion as to the stage of the individual S-curves so as to give estimates of when new technologies might be taking over. An additional problem in the analysis is to determine any major limiting factors to the curve (such as the depletion of the world's resources of a basic commodity or major social changes in behaviour).

Although the extrapolation of trends type of approach is subject to a large amount of error it does give, at a relatively low cost, some idea of the

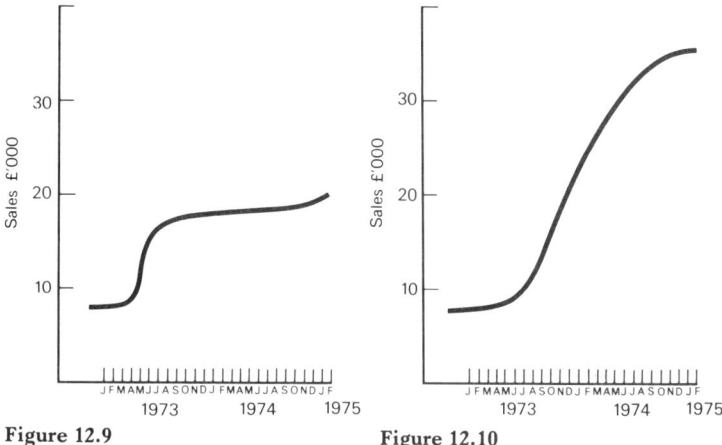

Figure 12.9 **Figure 12.10**

possible outcomes. The prior success of fitting S-shaped curves to product life cycles and to technological innovation gives some confidence in using them for at least estimating the shape, if not the extent and duration, of future growth. As with all qualitative forecasting, a considerable amount of human judgement is required and in practice many qualitative techniques are likely to be used in order to reach a consensus of opinion.

Time independent technological comparisons

This is another extrapolative approach, which is especially useful in technological forecasting. It is a method which forecasts a variable by deriving a relationship with some other time series; this other time series is either more easily forecastable (by quantitative or qualitative means) or is in some lead-lag relationship. This, of course, is the basic idea behind regression forecasting, but in cases where there are few data points no reasonably accurate statistical relationship is capable of being derived. The time independent comparison involves determining a relationship and then quantifying it to some extent. This quantification is subjectively based as the data is usually so sparse. Examples of this technique include, say, commercial engineering or metallurgical progress in some lagged relationship to military engineering or military metallurgical advances, e.g. any breakthrough in the use of a new material in military or space research use can be expected to achieve commercial application, say, ten years later. A possible relationship is shown in Figure 12.11. This method can only give very rough guides to future technological development, since it relies upon establishing what are likely to be at best only weak relationships and, further, the quantification of the association is likely to be fairly indefinite. However, it does provide one more tool in qualitative forecasting.

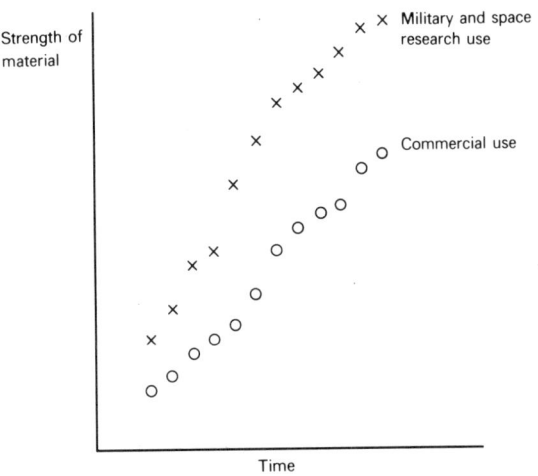

Figure 12.11

When the relationship becomes more precise, then statistical measures of association can be derived and greater trust may be placed on the forecasts. A frequently cited example is the maximum speed of aeroplanes (see reference 14). Here a fairly precise relationship was established between the maximum speed of military aircraft (speed doubling every ten years) and the maximum speed of commercial aircraft (speed doubling every twelve years). By forecasting the speed developments in military aircraft a conditional forecast of commercial aircraft capability can be obtained. The relationship can also be used by taking today's military aircraft speed capability and calculating how long it will be before commercial air-

Qualitative methods of forecasting 215

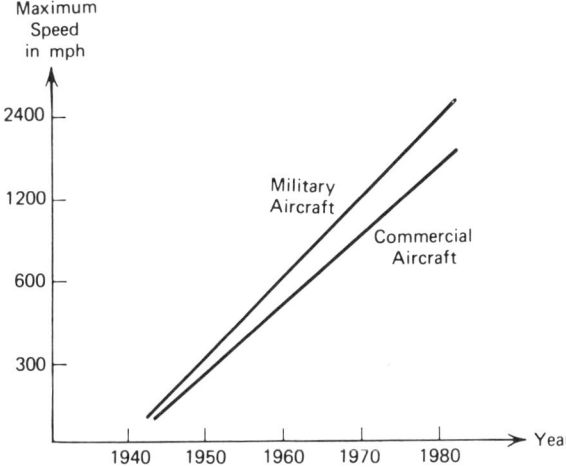

Figure 12.12 The development of the maximum speeds of military aircraft and commercial aircraft.
Source: *Technological Forecasting* by R. C. Lenz, Report ASD-TDR-62-414, Clearing House for Federal, Scientific and Technical Literature, June 1972

craft will reach this level (i.e. the degree of lag). Figure 12.12 shows the relationship between the maximum speeds of military and commercial aircraft. However, as seen from the figure, the data in this case appears to fit very well with a log linear trend, so the forecasts seem to be amenable to

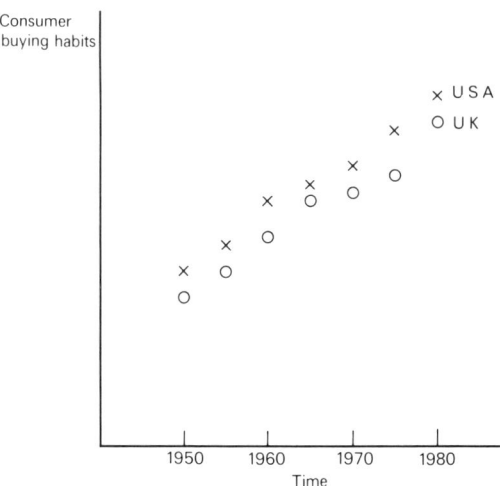

Figure 12.13

quantitative time series or regression methods (hence there is no need for any great subjective judgement).

The technique can also be used for other, non-technological forecasts when some relationship is acknowledged but no quantification is possible. Here subjective judgement and curve fitting by eye can give some idea of the possible outcomes. Examples might include consumer tastes in the UK being behind those in the USA or the tastes of the poorer section of society being in a lagged relationship to those in the higher income brackets. By examining the buying habits of Americans at the current time, some prediction can be made about the future British consumer buying patterns, although because of the imperfect correlation between the two variables the forecaster will attach a subjective relationship between them. In this way a forecast of buying intentions in the UK, say between 1980 and 1985, may be derived with some confidence by looking at current American consumer tastes. Figure 12.13 shows a hypothetical relationship, with the UK buying habits approximately five years behind those of the USA; this would provide valuable information for decision taking. These methods are therefore similar to regression models except that the statistical relationships are replaced by subjective ones (because of the poor statistical fit).

Morphological analysis

This technique involves a very detailed and precise breakdown of the present state of a particular technology, to evaluate target areas for development. Specific parameters to the development of the technology are analyzed and possible inter-relationships assessed.

The use of morphological analysis was initially developed by Zwicky when he was working in the field of jet engines. His published work on the subject provides a good insight into the application of the technique and will be briefly described here (see also Zwicky 1962 and 1969). The basic features entailed in morphological analysis are as follows:

1. The problem situation or functional capability desired must be stated explicitly and precisely.

2. All parameters and constraints to the particular variable must be identified and classified. Figure 12.14 gives the eleven basic parameters used by Zwicky in his analysis of jet engines (the number of alternatives within each parameter is given in parenthesis).

3. The parameters must be categorized into particular groupings. These are then put into matrix form.

The matrix shows all the possible combinations of the parameters although some are clearly impossible because they are self-contradictory (e.g. the distinction between internal and external is meaningless in the case of zero thrust augmentation). In Zwicky's jet engine research 36 864 combinations were given by the matrix, although when allowance was made for the impossible combinations the total fell to 25 344 feasible combinations. Some of these 25 344 combinations will have been already developed, but others will not and these represent potential developments of the technology or product. The management now has to look very closely at the potential combinations and subjectively forecast which are the most fruitful targets to aim for. To look at all the combinations of this type of analysis involves an enormous amount of time, so management has to use some subjective method to cut down the work.

1. Intrinsic or extrinsic chemically active mass (2)
2. Internal or external thrust generation (2)
3. Intrinsic, extrinsic or zero thrust augmentation (3)
4. Internal or external thrust augmentation (2)
5. Positive or negative jet (2)
6. Possible thermal cycles (adiabatic, isothermal, etc.) (4)
7. Medium (vacuum, air, water, earth) (4)
8. Motion (translatory, rotary, oscillatory, none) (4)
9. State of propellant (gas, liquid, solid) (3)
10. Continuous or intermittent operation (2)
11. Self-igniting or non-self-igniting propellant (2)

Figure 12.14

There are some analyses of the matrix which may in fact help cut down the potential developments (or cells, in matrix terminology) to feasible regions, that is advances which are more likely to be made in the near term. Firstly, there is the degree of technological advance required to reach the potential cell. If this cell has been formed by the combination of a number of advanced parameters, then it may be some considerable time before it is achieved. Secondly, if there are a number of potential uses awaiting a particular technical breakthrough or if further advances are awaiting this particular technical breakthrough, then the chances of the breakthrough occuring are very much greater because of the increased demand, therefore increased resources are devoted to its solution.

The morphological approach can also be used in a wide variety of other-than-technological forecasts; for example complex social and economic systems can be evaluated in such a way. Another example might be the possible uses (as opposed to the technical development) of a product. A matrix could be constructed relating to the characteristics of a particular type of material (toughness, weight, heat resistance, etc.) and the desired requirements of end use products (such as the qualities of materials desired by motor car manufacturers). This may well reveal present uses of the material which had never even been considered previously.

The main attribute of the morphological approach is that it makes a very detailed study of a technology or a variable and subjectively evaluates possible inter-relationships, potential uses and development opportunities. This can help reduce the missed opportunities that are currently available, as well as identifying at an earlier stage possible avenues for research and development. The technique is mainly useful as an analysis of a current product or technology and is therefore usually an exploratory model. Because the emphasis is on the future development of an existing variable, the technique is not quite as long-term a method as other types of qualitative forecasting.

Delphi method

This is a fairly common method used in long-term and technological forecasting. It basically consists of a group of experts giving their own opinions and views as to the possible outcomes of specified variables; these experts are kept apart but are told what the average opinion is. A consensus of the forecasts is then obtained and used as a forecast of the future. The method can perhaps be best explained by showing it in steps.

Step 1. A group of experts (the panel) on the subject under consideration are employed for its forecasting. These experts are preferably from both inside and outside the organization. For complex problems the panel may consist of experts in the various subsections of the problem, since there may be too few or perhaps no experts for the complete problem situation.

Step 2. The experts are sent the particular problem and asked for their answers. Typical problems would be the forecasting of, say, technological advances in the plastics industry up to the year 2000 or consumer acceptance of a new product over the next five years. The individual experts give their answers by letter. The reason for their being separate from each other is that it obviates the very probable bias of small group behaviour (e.g. persuasion, unwillingness to alter publicly expressed opinions and the bandwagon effect of the majority viewpoint). The experts prepare their forecasts by any method they wish and by incorporating any assumptions they think will be relevant: it is possible for the problem situation to specify various methods and assumptions within which the experts must operate. The experts send their completed forecasts back to the co-ordinating forecaster.

Step 3. The co-ordinator ranks the returns and the assumptions used in the returns. Another problem questionnaire is then sent to the experts asking whether they want to revise their opinions in the light of the results

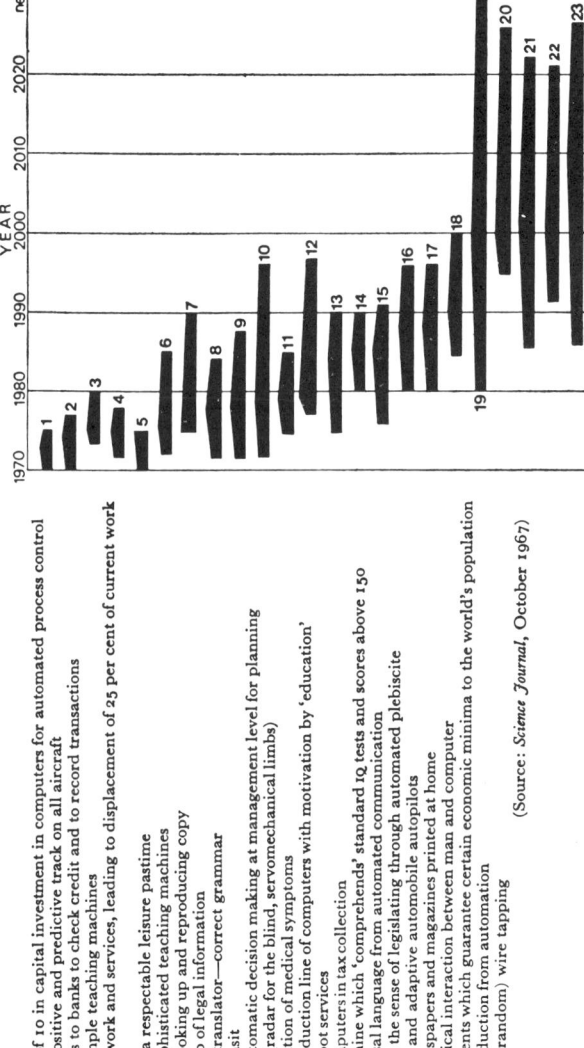

1 Increase by a factor of 10 in capital investment in computers for automated process control
2 Air traffic control—positive and predictive track on all aircraft
3 Direct link from stores to banks to check credit and to record transactions
4 Widespread use of simple teaching machines
5 Automation of office work and services, leading to displacement of 25 per cent of current work force
6 Education becoming a respectable leisure pastime
7 Widespread use of sophisticated teaching machines
8 Automatic libraries looking up and reproducing copy
9 Automated looking up of legal information
10 Automatic language translator—correct grammar
11 Automated rapid transit
12 Widespread use of automatic decision making at management level for planning
13 Electronic prosthesis (radar for the blind, servomechanical limbs)
14 Automated interpretation of medical symptoms
15 Construction on a production line of computers with motivation by 'education'
16 Widespread use of robot services
17 Widespread use of computers in tax collection
18 Availability of a machine which 'comprehends' standard IQ tests and scores above 150
19 Evolution of a universal language from automated communication
20 Automated voting, in the sense of legislating through automated plebiscite
21 Automated highways and adaptive automobile autopilots
22 Remote facsimile newspapers and magazines printed at home
23 Direct electromechanical interaction between man and computer
24 International agreements which guarantee certain economic minima to the world's population as a result of high production from automation
25 Centralised (possibly random) wire tapping

(Source: *Science Journal*, October 1967)

The length of each bar represents various estimates put forward by 'middle half' of the panel. In each case one quarter—the 'lower quartile'—proposed dates earlier than that at which the bar begins and another quarter—the 'upper quartile'—give dates beyond that marking the end of the bar. Each bar has a peak value which represents the median date estimated.

Figure 12.15 Forecasts of technological progress in automation using the Delphi approach

to date, asking for reasons why their final answers differ from the mean and asking for a more precise quantification of the forecast. This stage is then repeated as often as appears necessary, i.e. until the experts stop changing their viewpoints. The repetition of the process narrows down the range of possible futures and allows the co-ordinating forecaster to pinpoint the likely technological advances or other variables under consideration. There is of course some danger in asking the experts to review their forecasts in the light of the average opinion, since this may influence their judgement.

Figure 12.15 shows technological progress in automation as predicted by a panel of experts using the Delphi technique. The length of the bar denotes the range of estimates given by the middle half of the panel. The hump in each bar represents the median data prediction. Management can use the information in Figure 12.15 to make decisions as to

1. The direction and resources to be devoted to research and development.

2. The likely competition both from within the industry and outside it (i.e. whether other organizations are likely to achieve the break-throughs in technology more quickly).

3. Corporate planning. For example, the scale and expenses of the technological development suggested by Figure 12.15 may be too much for the expected returns, so the organization may change its direction of activities. Additionally, the quantification of the future shown by the figure provides long-term budgets for the company.

The main problems in the Delphi method are as follows:

1. When using large numbers of experts and especially those from outside, problems may arise in accurately explaining the problem situation and what the expert is required to do.

2. Ranking qualitative answers from respondents may prove difficult.

3. Problems may arise relating to small group bias, although these should have been kept to a minimum by a well developed system.

The technique can also be quite expensive if many leading authorities, including research institutes and organizations, are employed. These disadvantages are relative, however, since most qualitative forecasts suffer in a like manner. The Delphi approach's main difference from other qualitative methods is the use of a large number of independent experts to make forecasts.

Scenario

This is a similar approach to the Delphi method, again involving a panel of experts, but in this case they may be brought together in a room to take specific roles in a type of game (i.e. trying to 'play' the future in a short period of time). The roles given to the individuals may correspond with their individual skills. The scenario method assesses possible futures for the variable being considered and attempts to determine the likely constraints from technology and elsewhere. An organization can easily adapt or experiment with the Delphi and scenario techniques outlined above to suit its own requirements.

Both scenario and the Delphi approaches are viable as normative and exploratory models; when used as a longer-term forecast the approaches are generally normative (i.e. forecasting a future and then working back to today to assess the developments needed for this future). When the Delphi technique is used to forecast, say, the next five year's sales of a product this will usually be an explorative model (i.e. extrapolating the current state of affairs, forward).

Normative relevance trees

This is a development of normative scenario and Delphi forecasting. Here a range of possible desired futures for a specific variable is estimated by the forecaster or panel of experts; the desired future becomes an objective to which the organization strives. Management then has to evaluate the various alternative routes by which the objective can be achieved. A network or tree of the possible routes is drawn up representing the various technologies that will have to be solved or the social or economic constraints or problems to be overcome. The tree may show that certain technologies or other subgoals may be impossible or very costly. In this case an alternative route will be looked for; if none appears feasible then the objectives may have to be re-appraised. If possible, quantitative data should be applied to the tree or network and then critical path and project evaluation review technique methods can be applied to optimize the achievement of the goal. The type of quantitative data required might include say the dates when technological breakthroughs are expected, the costs involved and the returns from selling the product. Of course, in long-term forecasting such data is very much guess work and so certain formalized processes have been developed to aid forecasters.

One such method is known as PATTERN (Planning Assistance Through Technical Evaluation of Relevance Numbers) and was developed by Honeywell (see reference 18) to help planners in identifying the developments that were most important in the achievement of specific objectives. Firstly, a scenario of the future is prepared by a panel of experts (as in the Delphi approach) and this forms the objective (Figure 12.16 shows military and scientific pre-eminence as a major objective of the

222 Forecasting methods in business and management

United States). The various technologies that will need to be developed are then drawn in as a tree (Figure 12.16, adapted from Sigford and Parvin, shows eight particular levels). The forecaster now has an idea of how the national objectives are to be achieved and what technical deficiencies have to be overcome. The experts are then sent a copy of the tree and are asked to assign relevance numbers or weights to each element of it. This is usually done by obtaining the separate viewpoints of each expert, again obviating small group bias. The relevance numbers represent the importance of the item in the achieving or maximizing of the desired objective. As with the Delphi method, the co-ordinating forecaster can repeat this stage of the operation asking for revised opinions from the experts in the light of the

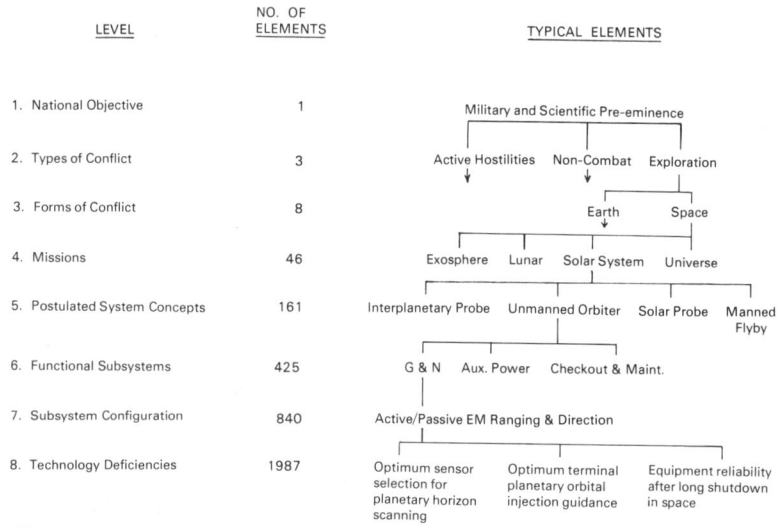

Figure 12.16 Relevance Tree (PATTERN).
Source: 'Project PATTERN: A Methodology for Determining Relevance in Complex Decision-Making', *IEEE Transactions on Engineering Management*, March 1965, by Sigford and Parvin

mean values so far recorded; other modifications can also be used, such as allowing group discussion. The mean of the experts' judgements becomes the relevance number for that element of the tree. Following from this, the total relevance number for each branch is obtained by multiplying the individual relevance numbers for each separate element. Hence the relevance for active hostilities would be reflected in the relevance numbers of all the elements below it. The tree therefore not only tells management which breakthroughs or developments are necessary in achieving the organization's objective but also gives the relative importance of each.

Another normative method is that of the impact study, which is concerned with the likely impact of any new probable technology, discovery or invention. Its sets out to identify all possible uses and markets for a specific project. This is of importance to management, since it gives predictions of the total markets and hence some idea of the total returns from a particular development or product.

The normative relevance tree methods have been applied at both government and corporate level: Figure 12.16 relates to the United States' objectives as a nation. A recent example in the UK has been the adoption of target growth rates (desired objectives); once these have been set, the various ways of achieving them have to be analyzed and this involves many subgoals. At the corporate level, the marketing department of a transport company may predict what will be the desired mode of transport in the year 2000 and this will become its objective. The company can then bring its various imaginative and technical brains to bear on how the objective can best be achieved. The relevance tree approach has as a major feature the detailed breakdown of possible avenues and routes to some desired future objective. This gives valuable information to the managers for a wide variety of technological and corporate planning decision making; it quantifies as well as possible the future events and uncertainties.

Qualitative techniques in technological forecasting

As will have been realized in this chapter, one of the major uses of qualitative techniques is in technological forecasting. The absence of directly relevant historical information and the long forecasting period make most quantitative methods infeasible for predicting technological change. Technological forecasts predict when a new process or product will be discovered or when an existing technology will achieve substantial commercial acceptance. This provides information for research and development decisions, marketing strategies and corporate planning.

The major published study to date of the use of technological forecasting in practice is that by Gerstenfeld (reference 8). He sent a questionnaire to the top 425 American corporations and received 162 valid replies. The questionnaire and a summary of the replies is given in Figure 12.17.

The author analyzed the answers by whether the adopting companies were fast growth or slow growth. He found that fast growing companies were most likely to adopt specific technological forecasting methods. No cause and effect relationship was attempted, however; the reasons for the difference between low and high growth rate companies could be that

1. Adopting the techniques might help make the corporation a high growth rate organization.

2. High growth rate corporations are most likely to be situated in fast changing industries and technologies, therefore there is a greater reward for using formal forecasting techniques.

---

1. *Does your company use a formal system of long-range planning or technological forecasting?*
   115 (71%)   Yes
   47 (29%)   No
   162 = 100%

2. *Have you ever had occasion to use:*
   23 (11·3%)   Delphi
   68 (33·6%)   trend fitting (S-curves)
   24 (11·8%)   Pattern
   25 (12·3%)   time-independent technological comparisons
   39 (19·2%)   PERT (for technological forecasting)
   24 (11·8%)   others (please name)

   Ninety-five firms of the 162 respondents indicated that they use at least one specific method of technological forecasting. Most of the firms stated that they use more than one method of technological forecasting. The total therefore adds up to more than the 162 firms being analysed. In order to determine the relative popularity of one method over another, the percentages are calculated by dividing the number of correspondents that indicated a specific method by the total number of methods used by all the companies.

3. *Please circle the average number of years into the future that you perform technological forecasting:*
   0 1 2 3 4 5 6 7 8 9 10 11 12 13 14 15
   The average answer for all companies was 7·06 years.

4. *How many people are in your technical forecasting or related group?*
   The average answer for all companies was 5 people.

Figure 12.17 Questionnaire and responses of 162 companies regarding their use of technological forecasting techniques

The future forecasting period used in technological predictions averaged 7 years. This is perhaps a rather short period and one would therefore expect many of the techniques to be explorative; it may be that longer time periods are now being utilized for forecasting. The longer time periods that were used were generally for the faster growth industries.

Summary

Qualitative forecasting is used when there is too little historical data with which to forecast, as well as for long-term forecasting. Although specific forecasts are subject to a fairly high degree of error, the use of ranges of outcomes gives valuable information to management on possible future outcomes. While qualitative methods rely upon fallible and often intuitive human judgement, the discipline imposed on management by the formal forecasting techniques discussed in this chapter greatly aids longer-term decision making and provides guidelines and budgets with which to compare performance.

References and suggested reading

1. Ayres, Robert U., *A Technological Forecasting Report*, HI-484DP, Hudson Institute, New York, 1960.
2. Ayres, Robert U., *Technological Forecasting and Long-Range Planning*, McGraw-Hill, 1969.
3. Cetron, Marvin J., *Technological Forecasting*, Gordon and Breach, 1969.
4. Cetron, M. J., and Ralph, C. A., *Industrial Applications of Technological Forecasting*, Wiley-Interscience, 1971.
5. Challis, A. A. L., 'The Impact of Technological Forecasting' in *The Role of Forecasting in Corporate Planning*, D. Ashton and L. Simister (editors) Staples Press, 1970.
6. Gerstenfeld, Arthur, and Blumberg, John, *Technological Forecasting and R & D Allocation*, Boston University Faculty Working Paper, November 1968.
7. Gerstenfeld, Arthur, *Effective Management of Research and Development*, Addison Wesley, 1970.
8. Gerstenfeld, Arthur, 'Technological Forecasting', *Journal of Business*, 1, 44, 10–18 (January), 1971.
9. Gordon, T. J., *Report on a Long-Range Forecasting Study*, The Rand Corporation, Santa Monica, California, 1964.
10. Helmer, Olaf, *Social Technology*, Basic Books, New York, 1966.
11. Helmer, Olaf, *The Use of the Delphi Technique—Problems of Educational Innovations*, The Rand Corporation, Santa Monica, California, 1966.
12. Jantsch, E., *Technological Forecasting in Perspective*, OECD, 1967.
13. Jantsch, E., *Technological Planning and Social Futures*, Cassell/Associated Business Programmes, 1972.
14. Lenz, R. C., *Technological Forecasting*, 2nd edition, Report ASD–TDR–62–414, Clearing House for Federal, Scientific and Technical Literature, No AD 408 085, June 1972.
15. Mansfield, Edwin, 'The Speed of Response of Firms to New Techniques', *The Quarterly Journal of Economics*, 77, May 1963.
16. Mansfield Edwin, *Industrial Research and Technological Innovation*, Norton, 1968.
17. Quinn, J. B., 'Technological Forecasting', *Harvard Business Review*, March–April 1967.
18. Sigford, J. V., and Parvin, R. H., 'Project PATTERN: A Methodology for Determining Relevance in Complex Decision-Making', *IEEE Transactions on Engineering Management*, 1, 12, 9–13 (March), 1965.
19. Zwicky, Fritz, 'Morphology of Propulsive Power', *Monographs on Morphological Research No 1*, Society for Morphological Research, Pasadena, California, 1962.
20. Zwicky, Fritz, *Discovery, Invention, Research*, MacMillan, 1969.

13

Data sources for forecasting

One of the most important factors that a forecaster has to consider is the availability of data. This relates to both the variable that is being forecast (requiring sufficient past data to form a time series) and independent variables (for use in causal models or as leading indicators). The importance of the data is that it has a major role in determining the type of forecasting model to use, as well as an important impact on the accuracy of the forecast.

The forecaster will also have to consider the variable to forecast; although the board of directors of the firm may want to know the profitability of a product, this may not be directly forecastable. In tackling such an assignment the forecaster may well elect to use unit sales data in the forecasting model (time series or causal model) and from the forecast produce a forecast sales value and hence the profits. There are likely to be numerous situations where the forecaster will find it appropriate to forecast one variable in order to get a forecast of another that management is really interested in (for example, forecasting physical sales and deriving a profits forecast from them). There are no specific guidelines in determining what variable to forecast other than to use one's business common-sense and experience. In particular the forecaster should be aware of the purpose for which the forecast is required, since this will help in the utilization of suitable data series and models. In analyzing the purpose for which a forecast is required the forecaster should identify the following characteristics:

1. The level of accuracy required. If it is imperative that the level of accuracy is maximized, then very accurate data is required (i.e. reducing the amount of aggregation and estimation used), probably of a very detailed nature.

2. The level of detail required and the frequency with which forecasts are required. If, for example, short-term sales forecasts of say 100 different items of stock are required, then a detailed breakdown of past sales on a daily basis must be obtained. This in turn is likely to suggest the use of a

time series technique (although causal model building approaches could be used for the longer-term forecasts.)

From this sort of analysis and from the knowledge of data sources, the forecaster will determine an appropriate forecasting technique to use. When this is done it is necessary to ensure that the data is properly collected and classified.

Data classification

Data can be conveniently classified into three types, each with certain characteristics:

1. Existing accounting information. This is the record of the firm's transactions and activities and forms the easiest and most accessible data to utilize. However, most accounting systems categorize transactions into various groupings and these are invariably difficult to disaggregate should the grouping be inappropriate for the forecast. For example, sales are often lumped together in accounting systems in monetary terms. This is inappropriate for the forecaster who wants to know physical unit sales, their monetary value by the type of product sold and a geographical split up of sales in order to know where to concentrate promotion. The disaggregating of data in accounting systems can be very costly and in some cases the forecaster may feel it necessary (in view of cost-benefit considerations) to use less appropriate, but readily available, data and even to modify the forecasting technique to take account of this. The forecaster should at the same time, however, seek to get the more appropriate data recorded in the accounting system so as to facilitate future forecasts.

2. Existing data which is not in the existing accounting/management information system. This may cover situations where the data is somewhere in the accounting system but is aggregated with other data or where the data is not in the accounting system at all (e.g. labour statistics for manpower and productivity forecasting). The obtaining of this data is usually fairly expensive and a good deal of care is needed in organizing its collection. The major advantage of collecting original data (where there is a choice between this and existing accounting data) is that it can be made to suit the particular forecasting technique chosen for the situation. If the forecasts are likely to be required in the future then the data collection should be incorporated in the day-to-day accounting/management information systems.

3. The use of published data sources and forecasting agencies who undertake consumer surveys. The popular sources of published data and the use of forecasting agencies are dealt with later in the chapter. The use of published data is generally cheap, the main cost being that of employing a

228 Forecasting methods in business and management

person to interpret the vast array of statistics that are produced. Published data often provides the variables which go into causal modelling and longer-term forecasting. Short-term forecasting by time series techniques rarely requires the use of published data apart from being a check or comparison yardstick on the forecasts. The limitations of using published data are dealt with in the next section and the use of forecasting agencies discussed on page 235.

Checking data sources

Before using any data in a forecasting system, the forecaster should assess its accuracy, since the accuracy and value of the forecast are dependent on the input data. In the case of internally generated information the forecaster should initiate a system of internal checks and audits on the data collection procedures, to assess

1. The adequacy and the possible improvement of procedures.
2. How well the existing procedures are being carried out. This will indicate the reliability of the data.
3. The accuracy of the data. This may involve some spot checking, although it is expensive.
4. The cost-benefits of the forecasts produced from the data. Alternative data sources should be assessed as well.

A tight internal audit, as outlined above, should ensure that the data is as accurate as is possible.

For published data sources the problem of assessing accuracy is more difficult, since the forecaster has no access to or control over the procedures involved with collecting and recording the data. A major investigation of the accuracy of economic observations has been carried out by Morgenstern (9) and he classified errors as originating from seven major sources: sampling methods, measurement errors, unknown and hidden data, errors and bias in questionnaire techniques, aggregation of data, classification of data and the time of recording data. Some of these are fairly obvious, while others need some explanation:

1. Sampling methods. Many published statistics relating to economic and business events are derived from samples. The forecaster should recognize this and also be aware that some of the sampling methods that have been used have been statistically unsound such that the inaccuracies may be high.
2. Measurement errors. These arise in the actual collection and recording of information. When large masses of data are collected it is quite like-

ly that some measurement errors will be made (this is evidenced by the fact that official statistics are sometimes corrected at a later time period).

3. Questionnaire errors and bias. Some data statistics are derived from questionnaire responses and a variety of errors and bias can arise from this type of approach. See the reference to Moser and Kalton (10) for a description of questionnaire techniques.

4. Because data is aggregated this may make it unsuitable for some forecasting purposes. The problems here include

(a) The aggregation is not always explicitly stated and so the forecaster does not know exactly what went into the statistic.

(b) Even if the basis of the aggregation is stated the quantitative breakdown is not often given.

(c) Different time periods may have been used in compiling the statistics.

Unfortunately there is not a great deal that the forecaster can do in determining the accuracy of data from published sources apart from seeing how well these have aided the forecasting process in the past. The forecaster should at least be aware of the possible shortcomings in published data and should monitor their ability to help in the firm's forecasting process.

Data banks

Over the past fifteen years or so there has been a vast increase in research into and development of accounting and management information systems (MIS), partly caused by the rapid growth in the adoption of computer facilities which enable sophisticated systems to be developed. While MIS is a subject in itself and largely outside the control of the forecaster, contact should at least be made with the MIS manager to ensure that data for forecasting purposes is being properly collected and recorded. In some advanced MIS systems they have introduced methods of creating a general data base from which any type of classification and categorization can be made (i.e. information is not immediately 'lost' into an aggregated category). In this situation each event or transaction is recorded separately along with its characteristics; a sale may be characterized by the customer, the type of product sold, the date when sold, the colour of the product, the location from where sold, etc. From this general data base any specific category can be constructed, such as sales by colour of product, sales of product A made from location 3, etc. Such a system has clear advantages for forecasters, especially those who need continually to reappraise model formats or who have a lot of one-off forecasts to make. As stated previously, MIS is a specialized subject and the interested reader should consult a standard text for a detailed description (for example Cushing (2) or

O'Brien (13)). The forecaster must, however, be aware of the importance of the data collection and recording process and should interact with the MIS manager to ensure an optimum contribution to the objectives of the firm.

Market surveys

This section gives a very brief review of market survey methodologies which can provide data for forecasting purposes. The general methods involved border on the qualitative forecasting techniques discussed in Chapter 12 and this is especially so when they are applied to longer-term decision situations.

Market surveys basically involve asking interested parties for their opinions and plans either in terms of an oral interview or a written questionnaire. Examples include

1. Asking customers their purchasing plans in the next so many weeks or other period.
2. Asking customers their reasons for purchasing specific brands of a product.
3. Asking customers the developments they would like to see in a product.
4. Asking industrial customers (production managers, purchasing managers, managing directors, research and development directors, etc.) their future purchase requirements and their capital expenditure commitments.
5. Asking middlemen (e.g. wholesalers, factors, retailers) their opinions on future market demand and possible technical developments that the final consumer would desire.
6. Apart from asking about the future, market surveys can also be used to help determine the total market for a product. If there are no existing statistics available then the total market computed by market survey methods allows the firm to estimate its market share.

The results from a market survey can be used in a number of ways in the forecasting process. For example, the data obtained could

1. Be used on its own to forecast, say, sales in the short or longer term.
2. Be used when a new product is being launched. In such cases time series and causal model techniques are often impossible to apply because of the lack of data, so resort must be made to market survey and qualitative methods.
3. Be used in conjunction with other forecasting techniques. If any wide discrepancies appear then these should be investigated.

4. Be used in helping derive the form of a causal model and its independent variables.

5. Be used in helping derive the qualitative factors (e.g. quality, colour, after-sales requirements of customers). These can be used as an input into a causal model and to help determine the research and development programme of a firm.

The forecaster or market survey executive has to be aware of the shortcomings of market research and of possible bias in its results. Although there are many different ways in which bias may creep in there are two fairly common instances which can be singled out. One is that private individuals' buying intentions (especially for non-durables) are very fickle and the results often do no more than specify an approximate level of sales; in such cases a better forecast may often be given by using the historical sales figure as a forecast for the future. The respondent may also give the answer that is thought to be required (e.g. buying the brand produced by the firm doing the survey) or which appears to be rational. In any event the market survey executive has to specify the form of the survey in as clear and unbiased terms as possible and treat the results obtained with some caution (possibly comparing the results with those produced by time series forecasting techniques).

The second common bias is that it may be in the customers' interests to give deliberately wrong forecasts. For example, a garage retailing motor cars may tell the various manufacturers that they expect sales will be higher than in fact they really think. By this strategy the garage makes sure there will be enough supplies if an unexpected sales boom occurs. The manufacturer holding excess stocks may also be in a position to sell more cheaply or offer some other incentive for the customer to buy. Again, the person in charge of the market survey must take care in both preparing the survey and interpreting its results. The interested reader can look at Heald's article (reference 6) which examines the relationship of intentions to buy consumer durables with the purchases actually made.

Examples of types of market survey

1. Surveys of private individuals' buying intentions and the qualities they desire in a product. In the case of non-durable products the results of such surveys have been found to be very dubious in all but the very short term (National Bureau of Economic Research (11)), i.e. they give poorer results than even simple time series techniques. For consumer durables the results are somewhat better although again this largely relates to the short term. Probability methods have been applied to consumer market surveys (see Juster (7)) but these have not gained much practical acceptance to date.

2. Surveys of industrial and commercial customers. These surveys are often more productive than those of private individuals, since the industrial customer is very aware of the need to insure supply lines and hence give accurate or over-optimistic forecasts of plans and intentions (the over-optimistic aspect was mentioned previously). In this regard industrial customers (via purchasing, production, plant, research and development, and general managers-directors) are often prepared to meet and discuss with the forecaster their future requirements as regards purchases and longer-term technical developments. If such meetings can be conducted with the majority of industrial customers then very valuable forecasting information can be obtained (and if advance orders can be gained then the uncertainty is reduced even further). Another advantage of such meetings is that some close friendship relationship may be built up with various executives of customer companies. This has fairly obvious advantages as far as the forecasting process is concerned.

If the forecaster relies on a questionnaire approach to industrial customers then the resulting information is generally worse than that obtained by personal meetings. The questionnaire approach is required, however, if the firm has many (say 100) customers, since personal meetings between the forecaster and the customers would be infeasible. (However, personal contact with the sales representative would be possible; see 4 below).

3. Surveys of wholesalers, factors, retailers and other middlemen. These will to some extent have prepared their own forecasts which could be passed on to the forecaster. The middlemen often have a fairly good idea of changes in customer demand, hence their opinions and forecasts can be quite valuable.

4. Forecasts by the firm's own personnel. In many situations the firm's salesmen are able to obtain valuable feedback on consumers' buying intentions and their product desires. In order to make maximum use of the opportunity and in order to reduce bias the survey needs to be formalized. The following points provide guidelines to the forecaster in forming a strategy:

(a) The questions should be preset. This means each salesman is asking the same questions and also the questions relate to data that management requires.

(b) Typical questions might include: future buying intentions (this may be a regular purchase, such as foodstuffs, or a periodical purchase, such as a motor car); the reasons for the brand purchase (i.e. price, style, quality); purchasing intentions over various periods, such as week, month or year (these intentions can be ranked by the amount of certainty the customer can place on them). If a causal model is being built then consumer surveys may help provide the data with which to quantify it. The consumer survey would typically give data on the more qualitative factors such as quality and style. If the consumers are asked for and give their answers in probabilistic terms this gives additional information to the forecaster and helps in implementing the various decision analysis techniques discussed in Chapter 11. Future customer desires can also be requested, which give management information on quality, styling and other characteristics that customers desire. This helps in product planning, research and development planning and, indeed, corporate planning. In addition, customers can be asked their reactions to changes in prices and credit terms. This gives management some idea of the elasticity of demand and may be the only way to obtain elasticities if there has been little variation in prices in the past. Finally, some idea of the impact of advertising on sales may be ascertainable.

(c) If some consumers appear to be very co-operative then the firm may send a larger questionnaire to them, containing questions which are both wider and deeper than the original salesmen's survey.

(d) The salesmen should be allowed some latitude to ask their own questions relating to the data required for the forecasting process, especially when, in addition to analyzing the results of the survey, they are asked to express an opinion on sales potential or market share.

(e) In analyzing the data, the trends of recent surveys should be calculated. It is these trends allied to actual outcomes which may provide the most reliable information. A comparison of past survey results and the actual results should always be made.

(f) Feedback on consumer satisfaction can actively be sought. Thus a questionnaire could be sent to the owners of consumer durables to see how satisfied they were with their purchase. This could include a question asking when the consumer is likely to replace his durable.

(g) Some consideration should be given to the training of sales personnel in consumer-survey techniques. Whether this is necessary depends very largely on the length and complexity of the questions to be asked. If they are short and easy to understand then no formal training may be required.

(h) In some circumstances the forecaster may feel that the above formalized method is unsuitable and may prefer to use salesmen's subjectively based forecasts. This can be done on a very subjective basis, by asking salesmen for their forecasts, or it can be conducted on a more objective basis by asking the salesmen to obtain forecasts from their customers and then make their own forecasts. In obtaining forecasts some care has to be taken in telling the salesmen what is required of them and, especially in the case of longer-term forecasts, to give them specific assumptions. Examples of the former include: forecast of unit sales in a specific period; forecast of unit sales in a particular area; forecast of total units sales; forecast of unit sales by product type. Examples of specific assumptions might be 'What is your sales forecast, given a 5% growth in GNP during the next year?' or 'What is your sales forecast given that credit controls of X amount will be introduced during the year?'

The forecaster should appraise the results with care. Particular attention should be paid to the past forecasting accuracy of each salesman. If a salesman consistently under- or over-forecasts sales then the forecaster may be able to derive an adjustment factor. Also salesmen with the greatest past accuracy can be given greater reliance in the future. Differences in the results between salesmen should be investigated; for example one salesman may predict a growth in sales of 50 per cent, while another may predict no growth at all. This also applies to substantial differences between salesmen's forecasts and predictions given by other forecasting techniques.

It is obvious that bias can creep into salesman's forecasts and even if the forecasting process is carefully designed this bias can still be present. Salesmen are often said to be over-optimistic in their forecasts because the very nature of their job (especially those concerned with private individuals or shopkeepers) requires them to be enthusiastic about the products they are selling. Additionally, they may forecast on the high side to show how much growth they can achieve and hence how successful they are (salesmanship is often a fairly precarious profession as far as employment goes). Conversely, salesmen may forecast on the low side if their remuneration is in some way based on beating a target which itself is partially based on the salesman's forecast. Thus by making a low forecast (saying, for example, that competition has increased) the target sales are set at a low level and by eventually beating the low target the salesman may earn large bonuses and be deemed to have been very successful.

The extent of such bias depends partly upon the personality of the salesmen, the remuneration and reward packages of the firm, and the training and education of the salesmen. The forecaster should attempt to educate and motivate the salesmen into giving responsible forecasts (including probabilistic forecasts), indicating how this will benefit the firm and themselves. Although this will reduce the bias in the salesmen's forecasts, it will not be possible to erradicate it completely.

The benefits of utilizing the salesmen in the forecasting process are that they are very near to the market and can provide valuable information for model building and for estimating qualitative factors. Also, by becoming involved in the forecasting process, the salesmen may gain greater motivation in their work. Industrial and technical product salesmen may be expected to make an even greater contribution to forecasting because they have a considerable (time-wise) contact with customers and can build up a good relationship.

5. Using what has been termed 'jury of executive opinion'. This is where many executives of the firm (salesmen, technical salesmen and others) are asked their opinions of future sales. The method is exactly similar to the Delphi and scenario techniques discussed in Chapter 12. The executives can be interviewed collectively or individually and they can be asked to express the reasons for their forecasts (they may be given assumptions within which they must forecast). The executives can then be told of the other executives' opinions and asked if they want to revise their own. This methodology can be used when forecasting the outcome of a new product launch, i.e. where qualitative judgement has to be used. The formalized use of jury by executive opinion is expensive in taking up managers' time and its regular use is usually confined to where qualitative judgement is required. The method can be adopted to include all the prior types of surveys; various time series techniques can also be incorporated.

In implementing market surveys the forecaster should recognize that they can be fairly expensive exercises if they are to be a part of ongoing operations, and if a survey relates to consumer non-durables then it should be repeated very frequently. Additionally there are various shortcomings and biases in the techniques and the forecaster needs to take care in constructing the survey so as to minimize these.

The use of outside agencies in carrying out surveys*

There are a number of market research agencies and economic and management consultants who will carry out surveys for client firms. In such cases a meeting is arranged with the consultants to discuss the objectives of the survey and then the consultants usually formulate a strategy and discuss this with management before finally adopting it. Amongst the advantages of using an outside agency are

1. The firm can leave its own staff free to carry on with their normal duties. If the firm's own staff are used then there is the possibility of a breakdown in normal operations.

2. Outside agencies usually have a wide range of experience in devizing and implementing surveys and hence better results may be obtained, and more efficiently, than if the firm's own staff are used.

3. The outside agencies may have done comparable surveys for other

---

* See numbers 8, 9 and 10 on pages 240 and 241 for organizations who have registers of market survey organizations.

firms and associations and they may utilize the results in the current study.

4. More reliable information may be obtained from survey respondents. If they are responding to the firm's salesmen or other executives, private individuals may feel they ought to give certain answers (e.g. they like the firm's brand of a particular product) instead of giving their true opinions. The use of an outside agency avoids this problem.

The disadvantages of using outside agencies are

1. If the surveys are to be done on a regular basis over a long time it is probably cheaper for the firm to organize its own surveys.

2. An explicit brief must be given to the outside agency. If the survey is conducted by the firm's own staff then it has a much tighter control of operations and is much more aware of the problems that accrue. When an outside agency faces such problems it deals with them as it sees fit without the firm ever knowing about them.

3. Often much of the work carried out by the agency will be duplicating data already in the possession of the firm. For example, the firm may have various statistics relating to market share which the agency may go out and collect itself, not being aware of the presence of the data within the firm.

4. One of the advantages of using an outside agency was that it may have done similar work for a competitor company and thus our firm gains from their experience. This of course can work the other way. If our firm gives any confidential or semi-confidential data to an agency this may well be used, although often subconsciously, by the agency when working for another client.

The forecaster has to weigh up the various advantages and disadvantages of using an outside agency or consultancy in any particular situation.

Some trade associations conduct surveys themselves and the results are usually available to members. One generally available market survey forecast is that run by the Confederation of British Industry published in *Industrial Trends Inquiry*. The survey sets out to measure businessmen's expectations as regards sales, productivity, profits, exports and various costs. While this is a very general survey, it is readily available; the national papers often summarize large parts of it. Another survey of businessmen's forecasts is undertaken by the Taylor Nelson Group and published in the *Financial Times*. This can be used as a guide to overall or industry-based business confidence.

Clearly market surveys do have some use in the forecasting process although their value is may be not as great as some would have us believe. The reader who is interested in following up survey techniques should consult the references to Cox (1), Kelly (8) Moser and Kalton (10) and Reichhard (14).

Sources of published data

This section provides a brief description of the major sources of business and economic data that are available to the forecaster. The information is likely to be of the greatest use in causal model building where it can help determine the values of independent variables; for example, statistics may be obtained on

1. Prices charged by other competitors or by an industry as a whole.
2. Growth in labour wage rates.
3. Growth in gross national product.
4. Social groupings of the population.

These four factors and many others could well be incorporated in a causal model and published data is likely to be the only source of such information.

Before going ahead with a description of the sources it is worth repeating what was said earlier about the use of business and economic statistics. The forecaster should pay special attention to the actual make-up and categorization of the data source: if there is any uncertainty about the relevance of the statistics to the forecasting situation, then the resulting forecasts should be treated with caution.

The major sources of data the business forecaster is likely to utilize are produced by the government and the Civil Service, independent economic consultants and trade associations.

Government sources of economic and business information

The following represent some of the most useful of government publications for the forecaster. They are available at government bookshops or from Her Majesty's Stationery Office, P O Box 569, London SE1 9NH. Many public libraries subscribe to at least some of the publications, while business libraries may subscribe to a large number.

1. The *Annual Abstract of Statistics* contains most of the aggregate economic and social statistics for the UK over a number of years.
2. The *Monthly Digest of Statistics* contains many of the statistics in the *Annual Abstract*, but updated monthly.
3. The above statistics on a regional basis are provided by
   (a) *Scottish Abstract of Statistics* (annual).
   (b) *Digest of Welsh Statistics* (annual).
   (c) *Abstract of Regional Statistics* (annual).
   (d) *Northern Ireland Digest of Statistics* (biannual).
4. *Trade and Industry* is a weekly publication of the Department of Trade and Industry and gives a wide range of statistics and economic and trade information.

5. *Business Monitors* are a set of publications giving statistics and current data on trade news, such as prices, stocks, exports, etc. Separate *Business Monitors* cover different industries, services and the distributive trades. The results of the annual censuses of production are also published in the *Business Monitor* publications in the form of a separate report for each industry.

6. *Census of Production.* The last of these was published in 1968. Annual updating is given in the *Business Monitors*. The census gives a wide range of information relating to industry groups.

7. The last set of input-output tables related to the year 1971 and are contained in 'Summary input-output tables for 1971', *Economic Trends* No 258, HMSO, April 1975. Unfortunately the publication of input-output tables always lags a few years behind the period to which they relate and this of course reduces their usefulness to the forecaster.

8. The annual *National Income and Expenditure* book (the Blue Book) contains a mass of information on income and expenditures. The annual *UK Balance of Payments* book (the Pink Book) contains information on balance of payments statistics.

9. *Economic Trends* is a monthly publication which contains articles, comments and statistics on the UK economy. It also updates the two prior ((8) above) annual publications on a quarterly basis.

10. The *Inland Revenue Statistics* and the *Report of the Commissioners of HM Customs and Excise* give regional data on incomes, taxation and wealth.

11. *Financial Statistics* is a monthly publication of the major financial statistics of the UK.

12. *Overseas Trade Statistics of the UK* is a monthly publication relating to overseas trade.

13. *Local Government Financial Statistics* is an annual summary of local government income, expenditures and services.

Labour and Wages

14. *British Labour Statistics: Historical Abstracts (1886–1968)* and *Annual Yearbooks* (1969 to 1971) provide an historical survey of labour statistics.

15. *New Earnings Survey* publishes the results of the annual survey of earnings.

16. *Time Rates of Wages and Hours of Work* is an annual publication.

17. *Department of Employment Gazette* is a monthly publication on labour statistics. This gives the most up-to-date information.

Agriculture and Food

18. *Agricultural Statistics: England and Wales* (annual).

19. *Agricultural Statistics: United Kingdom* (annual).
20. *Household Food Consumption and Expenditure* (annual).
21. *Food Facts* (quarterly).

Population

22. *Census of Population 1971* gives a detailed breakdown on households and population.

23. *Population Projections 1971–2011* is a forecast prepared on a national and regional basis by the government actuary.

24. *General Household Survey* covers a range of economic and social statistics. The latest results relate to 1971.

25. *Family Expenditure Survey* provides an annual report on the income and expenditure of households.

Retail Trade

26. *Census of Retail Distribution and Other Services 1971* provides statistics on retail outlets.

Transport (annual)

27. *Highway Statistics.*
28. *Passenger Transport in Great Britain.*

Social Statistics

29. *Annual Report of the Department of Health and Social Security.*
30. *Criminal Statistics* (annual).
31. *Education Statistics for the United Kingdom* (annual).
32. *Health and Personal Social Service Statistics* (annual).
33. *Scottish Educational Statistics* (annual).
34. *Social Trends* (annual) is a selection of key statistics relating to all aspects of social policy.
35. *Statistics of Education* (six volumes per year).

Department of Trade and Industry

1 Victoria Street, London SW1H 0ET, Tel. 01 222 7877. This department has a lot of economic statistics and business information; the data relating to overseas (exports, etc.) is especially useful. The department also keeps a comprehensive library (the Statistics and Market Intelligence Library is situated at Export House, 50 Ludgate Hill, London EC4, Tel. 01 248 5757). For a more detailed review of official economic and social statistical sources see the references to Edwards (3), (4) and Nicholson (10).

Independent economic and business services

Independent economic and business services often publish statistics and forecasts which the firm can purchase. These are often quite valuable, since they either forecast variables which government and civil service statistics have not, or they make unbiased forecasts of the variables which have already been forecast by official sources. Many of these organizations will also carry out specific research and forecasting work for the firm, although this is expensive (but often less expensive than if the firm carried out the research itself). If specific research or forecasting assignments are carried out then the forecaster will be able to state precise requirements and so suitable data may be obtained.

Among the major non-government sources of statistics are

1. *ASLIB (Association of Special Libraries and Information Bureaux)*
3 Belgrave Square, London SW1X 8PL, Tel. 01 235 5050. Aslib provides a service which advises on sources of information.

2. *The British Institute of Management (BIM)*
Management House, Parker Street, London WC2, Tel. 01 404 3456. The Institute publishes a range of statistical and business information, maintains a large business library and can advise on the sources of obtaining data.

3. *The Confederation of British Industries (CBI)*
21 Tothill Street, London SW1, Tel. 01 930 6711. The Confederation publishes the *Industrial Trends Inquiry* which contains statistical and business data. In addition, it produces economic and business forecasts and comments on economic policies. The CBI also provides advisory services to its members.

4. *The Economist Intelligence Unit Ltd (EIU)*
Spencer House, 27 St James's Place, London SW1A 1NT, Tel. 01 493 6711. This company provides consultancy services to clients (including market surveys), as well as publishing regular economic and business surveys of the economy, individual industries and market places.

5. *European Community Information Centre*
20 Kensington Palace Gardens, London W8 4QQ, Tel. 01 727 8090. Provides information on the European communities including industrial and business matters.

6. *The Financial Times—SVP Business Information Services*
Bracken House, 10 Cannon Street, London EC4P 4BY, Tel. 01 248 8000. This firm provides a consultancy service covering business, financial and marketing matters in the UK and some overseas data.

7. *The Henley Centre for Forecasting*
27 St John's Square, London EC1M 4DP, Tel. 01 253 4781. This centre publishes a number of regular forecasts on the economy and on business conditions. It also undertakes one-off type consultancy assignments for firms.

8. *The Industrial Marketing Research Association*
28 Bore Street, Lichfield, WS13 6LL, Tel. Lichfield 3448. This is the major

trade association of individuals who are engaged in industrial market research.

9. *The Institute of Marketing*
Moor Hall, Cookham, Berks., Tel. 062 85 24922. This is the professional institute for executives engaged in marketing. The Institute itself provides a wide range of information on marketing.

10. *The Market Research Society*
51 Charles Street, London W1, Tel. 01 499 1913. This is a major professional body for those engaged in marketing and economic research. The society provides an information service for members and subscribers.

11. *Maxwell Stamp Associates Ltd.*
55–63 Goswell Road, London EC1V 7PT, Tel. 01 251 0147. This firm provides economic statistics and comment on both regular and individual consultancy bases. They also provide consultancy services on overseas countries and markets.

12. *National Economic Development Council*
Millbank Tower, Millbank, London SW1, Tel. 01 834 3811. The council and its subsidiary industrial councils are made up of leading representatives of management, trade unions, government officials and independent members. The council publishes reports on the economy and in particular on individual industries and trades.

13. *National Institute of Economic and Social Research (NIESR)*
2 Dean Trench Street, London SW1P 3HE, Tel. 01 930 6711. Provides independent forecasts and comments on the UK economy. Its main publication is the *National Institute Economic Review* (quarterly).

14. *Newspapers*
Many national daily and Sunday newspapers carry business and economic commentaries and a perusal of these by the forecaster may be of some assistance. In particular, both the *Sunday Times* and the *Sunday Telegraph* publish economic assessments which have been built up on econometric models and the forecasts of leading businessmen. There are also many business and economic periodicals, such as *The Economist*, which contain useful information for the forecaster. The major newspapers and periodicals are found in libraries and the forecaster can soon assess which contain useful sources of information for particular needs.

15. *Taylor Nelson and Associates Ltd.*
457 Kingston Road, Ewell, Surrey, Tel. 01 394 0191. This organization provides economic and business statistics on regular one-off bases for individual clients. It undertakes the work involved in producing the *Financial Times Monthly Survey of Business Opinion*.

Trade associations

Most industries and markets have some sort of trade association representing them and many firms join such federations. These trade associations often act as a data collection agency and they publish an assortment of macro-statistics (i.e. covering the trade or industry as a whole) and comparative ratios (e.g. financial ratios, relative advertizing expenditures, relative selling prices). Access to these statistics, or to some of the statistics, may be restricted to the association's members. Again, the caveats about using external sources of data must be borne in mind and the forecaster should clearly establish the make up of any statistics. Some associations also carry out forecasting exercises which can vary from time series techniques to sophisticated econometric modelling. Clearly trade associations can provide very important data for a firm's forecasts and the forecaster should make as much use of these services as possible.

The list below gives an example of typical major trade journals (taken from Firth (5)), however the forecaster will be in a far better position to ascertain the most relevant trade journals. For a description of sources of UK marketing information see the Wills reference (15).

Industry	*Journal*
aircraft	*Flight*
	Flying Review International
banks	*Banker*
	Bankers' Magazine
breweries	*Brewing Trade Review*
building	*Building*
	Build International
	Construction News
	Construction Trends
	Development & Materials Bulletin (GLC)
	House Builder and Estate Developer
	Housing & Planning Review
	Housing Review
	Housing Statistics
	Monthly Bulletin of Construction Statistics
	National Builder
chemicals	*Chemical Age*
	European Chemical News
electronics & computers	*Computer Survey*
	Data Processing

engineering & machine tools	*Machine Tool Review*
	Machine Tool Engineering
	Metalworking Production
food	*Food World*
	Grocer
heavy electricals	*Electrical Review*
hire purchase	*Credit*
insurance	*Bests Review*
	Policy Holder
investment trusts and unit trusts	*Money Management and Unitholder*
	Unit Trust Year Book
mining & commodities	*Investors' Guardian*
	Mining Journal
	Mining Magazine
	Optima
	Platinum Metals Review
	World Metal Statistics
motors	*Monthly Statistical Review* (Society of Motor Manufacturers Trades)
office equipment	*Business Equipment Buyers Guide*
oil	*Oil and Gas International*
	Petroleum Press Service
	Petroleum Review
	Petroleum Times
paper	*World's Paper Trade Review*
property	*Estates Gazette*
rubber manufacturing	*Rubber Statistical Bulletin*
shipbuilding	*Shipbuilding and Shipping Record*
shipping	*Lloyd's Register of Shipping*
	Shipping World and Shipbuilder
stores	*Retail Business*
	Which?
textile, clothing and footwear	*Footwear Industry Statistical Review*
	Textile Monthly
	Wool Year Book
tobacco	*Tobacco*
	Tobacco Intelligence
	World Tobacco

The major sources of financial statistics relating to individual companies are those services run by Exchange Telegraph (Extel) and Moodies Services Ltd. These present summarized breakdowns of profits, assets and performance ratios for each company over a number of years. The *Stock Exchange Official Year Book* summarizes financial data and the capital structures of companies quoted on the Stock Exchange. Some agencies provide press-cutting services on individual companies. There are various business publications which are helpful to the analyst; the *Directory of Directors* gives the names of company directors and their directorships; *Who Owns Whom* lists parent companies and their subsidiaries; *Kompass* and *Key to British Enterprises* are directories of trade and industry categorization. The annual accounts of all limited companies are filed at Companies House and these can be inspected by the public for a small fee.

Two directories which contain an extensive list of sources of data are Hussey, D. F., *The Corporate Planner's Yearbook 1974–5*, Pergamon Press, 1974, and *European Directory of Economic and Corporate Planning 1973–1974*, Gower Press, 1974.

References

1. Cox, K. C., ed., *Readings in Market Research*, Appleton–Century–Crofts, 1967.
2. Cushing, B. E., *Accounting Information Systems and Business Organizations*, Addison-Wesley, 1974.
3. Edwards, B., *Sources of Economic and Business Statistics*, Heinemann, 1972.
4. Edwards, B., *Sources of Social Statistics*, Heinemann, 1974.
5. Firth, M. A., *Investment Analysis: Techniques of Appraising the British Stock Market*, Harper & Row, 1975.
6. Heald, G., 'The relationships of intentions to buy consumer durables with levels of purchase', *British Journal of Marketing*, Summer, 1970.
7. Juster, F. T., *Consumer Buying Intentions and Purchase Probability*, Occasional Paper 99, National Bureau of Economic Research, Columbia University Press, 1966.
8. Kelley, W. T., *Marketing Intelligence: management of marketing information*, Staples Press, 1968.
9. Morgenstern, O., *On the Accuracy of Economic Observations*, Princeton University Press, 1963.
10. Moser, C. A., and Kalton, G., *Survey Methods in Social Investigation*, Heinemann, 1971.
11. National Bureau of Economic Research, *The Quality and Significance of Anticipations Data*, Princeton University Press, 1960.
12. Nicholson, R. J., *Economic Statistics and Economic Problems*, McGraw-Hill, 1969.
13. O'Brien, J., *Management Information Systems*, Van Nostrand, 1970.
14. Reichhard, R. S., *Practical Techniques of Sales Forecasting*, McGraw-Hill, 1966.
15. Willis, G., ed., *Sources of UK Marketing Information*, Nelson, 1969.

14

The selection and implementation of forecasting techniques

We have examined a large number of forecasting techniques and the problem now facing the forecaster is to decide which is the most appropriate in the given circumstances. In order to do this the forecaster has to consider the requirements of the forecasting situation and the availability of the required inputs into each individual technique (such as data and expert personnel) and perform a cost-benefit analysis. The major common requirements of forecasting situations were described in Chapter 2, these being accuracy, the time horizon of a forecast, speed, regularity, detail and relevance. This consideration will in itself suggest possible techniques; for example if forecasts of the immediate future are required (say the next week or the next month), then time series techniques are the likely approach, in particular the simpler versions of Chapter 3. For medium-term forecasts of, say, 3 to 24 months the forecaster will have to take account of seasonal and cyclical factors (suggesting decomposition techniques or adaptive forecasting) and changes in the influencing factors such as credit restrictions (suggesting causal models). In the longer-term forecasting situations causal models and qualitative forecasting techniques are likely to be the appropriate methodologies; it will be rare for time series techniques on their own to be found appropriate beyond a period of, say, five years. Thus before we have even looked at any other factors, the time period requirement of a forecasting situation has suggested possible techniques to use; it should be noted that once we have looked at some of these other factors we may wish to alter our forecasting technique choice. (In some situations forecasts over various periods may be required for a variable; for example, sales forecasts for the immediate term are needed for inventory planning, sales forecasts in the medium term required for capital expenditure planning and sales forecasts in the longer term required for corporate planning. Different techniques may be employed for forecasting sales over these various periods.)

Similarly, the other requirements of the forecasting situation may suggest particular techniques or type of techniques. For example, if weekly forecasts of sales demands for say a range of 100 brand products are required for production scheduling and inventory planning, then this suggests the use of time series techniques and probably the simpler versions. This is because simple time series techniques usually give good accuracy in the very short term and because they are cheap to organize and operate (100 forecasts every week will be fairly costly, hence the cheapness of the technique becomes a major factor).

The forecaster should also consider the value of using several forecasting techniques in a given situation, although this is probably only worthwhile when there is considerable uncertainty. After considering the various forecasts given by the different techniques and the assumptions behind each, the forecaster can then derive a (probably subjective) final forecast.

Requirements for implementing a forecasting technique

Having assessed the forecasting situation the forecaster may have narrowed down the number of techniques that are suitable for the situation. The next step in identifying the appropriate technique is to see if the requirements for implementing the individual techniques can be met in the circumstances surrounding the situation. Amongst the major inputs of forecasting techniques are the availability of data, the time to build an acceptable model within the technique and the expertise required to undertake the technique. If, for example, there is no past data whatsoever (possibly a completely new product), then some type of qualitative forecast will be required. If quantitative data is available and a one-off forecast is required very quickly, then a simple time series method such as exponential smoothing is likely to be the appropriate technique. This is because it will probably take some time before suitable parameters to adaptive models can be found and even longer periods of time before causal models can be built. The availability of expertise may also restrict the use of some otherwise appropriate technique: the use of the Box-Jenkins approach requires some expertise and if this is not readily on hand then any forecast required quickly will have to use some simpler technique.

Examination of data

The next step the forecaster will take is to examine the historical time series of the variable to be forecast, assuming there is such a time series. From this analysis the general form of the time series should be noted and this can be used to indicate possible techniques. For example, is the time series approximately horizontal? (suggesting simple exponential smoothing); is it seasonal? (suggesting decomposition, adaptive modelling or causal models); does it show a fairly constant rise or decline? (suggesting double exponential smoothing, linear trend analysis or adaptive model); does it show a lot of erratic movement? (possibly indicating a complex pattern and therefore Box–Jenkins forecasting), and so on. Having obtained this rough idea of the type of data involved, the forecaster can now go ahead and formally test the applicability of the various time series methods which initially seem appropriate (ignoring causal models for the moment, i.e. identifying the best of the time series techniques). This is done by testing the technique on past data.

The testing procedure can take the form of either deriving the parameters of each model on all the past data (right up-to-date) or deriving the parameters on one set of past data and then testing its accuracy on the second set of past data. A third alternative is to use data produced by simulating the values of the variable being forecast: for a discussion of this technique see Brown (3). To clarify the procedural differences, assume there are 60 monthly observations available starting from five years ago. The forecaster can establish the parameters to the various techniques (i.e. the smoothing constant in exponential methods and the learning constant, K, in adaptive filtering) by using the five years data. The individual models are re-run until the optimum parameters have been derived by minimizing the forecasting errors (the mean absolute error or the mean squared error; see Chapter 2, p. 34). If the forecaster feels the pattern in the data is fairly constant then it may be assumed that the past forecasting errors will be approximately the same as the forecasting errors that will accrue in the future, i.e. the difference between the predicted and actual values. The forecasting errors of the various techniques are compared and the one showing the greatest accuracy is chosen for the forecasting situation (subject to cost-benefit considerations).

Alternatively, the parameters to the individual models could be established on the first 48 observations and then the forecasting accuracy tested on the last 12 observations (these being the actual values of the variable against which the predicted values are compared). Again, the technique showing the smallest error is chosen. This method is a more objective way of measuring accuracy and is to be preferred; the disadvantage with it is that it ignores the last twelve observations in deriving the parameters.

Once a technique has been chosen and put into operation the forecaster should carry out performance audits on its accuracy *vis-à-vis* the other techniques.

The forecaster must also consider the use of causal modelling, especially in the case of medium and long-term forecasting situations. Causal models automatically produce probabilistic results and if there is a lot of uncertainty about, and if the forecast is an input of a very important decision, then this is a significant attribute (such that it may negate the use of other techniques). This facility increases the robustness of the model in that it can be adapted to give accurate forecasts even in a period of changing conditions. Causal model building involves a fair amount of time and expense in its development stage, hence the technique is mainly used by medium to large organizations which are committed to formal planning techniques. The process of building and testing causal models is as described in Chapters 7, 8 and 9 and the testing of their accuracy is again done by measuring the errors. The error measurements are also the main criterion in deciding between a causal model and a time series model. Additional data problems accrue with causal modelling and accurate values of the independent variables are a vital necessity.

Qualitative forecasting

Qualitative forecasting methods can be used either on their own or as some adjustment to a quantitative forecast. The former is likely to occur when there is no quantitative data available (such as in a completely new product launch or research and development programme planning) or when the forecast is for a very long way ahead (such as fashion tastes in the clothing market twenty years ahead). The use of qualitative forecasting as an adjustment to some quantitative method can arise in any number of situations. Many time series techniques when used for forecasting beyond, say, two or three years are adjusted by the qualitative subjective judgement of the forecaster and management. Qualitative methods can also be used in estimating a range of outcomes for a 'single answer' time series forecast. Thus if exponential smoothing gives a value of, say, 12 500 units for next month's sales, then the forecaster, using some qualitative judgement, may be prepared to give a forecast to management that sales will almost certainly be in the range 12 300 to 12 700 units. In using qualitative or subjective forecasting the forecaster should keep a control on the procedures involved otherwise every forecast may degenerate to a very quick guess.

Using a number of forecasting techniques

Major decision situations may call for a lot of forecasts which can cover various time periods and the forecaster may have to use a wide range of techniques to obtain an overall forecast for a complex situation (this will probably be a probabilistic forecast). The forecaster must therefore be prepared to think of the overall purpose of the forecasting situation and plan the forecasting methodologies accordingly.

Cost-benefits of forecasting

Another consideration facing the forecaster in the choice of techniques is the costs involved. As described in Chapter 2, there are three types of cost; development costs, data acquisition and storage costs, and operating costs. The eventual determination of an appropriate technique will in fact be based on a cost benefit consideration but in order to assess the benefits the accuracy (and the importance of the accuracy) of each technique in the situation needs to be assessed. In determining this accuracy the forecaster will have to build and test the models and thus will at least have to meet the development costs (and probably any data acquisition costs). From here the further costs (although it should be noted that development costs are often the greatest expense) are compared against the benefits and the appropriate technique chosen. In practice many forecasters do not consider all the alternative techniques because

1. By experience they know, or think they know, the appropriate forecasting technique (or at least can narrow down the choice).

2. They know that some techniques are beyond the present capability of the firm (in terms of costs or expert personnel).

3. They may be unaware of a technique and do not have the commitment to investigating new methods.

The main practical basis for measuring the benefits of forecasting takes the form of calculating the resultant increase in profits. (Alternatively, utilities can be used: for a description of utilities in management decision making see reference 7.) Taking a simple case, management may forecast sales for the next month at £1 million, using only its judgement. On the basis of this inventory levels and the provision of sales personnel are planned. The forecaster, using a formal quantitative technique, may predict sales of £1·08 million and sales personnel would be altered accordingly. If the actual sales turned out to be £1·1 million, then by using the management's judgement there results a loss of £100 000 sales; by using the quantitative forecast, sales of only £20 000 would be lost (assuming that once inventory levels and sales personnel levels have been set they act as a rigid constraint on sales). If the profits generated by each £1 of sales is 20p then using the quantitative forecasting technique would result in a benefit of £16 000 (i.e. £80 000 increase in sales from using forecasting technique × 20p). Assuming this type of benefit accrued each month then it would be worth paying up to a maximum of £16 000 per month for the forecasting. Instead of the firm losing sales it may decide to carry higher levels of stocks to cover any plausible sales potential. However, by using formal forecasting the inventory levels could be lowered without any increase in lost sales and, since carrying stocks costs money, cost savings could be made.

Management can check the continuing benefits from forecasting by making its own judgemental forecast for the future each period. This will then be compared with the actual result and the result predicted by the forecasting technique. From this the increase in profits from using the formal forecasting technique can be established. These are then compared with the costs of the forecasting technique adopted or the costs of the forecasting department and decisions made as to whether to continue with formal forecasting. To date virtually all organizations have either maintained or increased their commitment to forecasting; there have been no recorded cases of firms closing down their forecasting departments.

In the case of non-profit making organizations or when the forecasts are long term it becomes more difficult to quantify the benefits of formal forecasting methods. For non-profit making organizations or departments the criterion for measuring the value of forecasting is the cost savings that are produced. For longer-term forecasts it becomes difficult to measure the efficacy of formal forecasting because a long time elapses (many years in the case of capital investment projects) before the actual result occurs. Additionally the formal forecasts (and the concomitant subjective management judgement) are revised over time as the actual event approaches, therefore it becomes difficult to decide how the performance should be measured. Longer-term forecasts are often made on major capital expenditure projects or major strategic planning exercises (where the expenditures or value of assets being decided upon are very large). Because of the large monies involved any increase in forecasting accuracy is usually justified and so the main criterion for deciding between forecasting techniques and whether to formally forecast or not is forecasting accuracy; the costs are usually so small, proportionately, that they can be ignored.

Summary of the guidelines to selecting an appropriate technique

The above considerations will help guide the forecaster in selecting an appropriate technique for any given situation. The major selection method is an analysis of the past forecasting accuracy of each technique, resulting in the choice of the one giving the smallest error. In many firms the number of techniques available for selection may be limited because of lack of full commitment by the top management. If this is so then the resources devoted to forecasting will be smaller than usual, as will be the commitment to using the forecasting output. A later section in this chapter gives a description of forecasting practices in use in the UK.

Data output

As acknowledged at the beginning of the book, virtually all forecasts turn out to contain some error and managers must recognize this when making their decisions. In many situations, such as longer-term forecasts, the error can be quite high and may result in a wrong decision having been made. In order to help managers with this problem the forecaster should attempt to obtain a range of forecasts for the specific variable, highlight the different assumptions on which these forecasts are made and assess the probabilities of these forecasts or assumptions occurring.

Some of the techniques discussed so far have in fact given probabilistic forecasts of the sort that can help management. These are the causal model building techniques described in Chapters 7, 8 and 9. On page 109 we discussed the standard error of the forecast and the interpretation of its meaning. The statistic tells us that we can be 95% certain that the actual value of a variable will be within $\pm$ 2 standard errors of the forecast of the variable, other confidence limits being similarly expressed. Thus in the example on page 128 the regression produced a forecast of 876 060 units and a standard error of 49 200 units. From this management can be 95% certain that the actual outcome will be between 777 660 and 974 460 units. The use of the standard error of the forecast is only relevant, however, if the regression coefficients and the values of the independent variables are correct. If the forecaster feels these could take different values then different approaches to determining probabilistic forecasts will have to be adopted.

If the forecaster feels the independent variable could take one of several values then the impact of each of these should be assessed. Thus in the

Table 14.1

		Relative price	Personal disposable income (£ million)	Absolute level of rainfall
	L	0.85	18 900	29.0
1976	M	0.90	19 065	32.6
	H	0.95	19 200	35.0
	L	0.85	19 600	32.0
1977	M	0.90	19 800	34.0
	H	0.95	20 000	36.0
	L	0.90	20 100	30.0
1978	M	0.95	20 550	34.5
	H	1.00	20 900	38.0

L = lowest estimate
M = middling estimate
H = high estimate

Note: Many more estimates could be included for each variable

raincoat example from Chapter 8 we could change the values of the independent variables: the figures from Table 8.6 (page 128) could take the values shown in Table 14.1. The forecaster or sales manager might think the price relative to competitors' prices will be 90% for 1976. However, the forecaster might think that there is a chance that competitors will lower their prices, such that the price relative could become ·95, or raise their prices so that the relative drops to ·85. This methodology is repeated for all the independent variables with the forecaster using as many values for the variable as is thought probable. From Table 14.1, there are now 27 (3 × 3 × 3) forecasts of the unit sales outcome for each year (assuming, as is quite likely, that the variables are independently distributed, i.e. the value of each one is not associated with the value of any other variable). The forecaster should attempt to attach probabilities to these different values for the variables; for example, the chances of the price relative being ·85 might be ·1, the chance of the price relative being ·90 might be ·7 and the chance of the price relative being ·95 might be ·2. From these probabilities can be attached to the forecast. The process is exactly the same as described in Chapter 11; Figure 11.1 also portrays a possible probabilistic forecast of unit sales given by the regression models. The techniques for obtaining subjective probabilities for the various independent variables are as described in Chapter 11; in some cases semi-objective data may be available in the form of past data.

It is also possible for the regression coefficients to change and this of course renders forecasts based on the old coefficients spurious. For example, a major move in the level of pricing or advertising is likely to change the price and advertising elasticities which are represented by regression coefficients. If the forecaster foresees the possibility of any major changes in the elasticities, then an attempt should be made to assess the new coefficients and their probability of occurrence even though this may end up as a very subjective exercise. The process is the same as that described above, i.e. examining the impact of each possibility. Eventually, when sufficient data has been collected relating to the new circumstances, a new set of regression coefficients can be established.

In some cases there may be a step jump in the variable, as in Figure 14.1. In this case the old regression coefficients may still be relevant but a new constant will be required. The forecaster should be aware of this possibility, since it will save a lot of effort in constructing new regression coefficients which turn out to be the same as the old ones.

In some cases the forecaster may feel there is the possibility of a new factor coming into play. One example might be the introduction of a new tax on a commodity. The forecaster should attempt to forecast the chances of this variable coming into existence and its impact. This assessment should then be incorporated into the forecast, probably as a subjective adjustment to the final forecast given by some forecasting technique.

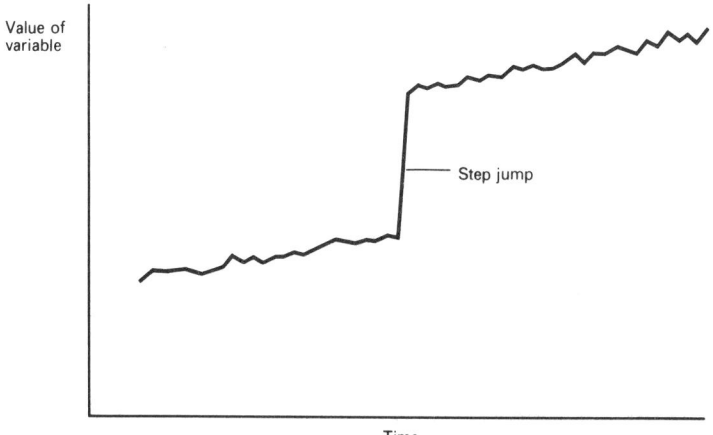

Figure 14.1

In the case of time series forecasting techniques there is no automatic way that probabilistic forecasts can be made. The forecaster could, however, adopt the following methodologies in order to give some idea of the range of possible outcomes:

1. If there are a number of time series techniques that have fitted the past data quite well then the forecasts from all of these methods could be given to management.

2. The parameters to a time series technique could be changed and the various forecasts given to the management. For example, the exponential smoothing technique could be adjusted for several values of α, the smoothing constant.

3. The forecaster can prepare forecasts from the time series technique and then make a subjectively-based probabilistic forecast from them. For example, if a particular time series technique gave a forecast of 4200 units then the forecaster might say there is a high degree of probability the outcome will be between 4150 and 4250 units. The forecaster could use various measures of past forecasting errors (such as standard deviations) as a method of computing the range of outcomes.

In summary, the forecaster should produce probabilistic forecasts, since these provide the sort of information that management needs if it is to make optimum decisions. The forecasts should relate to various economic assumptions that the forecaster and management feel may occur. Thus if there is a chance, even though small, that, say, a particular product may fail completely to sell, then the impact of this must be made clear to management. Only when management has a full picture of the possible outcomes can it begin to optimize its decision-taking in accordance with the firm's objectives.

The forecaster should, wherever possible, attach probabilities to the various forecasts that have been specified. In addition, the assumptions involved in reaching the various outcomes and their probability of occurrence should be explicitly stated; if these were subjectively arrived at this should likewise be stated along with any reasons for the values given. If there are sufficient forecasts made, then graphical methods (e.g. Figure 11.16) may be used to help highlight the figures for management; the forecaster should always be ready to help explain the meaning of probabilistic forecasts to managers and decision-takers. Although managers will now be faced with a mass of information from which they will have to reach a decision, they will at least have a good idea of the various possible outcomes.

As a final word, the forecaster should give some consideration to the communicating of the forecasts. Although management should be given full information, this should be given in as succinct a style as is possible; management does not want to be inundated with masses of paper and computer print outs.

Implementation of a forecasting system

In medium and larger-size organizations there will almost certainly be a need (on cost-benefit considerations) for employing a forecaster and some associated staff. Thus management will be faced with the task of locating and building up a forecasting department. If the firm already operates a central management services unit (e.g. operational research department, computer unit, etc.), then the forecasting department should be located there. If firms are extremely decentralized (e.g. separate subsidiaries being set up with their own boards of directors), then a small forecasting unit may be established in each subsidiary. In such cases the programming needs of the forecasting is usually done centrally.

In practice, however, the forecasting unit is often situated within one of the other management units of the firm, such as the operational research department, the accountancy/management information systems function, the sales department or the corporate planning department. The reason for this is usually that the manager of one of these departments is the first to recognize the benefits of formalized forecasting for at least that department's own functional activities. It is possible that the locating of a forecasting unit within one of the above mentioned departments would lead to poorer results than if the unit was given its own separate identity. This is because it may be subjected to the influence of the department in which it is located both as regards the forecasts it produces and the scheduling of the workload if there is a queue of work. For these reasons the forecasting unit should generally be kept separate; in undertaking forecasts for specific departments the forecasting unit will of course temporarily engage staff from these other departments to help them. In very large firms some of the functional departments may have their own forecasters who liase with the central forecasting unit in producing forecasts for their own departments. Examples of departments which may have forecasting expertise within themselves include the sales department (especially in the form of market research), the research and development department and the corporate planning department. In the case of small firms there may only be one executive who is involved in forecasting and that executive may be attached to another functional activity department.

In building up a forecasting department there are three main requirements:

1. The commitment of all levels of management to formal forecasting methods. This has to be a real commitment and not just an acceptance of a directive from the board of directors or a senior executive. In helping to get this commitment, training or information programmes should be introduced which explain the value of formal forecasting in decision-making situations. The commitment is important because the forecaster will require the help of line and staff managers in preparing forecasts and because forecasts will only be useful if they are actually utilized by management.

2. The recruitment of specialist and experienced staff and the provision of adequate facilities. It is important that the staff have a blend of technical competence, practical experience, the ability to understand management problems and the ability to communicate with management. While the first two attributes are well understood, the third and fourth attributes are often ignored in practice. However, in order to obtain a full commitment from management (as in (1) above), it is vital that these last two attributes are recognized and acted upon.

As regards the provision of facilities, this includes support staff (data clerks, programmers, computer operators, etc.), the building up of a library of computer programs and access to computer bureaus. It also includes the building up of liaison between the forecasting unit, the computer department and the management information systems function; the forecaster will have a lot of contact with these.

At the programming level, most computer manufacturers and many computer bureau specialists offer standard packages which contain a large array of forecasting techniques. These are generally satisfactory for most forecasting situations although some care is required by the forecaster in case there are any special circumstances surrounding the forecast or in the data. The existence of standard programs certainly reduces the cost of forecasting and has been a major factor in the growth of the use of sophisticated techniques in the past decade. But although standard computer programs ease the burden of forecasting, the forecaster and management still have to use a lot of skill and judgement in each situation; the computer only carries out mathematical functions.

There are numerous management consultancy firms who provide a wide range of forecasting services, such as

(a) Organizing forecasting systems for firms and getting them started.
(b) Doing one-off forecasting projects.
(c) Providing computing facilities and technical support staff. This may be a continuing assignment.
(d) Providing a complete forecasting system on a continuing basis.

In using outside consultancy services the firm must ensure that there is good communication so that both sides understand fully what is required and what is being done. Care must also be taken in selecting the consultancy; there are hundreds of firms and individuals offering their services, and many of them do not provide a comprehensive service or else have limited experience. In such cases the consultants may be utilizing a sub-optimum technique, this perhaps being the only one they know. For major forecasting problems (such as setting up a complete forecasting system) the firm should engage a large firm of consultants. A list of these is kept by the Institute of Management Consultants whose address is 23 Cromwell Place, London SW7, Tel. 01 584 7285.

If the firm does not have computing facilities and does not require the services of a management consultancy then it can make use of computer bureaux. There are numerous bureaux (many attached to management consultancies) which offer standard forecasting packages and training in the use of them. A list of the major bureaux and the services they offer is available from Computer Services and Bureaux Association (COSBA), 109 Kingsway, London WC2B 6PU, Tel. 01 405 2172.

3. The need for forecasting. In the vast majority of firms there will be a fairly obvious need for formal forecasting to be undertaken. However, there may be some organizations which have a very low requirement for forecasts, probably because they do not need to make decisions regarding the future. Possible examples might include various middlemen in industry

and commerce who match suppliers and customers but who do not have to carry stocks. In such cases formal forecasting may not bring sufficient benefits to outweigh the costs. With firms that do have a requirement for formal forecasting there may be some situations where forecasting is not necessary since it cannot be used to improve decisions. These situations should be identified if possible, so as to prevent the wastage of resources and save aggravating management who find the forecasts do not improve their decisions. Although smaller firms do not have a need for very sophisticated forecasting systems, they can nevertheless make very profitable use of the simpler techniques and methodologies; in many shorter-term forecasting situations the sophisticated forecasting techniques do not add much in the way of accuracy over the simpler methods. Small firms may employ just one full-time forecaster who uses a computer bureau; this can give very satisfactory returns.

There are no exceptional problems in the organization of the forecasting department beyond recognizing that it is there for managements' use, in contrast with some other management service functions which may be brought into a situation by top management (for example, sending in the operational research department to a situation which appears to be performing badly). However, there are a number of points which are worthwhile mentioning in relation to the organization:

1. There needs to be a fairly clear line of responsibility in forecasting situations. For example, while the forecasting department may suggest the appropriate technique, it may be the functional area managers who specify the assumptions which go into the model (e.g. the values of the independent variables in a causal model). In any event the line of responsibility needs to be identified; although mutual collaboration and agreement is required, there should be some executive who has the ultimate responsibility for seeing through the completion of the forecast.

2. There needs to be a performance audit, not only of the accuracy and the appropriateness of the forecasting techniques in use (and their alternatives), but also of the forecasting system as a whole. Such an audit may also ask for the opinions of functional management on the usefulness of the forecasting unit.

3. It may pay to assign the costs of the forecasting department to the functional departments which make use of it. This will allow these departments to perform some sort of cost-benefit analysis and will help prevent a ludicrous over-use of forecasting. (For example, in a causal model we can include various values for the independent variables and it is therefore possible for a manager to run wild and end up with thousands of forecasts, all of which have virtually no chance of occurring). The basis of

258 *Forecasting methods in business and management*

assigning costs is an accountancy and managerial matter; it could consist of the variable costs only or variable cost plus some overhead allocation.

Forecasting in practice and future developments

The purpose of this section is briefly to review the conclusions that have been reached in surveys into actual forecasting practices. Most of these have related to the USA and to sales forecasting in particular (this of course being the lynchpin variable upon which all plans are usually made, i.e. inventory levels, production schedules, labour requirements, the profitability of capital expenditures). The studies have largely used questionnaires or in-depth interviewing techniques of a sample of firms, with the results written up in the form of summary statistics or as case studies. The broad conclusions reached in the USA were that

1. There was a consistent and rapid increase in the use of formal forecasting methods.

2. The adoption of the more sophisticated techniques such as causal models and econometrics was also growing very quickly. In general it was the larger firms who were in the vanguard of the movement toward adopting the newer and more advanced techniques.

3. When subjective estimates had to be made by management these were being done on a far more systematic basis; they were using the qualitative forecasting methods described in Chapter 12.

4. The forecasting unit was becoming more formalized and more centralized as a staff function.

5. Firms were generally more than satisfied with the benefits they were deriving from formal forecasting.

For a fuller description of the American research into forecasting practices see references 6, 8, 9 and 11 at the end of the chapter; from these readings the reader will see the development of practices in the USA over time.

In the UK some research has been carried out into forecasting practices by the British Institute of Management (2), Jones and Morrell (5) and Targett-Adams (10). However, the most detailed survey was that conducted by Turner (12) in 1968 and 1969. He used both questionnaire (100 responses) and in-depth personal interview approaches (10 firms) in ascertaining the long-range sales forecasting techniques and practices used by British companies. The firms he approached were amongst the largest in the UK, they being those that responded from the Times 300 (the 300 largest firms ranked by capital employed). We can expect these to be the firms who utilize formal forecasting to the greatest extent.

Turner's findings were largely the same as those found in the USA, although he had no prior comparative UK surveys to fall back on to determine trends of acceptance of forecasting techniques. Specifically he concluded

1. That 90% of his sample viewed formal forecasting of sales demand as being a very important function in the firm.

2. That like American practice most firms treated the forecasting unit as a centralized department which undertook assignments for individual departments.

3. That again it is the larger firms which adopt the most sophisticated forecasting techniques and which give the greatest commitment to forecasting.

4. That although there have been no prior surveys in the UK there appears to have been a fairly rapid overall growth in the adoption of forecasting methods, this being gleaned from his discussions with management.

5. That simple time series methods were by far the most popular class of techniques in use.

6. That many firms reckoned that econometric modelling was beyond them. The main reasons for this were stated as being the problem of obtaining relevant data, the quantifying of qualitative variables, the time required to build models, the skilled personnel required, the cost, and, perhaps most important of all, the problem of having to forecast exogenous independent variables. Turner found however that when firms actually made a serious attempt at econometric modelling they often found the results to be satisfactory. The implication here is that many firms gave up econometric modelling without really giving it a decent attempt. This further implies that there has been a shortfall in training managers to consider the advantages and benefits of econometric modelling.

7. That he expected the trend towards formalized forecasting and the acceptance and adoption of sophisticated techniques would continue to increase in pace. He suggested that developments in techniques, the provision of technically competent personnel and the educating of management all required further effort in order to maximize the potential of forecasting.

From these findings it is apparent that there is immense potential from existing forecasting techniques which has still not been utilized by the vast majority of firms. While the research into and development of new statistical forecasting methods is an important task, it is felt that the utilization of currently available techniques in firms is perhaps the major problem. In meeting this problem two major items emerge; the provision of adequate trained personnel and the educating of management to become aware of the benefits of formal forecasting and become commited to its use in the firm. It is hoped that this book has contributed towards the latter and helped speed the intelligent consideration of more and more sophisticated forecasting systems by managers and firms. Although the results of formal forecasting may have been disappointing in many cases in the past, continual perseverance with them will surely improve forecasting to a level where there is an overwhelming support for it in virtually all decision-making situations.

References

1. Alexander, K. J. W., Kemp, A. G., and Rybczynski, T. M., eds., *The Economist in Business*, Blackwell, 1967.
2. British Institute of Management, *Survey of Market Forecasting Practices in Great Britain*, Information Summary 115, Sept. 1964.
3. Brown, R. G., *Smoothing, Forecasting and Prediction of Discrete Time Series*, Prentice Hall, 1962.
4. Butler, W. F., and Kavesh, R. A., eds., *How Business Economists Forecast*, Prentice Hall, 1966.
5. Jones, E. O., and Morrell, J. G., 'Environmental Forecasting in British Industry', *Journal of Management Studies*, Feb. 1966.
6. MacGowan, A. C., 'Techniques in Forecasting Consumer Durable Goods Sales', *Journal of Marketing*, Vol. 17, 1952–1953.
7. Moore, P. G., *Risk in business decision*, Longman, 1972.
8. Sord, B. H., and Welsch, G. A., *Business Budgeting*, New York, Controllership Foundation Inc., 1958.
9. Strong, L., 'Survey of Sales Forecasting Practices', *Management Review*, American Management Association, August and September 1956.
10. Targett-Adams, D. E., *Forecasting Business Conditions In The International Environment: A Study of Methods used by British Firms*, thesis available from Graduate Office, Centre for Business Research, Manchester Business School, Booth Street West, Manchester, M15 6PB.
11. Thompson, G. C., *Forecasting Sales*, A Conference Board Report, Studies in Business Policy, No 25, New York: National Industrial Conference Board Inc., 1947.
12. Turner, J., *Forecasting Practices in British Industry*, Surrey University Press, 1974.

Index

Accuracy, 109
Adaptive filtering, 82
Adaptive smoothing technique, 58
Additive trends, 51
Adoption of qualitative forecasting methods, 207
Agarwala, R., 157
Arrow, K. J., 157
Assessment of market share, 152
  advertising, 156
  distribution policies, 155
  estimates by salesmen, 158
  product quality, 154
  relative price, 153
Autocorrelation, 89, 121
Ayres, R. U., 211, 212

Ball, R. J., 157
Barometric forecasting, 173
Bass, F. M., 157
Batty, M., 96
Blumberg, J., 207
Box–Jenkins forecasting, 87
  autoregressive, 88
  autoregressive integrated moving average, 88
British Institute of Management, 240, 258
Brown, R. G., 1, 58

Causal models, 21, 98
Census II, 78, 79
Cetron, M. J., 207, 209, 210
Chow's method, 86
Classical decomposition analysis, forecasting with, 77
Classical decomposition model, 63
Coefficient of determination, 114

Company objectives, 3
Computer bureaux, 256
Computer Services & Bureaux Association (COSBA), 256
Confidence limits, 110
Controlled environment, 4
Corporate model, 5
Correlation, 99
Cost-benefit analysis, 245, 249
  non-profit-making organizations, 250
Cumulative probability distribution, 195
Cumulative sum (Cusum) technique, 93
Curvilinear analysis, 134
Cushing, B. E., 229
Cyclical factor, 72

Data banks, 229
Data classification, 227
  checking sources, 228
  data not in accounting system, 227
  existing accounting information, 227
  published data sources, 227
Decision analysis, 196
Decision events, 190, 192
Decision pay-off matrix, 196
Decision tree, 187, 188
Decomposing a time series, 64
Decomposition analysis, uses of, 64
Delphi method, 218
Dependent variable, 101
Direct requirements table, 162
Double exponential smoothing, 53
Double moving average, 56
Dummy variables, 135
Durbin Watson, 122, 125

Econometrics, 128

Elasticities, 134
Emshoff, J. R., 157
Envelope S-curve, 211, 212
Errors in economic forecasts, 228
  data aggregation, 229
  measurement errors, 228
  questionnaire errors and bias, 229
  sampling methods, 228
Expected values, 179
Explained variation, 115
Explorative model, 204
Exponential smoothing, 47
Exponential trend, 51
Extrapolation of trends, 208

F statistic, 118, 124
First differences, 135
Foran, 78, 79
Forecast, requirements of, 17
  accuracy, 17
  detail, 20
  relevance, 20
  speed and regularity, 19
  time horizon, 18
Forecasting of demand, 143
  advertising, 148
  changes in consumer tastes, 148
  complementary goods, 146
  consumer durables, 149
  goods not sold direct to the public, 150
  income distribution, 147
  new products, 151
  personal disposable income, 146
  population, 147
  price elasticity, 144
Forecasting with input–output tables, 160
  assumptions, 163
  existing tables, 168
  problems, 170
Forecasting loop, 3
Forecasting in practice, 10, 258
  corporate planning, 14
  finance, 13
  marketing, 11
  personnel, 11
  production, 11
  technological forecasting, 14
Forecasting techniques, attributes of, 24
  acceptability, 26
  accuracy, 24
  costs, 25
  data requirements, 25
  detail, 25
  interactiveness, 27
  speed, 24
  time horizon, 24
Full information, maximum likelihood, 132

Gerstenfeld, A., 207, 223

Heteroscedasticity, 120
Holt, C. C., 58
Holt's method, 57
Homoscedasticity, 120

Implementing a forecasting technique, 246, 254
  commitment of management, 255
  costing, 257
  data output, 251
  examination of data, 246
  responsibility for, 257
  staff recruitment, 255
Independent variable, 101
Indirect least squares, 132
Industrial Trends Inquiry, 236
Inequality index, 35
Input–output coefficients, 163
Input–output tables for 1971, 164–9
Instrumental variables, 132
Inter-relationships, 8, 129

Jantsch, E., 207, 211
Jones, E. O., 258
Jury of executive opinion, 235
Juster, F. T., 231

Lagged models, 136
Lead–lag relationship, 172
Leading indicators, 171
Learning constant, 83
Least squares, 104
Lenz, R. C., 215
Limited information, maximum likelihood, 132
Linearity, 119
Link relative models, 79
Log–linear, 124

Macroeconomic forecasting, 141

Index

Management information systems, 227, 229
Market surveys, 230
  forecasts by own personnel, 232
  individual buying intentions, 231
  industrial and commercial customers, 232
  types of, 231
  use of outside agencies, 235
  wholesalers, 232
Mathematical trend curve fitting, 59
Maximim, 196
Mean absolute deviation, 34
Mean squared deviation (error), 34
Measurements of forecasting error, 33, 46, 49, 56, 89
Mercer, A., 157
Minimax regret, 197
Morgenstern, O., 228
Morphological analysis, 216
Morrell, J. G., 258
Moving averages, 41
Muir, A., 57, 58
Muir's method, 57
Multicollinearity, 119

National Bureau of Economic Research, 231
National Institute of Economic & Social Research, 142
Nerlove, M., 157
Normal distribution, 122
Normative model, 204
Normative relevance tree, 221

O'Brien, J., 230
OECD, 142
Output distribution table, 162

Palda, K. S., 157
Parsons, L. J., 157
Parvin, R. H., 222
PATTERN, 221
Polynomial, 134
Prediction, 1
Preference theory, 182
Probabilistic forecasts, 111, 175
  interpretation of, 176
Probabilities, 176
  objective, 176
  subjective, 176
Probability tree, 185

Qualitative forecasts, 23, 175, 204, 248

Ratio trend, 51, 58
Regression, 99, 175
Research and development, 207
Risk analysis, 194
Risk averse, 183
Risk return analysis, 199

S-curve, 211
Salesmen's forecasts, 232
  bias in, 234
Sampling error, 112
Scenario, 220
Seasonal index, 66
Seasonal variations, 62
Selecting a forecasting technique, 246
  performance audit, 247, 257
  testing, 247
  using a number of techniques, 248
Sensitivity testing, 2, 175, 195
Sigford, J. V., 222
Simple correlation, 114
Simple linear regression, 101
Simple moving averages, limitations in, 46
Simplified input–output table, 160
Simultaneous equations, 128
  endogenous variable, 129
  exogenous variable, 129
  just-identified, 131
  over-identified, 131
  reduced form coefficient, 132
  structural equation coefficients, 132
  under-identified, 131
Smoothing techniques, 40
  data examination, 40
  for trend analysis, 51
Sources of published data, 237
Standard deviation, 110
Standard error of forecast, 109, 117

t statistic, 113, 125
Targett-Adams, D. E., 258
Taylor Nelson Group, 236
Technical capability trend, 209
Technological change, 204, 205
Thamara's method, 87

Theil, H., 35
Three-stage least squares, 132
Time-independent technological comparisons, 213
Time series models, 21
   appropriateness of, 39
   influences on the adoption of, 38
Time series patterns, 27
   cyclical, 30, 62, 245
   horizontal, 29, 39, 40, 47
   seasonal, 29, 41, 52, 61, 245
   trend, 30, 40, 61
Total variation, 115
Tracking signal, 85, 95
Trigg, D. W., 95
Trigg and Leach's method, 85

Turner, J., 258
Two-stage least squares, 132

Uncertain events, 190, 192
Uncertainty, 8
Uncontrollable environment, 4
Utiles, 183
Utility theory, 182

Von Neumann, 122, 125

Weighted moving averages, 47
   decimal, 47
   fractional, 47
Winters, P. R., 59

Zwicky, F., 216